DAVE GROHL

NOTHING TO LOSE

DAVE GROHL

NOTHING TO LOSE

Michael Heatley

REYNOLDS & HEARN LTD
LONDON

First published in 2006 by
Reynolds & Hearn Ltd
61a Priory Road
Kew Gardens
Richmond
Surrey TW9 3DH

© Michael Heatley 2006
This edition © Michael Heatley 2010

A CIP catalogue record for this book is available from the British Library.

ISBN 978-1-904674-11-5

Designed by Peri Godbold.

Printed and bound in Malta by Melita Press.

CONTENTS

Picture Credits

INTRODUCTION

Singing drummers... Well, there's Phil Collins, Ringo Starr, Don Henley, Roger Taylor and, er – that's more or less your lot. It would have taken a seer of Petulengro-esque proportions to predict that the long-haired sticksman thrashing away at the back of Kurt Cobain as Nirvana blasted forth their era-defining grunge anthems would add to that number. The similarly configured if slightly less hirsute Animal of *The Muppets* might have seemed a better bet...

Dave Grohl has confounded stereotypes and exceeded expectations to emerge as frontman with Foo Fighters, a band that started off as a solo studio project yet has become perhaps the first supergroup of the current millennium. It's a band whose popularity is inextricably bound up with Grohl himself – indeed, until the recruitment of former Alanis Morissette drummer Taylor Hawkins some two albums in, few but the committed could have named you another member of the outfit.

Foo Fighters were christened after the nickname given to mysterious silver balls of light seen by both the Allies and the Germans over the Rhine in December 1944 and, though officially explained as electrical phenomena, believed by pilots to be of extraterrestrial origin. In similar fashion, Grohl named his record label Roswell after the town in New Mexico where, legend has it, a UFO crash-landed in 1947 and where evidence of the unidentified visitors is still stored in top-secret conditions. After using a flying saucer on the cover of Foo

Fighters' debut single and a space-age ray-gun on the first album sleeve, Dave was later to play down the UFO connections.

Google the name Grohl and you'll find over 1.6 million references. And while not all of them are attributable to our man, there aren't that many alternatives. Not bad for a drummer. Yet drums were always a means to an end for a man whose first instrument was the guitar. And since starting Foo Fighters, drums have proved his passport to freedom when the pressures have been too great. He will always be in demand as the world's highest-profile session drummer, and there's little doubt that, should Led Zeppelin ever decide to take one final live bow, their former teenage fan from Springfield, Virginia would be their first choice to take the place of the late, great John Bonham.

Of course, it's Dave's brief spell in Nirvana that guarantees him a place in rock history – even if, at the time of writing, he's spent more than three times as long with Foo Fighters. The band once claimed by their leader Kurt Cobain to be 'musically and rhythmically retarded' showed that, as with the first punk wave, rock music had to take a step back to move forwards. And it remains the fact that, since the release of the seminal *Nevermind* album in 1991, bands and albums have regularly been classified as pre- or post-Nirvana.

If Grohl has learned one thing from the Nirvana experience, it is this: engage with the media, but set the boundaries at the outset. This 'nice guy' tactic has enabled him to weather a divorce with surprisingly little fallout, and has kept his name off the front pages of the tabloids in more cases than most. Privacy is priceless in this day and age of internet and rolling news TV, and his way of dealing with the media has been an object lesson honed, without doubt, from first-hand observation of his former band mate's trials and tribulations.

It's certain that Dave Grohl has surfed to success on a wave of public approval. He's everyone's big brother, best friend, whatever. Foo Fighters' videos have displayed a choice sense of humour that has undoubtedly played a major part in converting the uncommitted, and there seems no reason that their current 11-year record of success cannot be substantially extended in the future.

In an era of increasing categorisation, Foo Fighters have proved adept in keeping their feet in several musical camps. Their videos ensure heavy rotation on MTV, VH1 and other, perhaps poppier cable television channels, while the Nirvana connection ensures they will never be ignored by the heavy metal fraternity. And the singles appear to have enough hooks to capture the ear of radio programmers – even those of Britain's dance-obsessed Radio 1. One corollary of this has been the Foos' ability to sweep up Grammy awards without being regarded as having 'sold out'. Instead, there's a knowing wink as if to suggest that they have somehow subverted the established order – the band that cleans up yet retains credibility.

A special relationship has been forged with the United Kingdom thanks to certain sympathetic characters like Radio 1's Steve Lamacq and Jo Whiley and journalist Everett True. The country also hosted several landmark Nirvana gigs, so Dave has always enjoyed playing to his British admirers. And a summer 2006 gig in Hyde Park to 60,000 fans should cement their position as one of the country's top live draws, following in the footsteps of Roger Waters and the Who.

In 2005, *New Musical Express* asked Grohl, relaxed and happy in his 606 Studio in Northridge, California, whether he was most proud of his achievements with Foo Fighters or Nirvana. Coming from the man who once said, 'At the end of the day, will I always be remembered as the guy who played drums in Nirvana, no matter what I do after the fact?', the answer was predictable, the reasoning fascinating. 'Definitely the Foo Fighters,' he told writer Ian Winwood, 'because it's so much more personal to me. When I think of Nirvana it's such a blur. You have to remember that I was only in that band for three and a half years and all that stuff happened in such a short space of time. It doesn't even seem like reality to me a lot of the time – that and the fact I was their sixth drummer ... But this thing is a labour of love.'

Enjoy the fruits of those labours – and this account of them.

BEGINNINGS

D avid Eric Grohl was born in Warren, Ohio, a town of less than 50,000 inhabitants, on 14 January 1969. His mother Virginia's ancestry was Irish, his father James' German, hence the name. His home was near Kent State University, the seat of learning where, the following year, four students protesting against the Vietnam War were shot by National Guardsmen. Neil Young wrote 'Ohio' as his impassioned response.

Dave spent most of his childhood in Springfield, Virginia, where the family moved (from Columbus) when he was three; father James was a newspaper writer for the Scripps-Howard group and needed to be near Washington DC for his work. (With impeccable timing, they relocated just before the Watergate scandal broke.) Dave has since described his parents as being at opposite ends of the political spectrum, his father a strait-laced conservative and his mother a liberal freethinker.

His parents had already produced a daughter, Lisa, three years Dave's senior. But the happy four-square average American family was to be fractured when his parents divorced; Dave was just seven. Prior to this sad event, Dave had witnessed his first live music when, at the tender age of two, he had visited the Ohio State Fair with the family and seen the Jackson Five.

After the divorce, James headed back to Ohio while Virginia, a schoolteacher, found herself the sole breadwinner.

She was forced to take on extra jobs to make ends meet, and Dave recalls 'tough times when we'd eat peanut butter and pickle sandwiches.' The pair's relationship strengthened in adversity, to such an extent that Dave has included his still young-at-heart mom in the band's backstage activities on Foo Fighters tours.

'My mother worked three jobs to support my sister and me,' he's since explained. 'She was a high-school English teacher. She worked at a department store at night. And on the weekend, she did estimates for a carpet-cleaning company. She worked her fingers to the bone just to make sure we survived. Now she's retired, and I bought her the house we grew up in, and I added on a whole extra wing. She comes out on tour at special locations, like Australia. We had a blast. We went to wildlife preserves and petted wallabies.'

Back in the mid-seventies the inevitable consequence of the one-parent family situation was that Dave had much unsupervised time on his hands. A fair proportion of that, if he is to be believed, was spent lying on his back in the garden late at night hoping to spot a UFO: 'I wanted them to abduct me. It was like, Take me! Take me! Please get me out of here.'

Another interest was ice hockey, and his first role model was selected from the sporting sphere – Jim Craig, the American ice-hockey team goalkeeper. 'Jim was, no doubt, the biggest hero in my life when I was a kid. When I was young, I played hockey, I played lacrosse and stuff, and for some reason, [during] the Olympics that year, when the US team won, he in particular made such an impression on me. He's the only person I remember being like a hero to me when I was young.' The Foo Fighters song 'My Hero' may well have been inspired by Craig.

Many years later, when Foo Fighters played the 2002 Winter Olympics, Craig called him on the telephone at a point when

Dave was experiencing greater than usual pre-gig nerves thanks to a prolonged lay-off. 'He gave me this pep talk that, I swear to God, changed my life. I can't remember exactly what he said, but it was something along the lines of, "Well," in his Boston accent, "tonight you'll do what the US hockey team did in 1980." It was so awesome! Unreal.'

Grohl rates his academic progress as 'pretty good until I got into high school. Then I started smoking pot and didn't give a shit about anything.' He claims to have got along with every conceivable social stereotype – 'the jocks, the stoners, the geeks, pretty much everyone.' At the tender age of 14 he graduated from pot to mushrooms one Christmas when a friend gave him some as a present. Somewhat unwisely, he took them at the family Christmas party, but his 'running round the party having the time of my life' was curtailed when a friend of his mother took him aside and accused him of 'being on cocaine'.

He wasn't raised in a religious household – 'There wasn't a whole lot of church going on' – but festivals were celebrated with family feeling. Christmas, for instance, meant 'a whole lot of whisky and a whole lot of presents. There'd always be a huge party – we would never need to send out invitations, a hundred or so close friends would come over and it'd turn into a raging keg party. Those parties were always pretty epic.'

School rapidly moved from a compulsory to an optional activity with the onset of puberty, but Dave, now the man of the house, wasn't one for rocking the boat. 'I could look after myself easy, so I focused on making sure the family was happy – I've been doing that ever since.' The teachers at Fairfax County High saw much unrealised potential: 'My old report cards were concerned with my hyperactivity,' he'd later remark. 'The teachers all said, "David could be a very good student if he could just stay in one place and sit still." There were lots of requests for my Mom to come in and talk about it.'

His father, a sought-after speechwriter for Republican politicians who once turned down a job with presidential hopeful Bob Dole, was watching from a distance and would give his son 'the State of the Union address ... if I fucked up.' Dave would later admit that, while he was somewhat intimidated by his dad, he probably grew up with a more tolerant attitude in his absence. 'I've learnt to accept the relationship we have, and he's a great guy, but growing up without a strong male influence had a strong influence on me. When I was 12, I was in theatre groups and they were predominantly gay. People often shy away from – or are scared of – people who are gay. And, growing up in rural Virginia where everyone's either a farmer or works in the Pentagon, to be so accepting of gay people was a real bonus.'

Dave describes the Grohls as 'a very close family' and suggests his parents' divorce came too early in his life for him to fully understand it. 'It just seemed abnormal for all my friends to have a father; I thought growing up with my Mom and sister was the way it was supposed to be.' He describes Virginia as 'strong, independent, sweet, intelligent and funny ... just the best.'

Grohl's first musical jolt, like many of his generation, came from the nationally networked television show *Saturday Night Live*. 'The B-52's played 'Rock Lobster' on one show I was watching in 1979 – they totally blew my mind.' Unknown to him, Kurt Cobain was also enjoying this experience and finding it (plus the appearance of fellow New Wavers Devo) equally life-changing.

So what was it that attracted him to the B-52's, that wacky quintet from Athens, Georgia? 'Those guitars! Two strings! How cool! Those drums! Slap slap slap! Dead easy! The women looked like they were from outer space and everything was linked in – the [record] sleeves, the sound, the clothes, the iconography, the logo, everything. I think when you're a kid, that's what you're after, a real unified feel to a band, and that's what the B-52's offered. Their songs were so easy to learn, they got me into playing really easily. This was definitely the first thing after Kiss or Rush that totally absorbed me like that.'

Mom Virginia had, in her youth, been the singer in an unaccompanied vocal group, and his father had played the flute, so when Dave showed some musical ability she was happy to indulge him. Dad, however, was as disciplined a flautist as he was a journalist and encouraged dedication. 'He thought that unless you practiced for six hours a day, you couldn't call yourself a musician; that work ethic had a big effect on me,' Grohl says. 'My dad was a really straight dude but he was a jazz freak. I was always surrounded by culture and music and literature so I was definitely the exception in my neighbourhood. I didn't grow up a complete idiot.'

Perhaps surprisingly, the Grohls didn't have a record player of their own, but Dave's mother, being a teacher, could bring home the school turntable at weekends so they could listen to albums. They tended to be his mother's choice, the Beatles, until he gathered together enough pocket money to buy his own. Everyone remembers the very first record they bought. In Dave's case, aged seven, it was a K-Tel compilation of recent rock hits. Catching an earful of Edgar Winter's chart-topping 1973 instrumental 'Frankenstein', with Ronnie Montrose on lead guitar, was 'the first time I had heard music that turned me on. I thought was the coolest thing in the world. That was my favourite.'

A nylon-stringed Spanish guitar had always been in the house since his mother bought it for his father as a Christmas present. Dave had managed to figure out some Beatles tunes without help – mother having bought him the complete Fab

Four catalogue on sheet music, he even managed to perform favourite song 'Rocky Racoon' to a theatre full of high school students. The Beatles' Red and Blue compilation albums were childhood staples, with 'Paperback Writer' succeeding 'Rocky Racoon' as his favourite. 'It had that nasty groove to it. I thought it was great they could look like such gentlemen and sound like such bad asses.'

His first youthful crush was on tomboyish Ohio singer Chrissie Hynde from the Anglo-American group Pretenders, though he insists that 'I was never big on girlie posters in my room, I was more into rock – Sex Pistols and Kiss.' With all this pop-related activity going on, it was all but inevitable he would be allowed to take lessons – if only to stop him churning out his favourite riff, Deep Purple's 'Smoke On the Water', time and time again on those six nylon strings. Next stop? An electric...

The occasion was his 12th birthday, the instrument he was given a Silvertone. These bargain-basement guitars have acquired iconic status, due to so many household names having picked their first solos on one, plus the quaint fact that some of them had a tiny amplifier incorporated in their cases, thus obviating the need for a further expensive purchase. The Silvertone's slightly more expensive relation, the Danelectro, has been toted by the likes of Led Zeppelin's Jimmy Page, but it is the Silvertone, with its body made of Masonite chipboard instead of real wood, that has the bigger place in rock 'n' roll mythology. Though Dave quickly graduated to a Les Paul (albeit a 'Memphis' copy rather than the unattainable Gibson original), the Silvertone retains a place in his affections.

Talking of Jimmy Page, his band Led Zeppelin was never off the stereo of Dave's Volkswagen Beetle. He'd drive to school, 'very stoned', listening again and again to Zep's track

'Friends' from their 1970 third album. He believes it swept him into 'my own little trance-like state, like Sting with those shamans in the Amazon. But all I had was a bong and a Led Zeppelin tape.' Interestingly, the acoustic/electric dichotomy Zep displayed on that album would eventually surface in Foo Fighters' music, especially 2005's partly acoustic *In Your Honour*.

Dave has gone on record as stating that 'Heavy metal would not exist without Led Zeppelin – and if it did it would suck.' A collection of linked-circle tattoos on his wrists and arms inspired by drummer John Bonham only serve to emphasise the point. But his first musical venture was, technically speaking, a drummerless duo, the H G Hancock Band, which he formed with his best friend Larry Hinkle.

The pair celebrated their bond in a rather permanent way in the shape of a tiny X-shaped tattoo on each boy's elbow. 'Larry and I decided we would be 'brothers' and both put these crosses on our elbows when we were about 12 years old. But I completely forgot about it and then about eight years later I was sitting in traffic with my arm out the window; I looked in the side mirror and saw this fucking 'X' on my elbow. I was like, "What the hell is that?" It took me a couple of minutes to remember. Clearly, the stupidest tattoo I ever had.' It rivals, in that sense, 'a Black Flag tattoo that I made myself when I was 11 with a biro ballpoint pen.'

Led Zeppelin also made an indelible impression after Dave heard the anthemic 'Stairway to Heaven' at the age of seven or eight. 'My mom would always tune into the same radio station ... Zeppelin was the first band I actually listened to, and I was obsessed with 'Trampled Underfoot' and 'No Quarter' for about a year. Everything about that band is mind-blowing.' He also admits to a soft spot for the melodic pop of Abba, while Australian hard-rockers AC/DC would also make their way onto a personal playlist dominated by the likes of Rush and the ubiquitous Kiss.

He attended Thomas Jefferson High School for Science and Technology in nearby Alexandria and was popular with his schoolmates, who voted him class vice-president. This allowed him the privilege of playing a few minutes of music, typically Bad Brains or the Circle Jerks, through the school intercom. But his self-confessed over-reliance on dope ('from the time I was 15 to 20 I smoked four or five times a day ... and a lot') was reflected in his academic grades and he was moved at his mother's request to a local Catholic school, Bishop Ireton, where hopefully he would mix with a 'straighter' crowd.

Indeed, he has described his two years at the school as 'a pretty scary memory. Why did I go? I was a naughty boy – just didn't care about anything, really. One enduring memory of that school is getting really stoned and then sitting down and having to go through the whole morning-prayer thing. I was so high it kinda sent me into a panic attack.' Maybe the dope compensated for Dave's tendency to be 'super hyperactive'.

Dave's way of falling asleep when he was a teenager was to talk to his tape recorder about his problems. He'd then rewind the tape and fall asleep listening to himself. Unconventional perhaps, but it seems to have worked. He has, he later revealed, adopted a similar confessional approach to songwriting. 'There are some things that you don't want to say out loud, but for some reason when there are 10,000 people saying it with you, it makes it all right.'

So much for going to sleep. A family vacation in 1982 at age 13 would prove something of an eye and ear opener. The Grohl family was unaware, as they took their annual trip to Evanston, Illinois to visit their relations the Bradfords, that one of them had undergone a life-changing experience. 'Cousin Tracey had turned into punk Tracey – spiked hair, chains, the whole thing! The next few weeks changed my life forever! Her record collection was amazing.' Next step was to see his first rock show, comprising Naked Raygun and ROTA, at a local club called Cubby Bear's.

'I immediately ran to the record store and bought the Dead Kennedys' song 'Nazi Punks Fuck Off' – a pure, simple blast of hardcore noise.' He 'totally fell in love with this unbelievable underground network she was part of ... it was fucking wild, man. From then on that was it.' Suddenly cover versions were out and punk rock was in, leading to a renewed attack on the guitar with more aggressive sounds in mind. 'Sitting on the couch watching TV, I'd always have my guitar in my hands,' he says. 'My mom was like, "Put that down and do your homework!"' He put it down all right, but picked up a couple of sticks instead.

The inspiration for his new-found percussive direction seems to have been seeing Devo, a robotic-style band from Akron, Ohio whom he thought had 'been beamed from some parallel universe. Everyone in my year at school wanted to be in Devo, they were these aliens you really wanted to know, really wanted to be part of. Plus they were from Ohio, which is where I'm from, and it was really inspirational not only to have a band take New York by storm from Ohio, but also for them to be that far out, recreate themselves that much. Plus their songs were dead simple to learn. They kinda made me start playing drums.'

The switch from guitar to percussion resulted in him taking lessons at school – but, as money was tight and the house was so small, a kit to play on at home would have to wait. While he scrimped and saved, an improvised practice pad was fashioned out of pillows and beaten with a pair of oversize marching-band drumsticks he'd mysteriously acquired: Dave acknowledges the fact he had to hit hard to hear anything at all may account for his powerhouse style of today. Once correctly equipped, he cut his teeth on Rolling Stones and Who songs in a local band. Dances, birthday parties and even a nursing home were among the venues they rocked with their selection of classic rock covers.

At this point, Dave Grohl looked like any other spotty American youth of the time – right down to a haircut he refers to as a 'soccer rocker – mullet seems a little derogatory! I was 13 and listened to the Police. Everybody on the soccer team had a haircut like Sting's in 1983.' Soon, like all teenage kids of that age, he fell in love. He was 16, but the object of his affection moved to Arizona with her family not long after they started going out together. 'It broke my heart. All I wanted to do was drop out of high school and drive to be with her.'

Not long afterwards, he lost his virginity to a junior on the basketball team. But it was far from a joyful experience, and one played out in near-total silence. 'I was a freshman, and I never saw her again. She ruled me like a caged animal. It was like *2001: A Space Odyssey*, just silent until the monolith came crashing down.'

As ever, though, he could take solace in his musical pursuits. Indeed, he would later reveal that the art of drumming and lovemaking are in, his view, related. Both have to do with 'groove and power. The most important thing about fucking is your time and your rhythm, knowing when to back off and when to let it go ... You go from something beautiful and gentle and delicate to just slamming someone around.'

His role model – as a drummer, rather than a lover – was inevitably Led Zeppelin's John Bonham: 'I would learn every drum-fill, every roll, every single thing he did.' The thing that attracted him was the fact that 'Bonham couldn't have given a shit about the conventional restraints of being a rock drummer. He influenced me and thousands of other drummers to play the drums with soul and feeling rather than with just proficiency.'

Bonham, of course, had died in 1980 after a marathon drinking session. Zeppelin had died with him, and the music scene was in a state of flux. British punk had just about burned itself out as the 1980s kicked off, and as the New Romantic likes of Adam and the Ants planted their standard atop the British charts it was left to the United States to take punk's ideals into a new dimension. Washington would become something of a bridgehead and, being within reach, would be where Dave would experience live music both as a spectator and, later, a performer.

This wave of new American punk, headed by such bands as Naked Raygun and Bad Brains, taught him an important lesson – 'that you didn't have to be Eddie Van Halen to play incredibly powerful, intense stuff. And that was [an] incentive for everyone to do it themselves.' Bad Brains were a band that did just that. A hardcore, Clash-esque outfit of black Rastafarians, they made a point of playing gigs in Washington's less affluent neighbourhoods in a successful attempt to amass a grass-roots fan base. And the young Grohl was happy to pledge allegiance.

After witnessing Bad Brains live, he rated their show 'one of the most intense, powerful experiences you could ever have. They were just, oh God, words fail me, incredible. They were connected in a way I'd never seen before. They made me absolutely determined to become a musician, they basically changed my life, and changed the lives of everyone who saw them. Nobody else blew me away as much as Bad Brains. I'll say it now, I have never ever, ever, ever, ever seen a band do anything even close ... Bad Brains are one of those bands that everyone who's ever heard them has come away with a real extreme reaction, either love or hate. I loved 'em. The fact that there were four black guys, coming on to a predominately white scene that they then just surpassed and destroyed with everything they did, just staggered you.'

Another unusual musical touchstone, and one that would also stay with him for life, arrived in the shape of British Goth-rockers Killing Joke around 1982 or 1983. Their eponymous debut album from 1980 has often been quoted as one of his all-time favourites; what's more, Foo Fighters have often played its opening track, 'Requiem'. 'Killing Joke's music is everything I love,' Dave has pointed out. 'Relevant, melodic, energetic, and powerful. It's one of the great things about bands that had a political stance, whether it was the Clash, or MC5, or Fugazi. It makes you think. And you have all of that on top of the melody and power of the music.' He'd later describe frontman Jaz Coleman as 'one of my vocal heroes, it sounds like he drank a bottle of sulphuric acid and decided to get onstage and belt it out.'

It was finally time for Dave to leave the musical sidelines and become a participant. And his breakthrough from spectator to stage came quite by chance. A trip to Washington in the summer of 1984 led to a meeting with Brian Samuels, a teen punk who played bass in a band called Freak Baby. A successful audition saw Dave join as a 15 year-old second guitarist, and a run of high-school gigs followed.

Dave had encountered an influential person in his musical development when the band had cut a demo tape at Arlington, Virginia's Laundry Room Studios. This was Barrett Jones, whose parents owned the house in which the studio was situated. 'I pretty much recorded every other band he was in,' commented Jones. 'We were always doing music together when he wasn't touring or something like that.' Dave even took a turn behind the traps of Jones' band Churn as their relationship grew.

After six months in the Freak Baby ranks as rhythm guitarist, Dave switched to drums when an impromptu post-rehearsal thrash impressed his bandmates. Original drummer David Smith took up the four-stringed task with gusto, having started his musical life on the instrument before going behind the traps for want of anyone more skilled. Dave's distinctive style, which would stand him in such good stead later, quickly began to evolve: 'I had no idea how to set up the drums, but I loved to just beat the hell out of them.'

Bryant Mason (lead guitar) and Chris Page (vocals) agreed that this radical instrumental switch added to the band's power, and Brian Samuels, the man who'd introduced the out-of-town newcomer, found himself no longer part of the grand scheme. Rechristening themselves Mission Impossible to mark the change, they stepped up a gear gig-wise and started supporting bands of the status of Troublefunk and Fugazi.

'We were living our hardcore dream,' said Grohl, who made his first appearance on record when the band cut a 7-inch single shared with a band called Lunchmeat, the 'Thanks' EP on Sammich/Dischord, only 500 copies of which were pressed. They'd changed their name again, to Fast, by the time they broke up in August 1985; Page and Mason looked to the future and opted to go to college rather than remain part-time punks.

Local drummer Dante Ferrando, now the owner of Washington's Black Cat nightclub, was immediately impressed by the young Grohl, who made up in power what he as yet lacked in technique. 'He was pretty young, and the stuff he was playing was simple, but he did it with so much power and precision. I remember someone telling me he'd only been playing live about eight months, and could I believe it? I was envious because I'd been playing for years and couldn't play like that.'

Mission Impossible also opened for the Obsessed, a band that left just as indelible mark in Dave Grohl's musical brain as he himself had in Dante Ferrando's. He describes them as 'full-on dirge-rock metal craziness', admitting that their audience of bikers was 'pretty wild' as well. 'Plus you'd get all these hardcore skater kids there too. The Obsessed pretty much blew away any other band I've ever seen.'

The only downside of playing to an audience for Dave was a tendency to have anxiety attacks before shows. This feeling would intensify as the numbers he played to rose, but at age 13 or 14 he tried following a friend's advice and hypnotising himself out of it. It wasn't a practice to be recommended, as he later explained. 'Somebody told me you could hypnotise yourself by staring at a mirror for hours on end,' he revealed. 'I did and it freaked me out for the rest of my life, really badly.'

Early jobs as a schoolboy included employment in a nursery and as a stonemason. But the worst, by some way, was a spell working at a pizza parlour called Shaky's. 'That job fucking sucked,' he recalls. 'I was working the whole summer, working my ass off, smelling of pepperoni, just to buy my books for school. And I knew that I would eventually just fucking discard them all anyway. Was I hygienic? Well, I was 16, and I'm sure my hands had been in places the pizza lovers wouldn't want to know about.

'I didn't really have that slacker thing. Yeah, I'm a high school drop-out and I might have shown up late when I worked at Tower Records when I was 18. But playing in a band doesn't seem like work to me. It's my greatest passion. It's the one thing I can't do without.'

Freak Baby/Mission Impossible/Fast had shared bills with an impressive outfit known as AOC and, on their demise, Dave nipped in smartly and recruited bassist Reuben Radding for his next project, the improbably named Dain Bramage.

The object was to 'experiment with classic rock clichés in a noisy, punk kind of way,' and Radding, whose influences included art-punks Television and Gang of Four, was a suitably noisy vocalist. Dave Smith from the now defunct Freak Baby/ Mission Impossible/Fast completed the line-up, which played its first gig in December 1985 at Virginia's Burke Community Centre.

'I don't know where the hell we got that name Dain Bramage,' he laughs. But the band did have a connection with his future in introducing him to a looser, more spontaneous way of working and writing. 'You know, I remember when I joined Nirvana I thought, "Wow, this is just like Dain Bramage." Not in the music that we wrote but in the way the band wrote music. Every Dain Bramage practice, we'd walk in, plug in, and we'd just go. For about half an hour. And ridiculous as it sounds, sometimes songs come from that. 'Come As You Are', 'Smells Like Teen Spirit' or 'Drain You', they came from jamming.'

Dave told Nirvana's official biographer Michael Azerrad that Dain Bramage's mix of hardcore punk with snatches of music reminiscent of Television or Mission of Burma was not well received: 'Everybody just hated us.' Apparently, if you weren't on the Dischord label, co-founded by Minor Threat/Fugazi mainman Ian MacKaye, you weren't at the races. It was, however, at this time that Dave managed to establish a drumming style he could truly call his own – even if he admitted it was a mix-and-match job culled from his favourites. 'You take pieces from other drummers like the drummer from Bad Brains, to John Bonham and the drummer from Devo and it eventually becomes this big mush. That's me – just one big rip-off!'

After recording the obligatory demo tape with Barrett Jones' assistance, the band used it to attract the attention of

Corrosion of Conformity's Reed Mullin. He in turn introduced them to Los Angeles indie label Fartblossom, and the result was an album, *I Scream Not Coming Down*, produced by Jones. 'None of this stuff was ever really released in anything more than 500 or 1000 copies total, and it never really got distributed,' Jones later stated of an album Grohl described as combining 'rock, art punk and hardcore – I still like it'.

All was going well for Dain Bramage. But temptation too strong to resist came Dave's way in the shape of Scream.

THE ROAD TO NIRVANA

Washington DC-based band Scream had become something of a hardcore legend since its foundation in 1979, brothers Franz and Pete Stahl being its mainstays on guitar and vocals respectively. Their musical inspirations ranged from UK punks like the Damned and Subhumans to heavy metallers Black Sabbath and Venom, with a twist of homegrown hardcore heroes Bad Brains.

The band's first album, *Still Screaming*, was produced in 1982 by Minor Threat/future Fugazi man Ian MacKaye and Eddie Janney and released early the following year. It was voted record of the year by readers of *Suburban Voice* magazine, while the band's third album, 1987's *Banging the Drum*, is still considered a US punk hardcore classic nearly two decades later.

It was Scream's second album, however – *This Side Up*, released in May 1985 – that made the biggest impression on Dave Grohl. If Bad Brains had been top of his hardcore hit parade, then this was the release that propelled his new bandmates into second place. 'This is the album where Scream went from being a hardcore band into being a rock band,' he enthused. 'They sounded like Aerosmith. I loved that. They were also from Virginia. I had roots in Virginia ... They lived near to me, but I wasn't sure where and I loved the fact that I could be walking past them every day without knowing it.

'I liked the fact that they had long hair, that they weren't straight edge, that they played this kinda hard-rock/hardcore thing. It made me realise there was a place for me making music, even though this was long before I joined any bands.' (Straight edge was a term used to describe bands and fans, notably Minor Threat, who abstained from drink and drugs.)

Kent Staxx had vacated the drum stool in the spring of 1987, the year of the third album's release, allowing Dave to complete the line-up. The catalyst had been a flyer stuck on the wall of a local music store: 'It said Scream was looking for a drummer. Man, I'd worshipped those guys, seen them a billion times. I had to call.' He was rejected at his first phone call on the grounds of age, even though he'd lied to add three years to his real 17. But he persisted, and received the longed-for invitation.

There were, of course, other options: digging ditches, raking gravel, roofing, working at a petrol station or in a furniture warehouse. 'Those are what I call 'Virginia jobs' – real jobs,' said Dave, admitting that he was 'a drop-out who was destined to work in a furniture warehouse. That was cool, I liked it while I was there. I was happy with that. But this career, music as a career, just wasn't an option. It was never on the cards. So to me, it's like I've been winning the lottery every year of my life since '81.'

Franz Stahl likened Dave's arrival in their basement to 'an infusion of energy', to what would happen later with Foo Fighters when Taylor Hawkins joined their ranks. For Dave, it was a long-awaited vindication of his music-centric lifestyle choice – not to mention a flashback to his pillowcase drum-kit days. 'Scream were among the records I used to play drums to on my bed when I was first learning. I knew all their songs by heart.'

The audition was a breeze. 'When Franz asked, "What do you want to play, some Sabbath or some Zep?" I said Nah, let's play ... and rattled off the names of all their songs!' Dain Bramage were still a going concern, however, and, though Smith and Radding aimed to replace their departed member, their demise occurred in a matter of days. 'After you've spent a couple of years with Dave Grohl as your drummer,' Radding told his band's website, 'it's easy to feel like no other drummer exists.'

If Grohl had been able to change horses with few, if any, recriminations, his parents' reaction when he dropped out of school to play full-time music was predictably sceptical, despite their own musical backgrounds. 'They are parents, there is resistance. I think they believed in my love of music and they had faith that I could probably do something good.' It has even been suggested that Grohl had been asked to leave his seat of education due, perhaps, to the fact he was 'so stoned I had no idea what I was studying.'

He later admitted, 'I think if I were to have a child and my child pulled a stunt like I did when I was 17 or 18 years old and split school to go jump in a van with four other guys and tour Europe and sleep on people's floors – and, you know, seven dollars a day, that doesn't go far. If I were to have a child that did the same thing, I would be concerned as well. Because 99 times out of 100 it doesn't pay off. It doesn't. I really feel like I won the lottery, man. I got to go out and do what I love to do. It's ridiculous to keep saying it, but it's absolutely true.

'Both of my parents were always really supportive, but my mother especially. I think when I was young she knew that there was something about me that was going to be all right. She had faith in me as an individual. And even when I was young I had this independent spirit. I felt like I don't need to take that conventional four years of high school, four years of college... I just kind of figured I would be all right. When I told her I was leaving school, she said, "All right. Well, you better be good at this." I'm like, "I'll try."'

Dave had anticipated resistance from his father 'because, well, because he was a Republican speechwriter. I think my dad wanted me to ... go to the army or something like that. But once I started earning more money than him, though, he accepted it. Both my parents were proud. They might not have put my records on at night with a glass of Chardonnay, but they thought it was a constructive application. And I'm forever indebted to both of them.'

He immediately took to life on the road with Scream: 'The feeling of driving across the country in a van, stopping in every city to play, sleeping on people's floors, watching the sun come up over the desert as I drove, it was all too much. This was definitely where I belonged.' The seven dollar a day expenses (or 'per diem', as parlance has it) would buy cheap food, but cigarettes were strictly rationed and 'bargain brand' if they could be afforded at all. An advance of three days' per diems would be enough to score some pot, but it didn't necessarily guarantee a nutritious diet.

An added advantage, though, was guitar lessons 'on the side' from Franz Stahl: 'I've spent more time with him than with any other guitarist in my life, he taught me so much about playing.' The friendship forged as they explored the fretboard together would be an enduring one that would transfer into another musical situation as time went by. In all, it was a great education for someone who, by his own admission, had 'never been past Chicago.'

Things kicked off with 'a good two-month tour, everywhere from Fender's Ballroom in LA to the Botanical Center in Des Moines. Whether it was learning how to perform live, how to live within the confines of a Dodge Ram or learning how to score chicks, I learned everything. I didn't have a car until I was in Nirvana. Cigarettes were cheap, and Taco Bell was everywhere.'

The lie he'd told at the audition was inevitably uncovered. But by that time the newcomer had more than proved his worth. 'When Pete found out my real age and that he was ten years older than me, he became my father figure,' said Grohl. 'We'd be on the road for months in a van, and he'd be teaching me how to behave on the road, how to survive without burning out, how to have fun, when to be serious.'

Not so bassist Skeeter Thompson, who would attempt to rile his young rhythm section partner by pinning him down and 'putting his stinking feet in my face.' Whether he did this to Grohl's predecessor, Kent Staxx, is not recorded, but Staxx's decision to return to his family in Virginia and pursue a career in carpentry had certainly put Scream's future in jeopardy until Grohl made that fateful phone call.

Though Scream had cut three albums in their six years of existence, this had not proved sufficiently lucrative and they had to rely on consistent touring to bring in the money. They also needed to cultivate a following in Europe, where audiences were perhaps less parochial than the States. Their unwillingness to adopt an image hadn't helped them take off on the hardcore scene at home, while their inability to conform to a musical stereotype also worked against them. 'We were a punk-rock band,' says Grohl. 'But we were also a hard-rock band. Franz was playing all this great metal guitar stuff, then he'd go into these incredibly fast hardcore punk riffs, and people couldn't figure it out.'

Dave's first venture into the studio with Scream came in 1988 with *No More Censorship*, their first album for reggae label RAS (Real Authentic Sounds) after leaving the hardcore Dischord imprint. While RAS were hoping to diversify into the rock market, Scream had followed Bad Brains' lead and

31

included reggae rhythms in their musical vocabulary, a first for the young drummer. He also enjoyed his first trip to Europe when they crossed the Atlantic to play Dutch dates in February. A souvenir album, *Live at Van Hall in Amsterdam*, emerged on the Konkurrel label in 1989.

A Grohl-penned song, 'Gods Look Down', was recorded with Scream, and was the first evidence of his writing ability. It was also to be the first song he recorded by himself with Barrett Jones. 'Dave's version,' in Jones' opinion, 'is so much better than what Scream ended up recording.' The latter appeared on the album *Fumble*, recorded in December 1989 at Inner Ear studios, but it remained unmixed and on the shelf until a reunion tour took place three and a half years later. The song also suggested a need on Dave's part to be more than just the man driving the band from the back.

Grohl visited Europe no fewer than three times with Scream, and remembers driving through Italy in the summer enjoying the sounds of the Ry Cooder soundtrack to *Paris, Texas*. A huge contrast to Scream's output, it remains for Dave 'the most beautiful acoustic album ever made.' He remembers these heady hardcore days fondly, turning up to a squat in Turin, Italy 'and they're burning the mattresses 'cause they have scabies all over them. You walk in with your gear and they're still trying to figure out how to steal electricity from the building next door. And someone's building a stage. That's how it was every night! Some of it was really fun. The sense of community, it was really strong. They couldn't pay us any-thing. They might give us only gas money, but they'd make you the biggest bowl of pasta you've ever seen in your life and smoke you out! It was great.'

It was around this time that Dave, along with many thousands of American youths, experienced (as a spectator) the Monsters of Rock package tour, which slammed together metal gods Van Halen, Metallica, the Scorpions and Dokken. It was his first big concert, but far from being impressed by the sheer scale of it, he found the whole thing 'comical', promising he would never have anything to do with that kind of over-the-top event. It was certainly light years away from the life he was living as a full-time musician, but he wouldn't have swapped places. And it sowed the seeds of suspicion that would bloom when Nirvana hit the big time a couple of years later, trading small clubs for bigger venues.

In the spring of 1990, Scream made what was to be their final European tour, playing 23 shows in just 24 days. Skeeter Thompson in particular found the pace too demanding and returned home midway through. His replacement was J Robbins, singer-guitarist of Washington band Jawbox, who'd played bass in previous outfit Government Issue. Though Thompson would return to the ranks, it was a foretaste of things to come. A self-titled live album on the Your Choice Live Series label was cut at the Oberhaus in Alzey, Germany, in May 1990 – a final sonic souvenir of Dave's time in Scream.

Having tasted the authentic rock 'n' roll lifestyle and developed a taste for it, Dave then did something many might think was out of character: at the age of 20, he gave up drugs. He'd augmented weed with acid, which was 'fun for a while but gave me panic attacks.' His decision means he's 'one of the few people I know who hasn't done coke, speed or heroin.'

He'd later expound at greater length on his philosophy. 'I never fancied coke at all, because a friend of mine had a heart attack outside a 7-11 when he was 18 doing coke. So it's always been this evil, deadly drug – plus if I started doing it, I'm the kind of person who would just fucking blow every cent I had to shove the world up my nose, I'm hyperactive enough. I'm not one to preach to kids because I'd hate for anyone to tell me not to experiment with things.'

The newly straight Grohl was prepared for what came next. He'd long been a fan of the Melvins, who'd been a staple of his musical diet when in the Washington area. When they re-formed he started corresponding with guitarist Buzz Osbourne, and the pair were firm friends after meeting up on the same bill in San Francisco.

It was Buzz who alerted him to the fact that Nirvana were seeking to replace their drummer, Chad Channing. He had a copy of *Bleach* and, after a couple of days' consideration, made the call – only to be told the vacancy had been filled by Mudhoney's Dan Peters. But that union was clearly going nowhere, and the very same night saw Dave accept bassist Krist Novoselic's invitation to fly up to Seattle and audition. His drums were artfully packed in one large cardboard box. 'All I really had was a suitcase and my drums, anyway, so I took them up to Seattle and hoped it would work. It did.' The rest, as they say, is history.

The fact was that Scream were on their last legs anyway. Peter Stahl came back from the final tour to find himself potentially homeless thanks to an eviction notice. Bassist Skeeter left the ranks in mid-tour for a second time, putting their future in doubt. But Dave's defection made their demise doubly certain. In truth, the band had enough diehard fans to sell a few thousand records per year and stay on the road indefinitely – providing they could live on next to nothing. Hardly a sustainable lifestyle. A couple of major record labels 'came sniffing around,' said Grohl, 'but nothing ever happened.'

But strong bonds had been fostered over many miles of hard travelling, and opting out still felt like betrayal. When a magazine, some years later, asked Grohl what was the worst thing he'd ever done to someone, he revealed that the matter still troubled him. 'Probably when I left Scream to join Nirvana. It – it wasn't really screwing them over, but we were like brothers. We were on tour and broke up in LA when one of the members went home to DC without saying anything to anyone. So we were stuck. Fortunately, we had a Canadian roadie who was getting his unemployment cheques shipped down to LA, so we could buy beans and hot dogs. It was just a drag. Someone called and said Nirvana was looking for a drummer and they thought I was good. I had to leave my friends and move to Seattle. It was painful.'

He would have the option of salving his conscience later, however, by hiring Franz as Pat Smear's replacement in Foo Fighters. Certainly their relationship had been close, Dave reckoning that both Stahls had been 'like brothers' to him. And Franz would confess, 'My brightest moments playing music were with Dave.' Grohl gave a slightly different version of events to Q magazine in April 1992: 'We were staying in this house in Laurel Canyon with three mud-wrestling girls for a week and a half; we had two shows booked, and the guarantees were like for $100 a show. Then our bass player's girlfriend wired him $800 dollars over the telephone and he disappeared. He flew back to DC – end of band.'

It wasn't that Dave Grohl saw a gravy train in Nirvana; in fact, he admitted in 1997 that he 'wasn't the biggest fan in the world.' The fact they sounded a bit like the Melvins certainly counted in their favour. Nevertheless he thought *Bleach* was 'pretty cool', being attracted by its 'really hilarious' lyrics. At the time he headed for Seattle he had yet to see them play, though guitarist/leader Kurt Cobain and Novoselic had caught a Scream show in San Francisco and were apparently highly impressed with his performance behind the traps.

He remedied the situation by catching a Nirvana show, playing to an audience of 2000 – rather more than Scream had been attracting. But what impressed Dave most was that they 'weren't punk rock kids. Kurt would say, "The next song is called 'About a Girl'," and the place would freak out.' He was impressed, it was safe to say, and the idea that he would be able to afford to smoke two packets of cigarettes a day and collapse into his own bed sold it. 'With Scream,' he explained, 'I was sleeping in the van, on floors.'

The fanzine *Backlash* had been first to give Nirvana the oxygen of publicity back in August 1988. It was probably fitting that Nirvana also featured in the last ever issue, in March 1991, when editor Dawn Anderson and photographer James Bush came to find out the story behind Dave's recruitment and the band's plans now they had signed to the mighty Geffen Records' 'alternative' DGC imprint. The pair showed up at Kurt's house at two in the afternoon, only to find him asleep in his clothes. Krist roused him and the interview was conducted with Nirvana's mainman, if not in his pyjamas, then certainly in a less than photogenic state.

The newly arrived Dave more than contributed to the four-way conversation. He first explained the transition to Nirvana from Scream. 'The [Scream] tour sucked, we weren't making very much money and the bass player started getting back together with his girlfriend over the phone. We woke up one morning and he had gone; she wired him money and he flew home. So we were stuck in Hollywood. Then I talked to Buzz from the Melvins and he said: "I think Nirvana may call you because they need a drummer." They didn't call so I called them. And I've been playing with them ever since.'

*   *   *

So what kind of band was Dave joining? To better understand Nirvana's pre-Grohl history, you have to go back to Aberdeen –

not Scotland, but a small town on America's northwest coast so boring that spray-painting obscenities on the wall was the highlight of the week – where Kurt Cobain and Krist Novoselic got together.

Kurt had graduated with honours from six-year-old John Lennon fan to 17-year-old runaway, sleeping rough by night and living in the public library all day (it certainly helped his lyrics). His parents divorced when he was eight, and he spent much of his youth with his mother, relatives or friends – something of a loner, by all accounts.

Guitar and drum lessons gave him an outlet for his restless energy and, in retrospect, put him on the path to rock stardom, while his listening habits ranged from the heavy – Led Zeppelin, Kiss and Aerosmith – to the new-wave punk of the Sex Pistols and Black Flag. Meanwhile he kept body and soul together by taking low-paid 'McJobs'; being a lifeguard at the local swimming pool was one of the few pre-fame jobs it seems he actually liked. The parallels with Dave Grohl were clear.

In all honesty the American northwest is no great shakes to grow up in. The grey skies and constant rain resemble Manchester, England, where Joy Division first got together – and the bleakness of much of Washington State is hardly more optimistic. Director David Lynch shot that blackest of soap operas, *Twin Peaks*, in the hills around North Bend and Snoqualmie. The other rather sinister fact the area is associated with is that it was the killing ground of serial killer Ted Bundy.

Then, of course, there was the famed high school scene where men aren't just men but sportsmen. It would have been hard for Kurt, a scrawny, unathletic kid, to mix it with the macho gridiron types. 'I decided at seven,' he later revealed, 'that all my surroundings sucked, that there was no sign of anybody who would be into art or music.' Becoming a rock star became his ambition because 'that would be my payback to all the jocks who got girlfriends all the time.'

But when *Rolling Stone* sent writer Michael Azerrad – later to become Nirvana's official biographer – to Aberdeen to research a cover story in 1992, Azerrad found some interesting characters. Raising the subject of Nirvana in a local bar, two of his drinking companions mused at length on whether the singer was homosexual – a 'faggot', in their words. One of them went further. 'We deal with faggots here,' he stated unapologetically. 'We run 'em out of town.' With such attitudes the rule rather than the exception, it's unsurprising that Kurt – an artistic soul who lived for painting and drawing as well as music – felt constrained.

Kurt was apparently an uncontrollable teen who, after dropping out of high school, worked as janitor or maintenance man and delighted in enraging Aberdeen's elders by spray-painting slogans like 'God is gay' (a phrase that later cropped up in the song 'Stay Away') on their cars.

It was while roadying for local band the Melvins that Kurt ran into 6' 7" teenager Krist Novoselic, two years his senior, whose family hailed from Croatia (then part of Yugoslavia). The gangling youth had moved to Aberdeen from his birthplace of Compton, California, in 1979. His roots made him an outsider, as Kurt himself had become, and the two joined forces – initially to play the local bars for beer money. 'I started Nirvana, because there was nothing else left to do. I didn't like sports, so a band seemed to be the last resort for something to do socially.'

It may have started as something for fellow teen spirits to occupy their time, but Cobain and Novoselic were soon applying a musician's yardstick in an attempt to find a drummer they were happy with. Original choice Aaron

Burckhard was replaced by Dale Crover – but since he was also a member of the Melvins, they had to replace him with Dave Foster.

Foster was the man in possession when they played their first gig in public on 24 April 1988 at the Vogue, but resigned his position soon afterwards when he lost his driving licence – a liability for someone with a kit to transport. Aaron Burckhard was allowed a second chance but seemingly hadn't improved, as an advert soon appeared in local magazine, *The Rocket*, seeking a drummer who could 'play hard, sometimes light, underground, versatile, fast, medium, slow, versatile, serious, heavy, versatile, dorky, nirvana, hungry.'

Enter Chad Channing, previously of the band Tick-Dolly-Row, with whom Nirvana had shared a stage. He was the occupant of the drum stool when, in the summer of 1988, they cut their first single: 'Love Buzz', a song originally found on the B-side of a 1970 Number One, 'Venus', by Dutch group Shocking Blue. They discovered it in their parents' record collection one crazy evening, but no one from Amsterdam to Aberdeen would have recognised the result.

A Seattle record label, Sub Pop, had found success releasing records by loud rock bands Green River and Soundgarden, and when the label heard a tape by the early Nirvana they decided to take a chance and record them for their 'Singles Club' series of releases. The flip side, 'Big Cheese', was rough, raunchy and a taster of delights to come.

Nirvana cut their first album, *Bleach*, for just $606 – the self-proclaimed idea that you should 'get the fuck out of the studio before you're sick of the songs' resulting in some fabulously spontaneous first-takes. The album sold 30,000 copies – small by worldwide standards but enough to help them get a foothold on the college live circuit. But by the time Nirvana headed out onto the US tour trail in June 1989, second guitarist Jason Everman had been dropped, to resurface as bassist with Soundgarden. It's said he contributed the money for the recording, though he didn't actually appear on the album.

The album was an object lesson in 'less is more', the songs shining through despite being sparsely produced. Kurt (his name was spelled Kurdt on the sleeve) clearly had a complete vision before he went into the studio, and both the songs and their performance reflect this. When released in June 1989, *Bleach* was described by its author as 'Black Sabbath playing the Knack, Black Flag, Led Zeppelin and the Stooges with a pinch of Bay City Rollers.' The same Cobain-penned press release cited divorce, drugs and cult 1960s TV cartoon show Marine Boy as other crucial influences. He also jokingly criticised the indie scene, claiming it was playing to the interests of commercial labels. 'Do we want to change this?' he continued. 'No way! We want to cash in and suck butts up to the big wigs in the hope that we too can get high...'

Each of the 13 songs on *Bleach* had something to say, the gritty 'Blew' and melancholy 'About a Girl' among the highlights. The single 'Sliver' found Kurt baring his soul on his parents' divorce and its shattering effect on his young life. Songs like 'School' and 'Negative Creep' introduced yet more fans to the patented Cobain scream, and it was his voice as much as his incendiary guitar playing that made Nirvana's sound so gut-wrenchingly exciting. Yet there were already reservations about drummer Channing. Indeed, it was said that the reason two tracks, 'Paper Cuts' and 'Floyd', had been retained from earlier sessions with his predecessor, Dale Crover, was because they felt the drumming was superior.

Bleach was released in mid-June to complimentary reviews. ('So primitive they make Mudhoney sound like Genesis,' said *New Musical Express*.) But as the sales and hype rose, cash-flow problems at Sub Pop threatened to sink the label. They were being forced to pay out for pressing before sales money was received and thus had to postpone recording projects and offer bands future royalties instead of immediate payment. T-shirts reading 'What part of "We have no money" don't you understand?' were part of their marketing.

Founders Jonathan Poneman and Bruce Pavitt had a great ear for music but were no businessmen. 'It was sheer dumb luck that people kept giving them a whole bunch of money,' said journalist Everett True, an early chronicler of the Seattle scene. At one point, a wired, overwrought Cobain came storming into Sub Pop offices demanding to see more money and, in lieu of cash, started hauling away boxes of albums. His attitude was part of a repeating pattern where he would become paranoid and distrust those who had helped him. 'We weren't being promoted very well,' he'd later complain, adding: 'I challenge anybody to find a *Bleach* ad.' The situation was far from stable.

Nirvana have often been described as godfathers of grunge. But what exactly is/was grunge? The term (describing loud, distorted, punk-influenced rock) had been coined by Mark McLaughlin, better known as singer Mark Arm. A native of Aberdeen like Kurt, he had 'invented' grunge while writing for a Seattle fanzine in the early 1980s and, with groups Green River and, later, Sub Pop act Mudhoney, he did much to popularise it. Kurt apparently idolised him, but the feeling was more or less one way. However, to be termed a 'grunge' band at the start of things would not have been perceived as anything other than a compliment.

Grunge's potential audience in Britain grew out of press coverage of summer 1989's Lamefest, promoted by Sub Pop. The label had paid for plane tickets to bring over some British journalists who obligingly returned with tales of the 'next big thing'. Kurt was typically dismissive of the 'flattering hype from multiple occupational English journalists that catapulted the Sub Pop regime to instant fame.' And while Nirvana themselves were described as 'guys who, if they weren't doing this, would be working in a supermarket or lumber yard or fixing cars,' they would nevertheless soon reap the reward of their Sub Pop connections when they first visited Britain as part of the label's roadshow.

The original audience Nirvana attracted bought into the image and lifestyle as much as the music: this was just as well, for it was often only T-shirt sales that gave the band their essential 'gas money' to get home after a gig. Dave Grohl was hardly in awe of his new bandmates. If anything, the opposite was true. 'Everybody out there worshipped Washington. When I went up there to meet with Kurt, the first thing he says to me is "Wow, you're from Washington. Did you get to see [DC punk bands] Minor Threat and Rites of Spring?" It was weird after that to see what people made of Seattle and that scene. As far as I'm concerned, all that had already happened in DC.' But after joining the ranks in late 1990, Dave Grohl was to have a major hand in what happened next.

THE *NEVERMIND* PHENOMENON

S o why exactly did Chad Channing leave through the same revolving door that propelled Dave into the Nirvana ranks? In point of fact, it didn't quite happen like that. The Melvins' Dale Crover (again) and Mudhoney's Dan Peters were used as musical band-aids to ensure the relentless gig schedule continued, suggesting that the parting of the ways had been less than premeditated. It's said that Peters learned of his replacement when Kurt injudiciously let the news slip on the local KAOS radio station.

Kurt, having been a drummer himself in the past, had increasingly instructed Chad what to play, while *Bleach* producer Jack Endino felt he had never adequately filled the shoes of Dale Crover: 'When Chad first joined the band he had to sweat it a little bit; it took him a while to get into the groove of it.' The 'Love Buzz' single required a good deal of production trickery to overcome the fact that 'he wasn't hitting very hard ... he was barely touching the drums.'

Channing had, however, improved by the time *Bleach* was recorded, and appeared on the demos for *Nevermind*. The only difference, according to Endino, between these and the finished article in percussion terms was that 'Dave was a much harder hitter ... than almost anybody. He's an amazing drummer ... so what are you going to do?'

In Michael Azerrad's *Come As You Are*, the officially sanctioned Nirvana biography, Chad expressed the feeling that he wanted to participate more in proceedings 'and become part of what was going on ... it was then I realised that it really is Kurt's show, and that what he says goes and that's it, no questions asked.' Chad lived on Bainbridge Island, a 35-minute ferry trip from downtown Seattle, and Kurt and Krist did the decent thing and gave him the bad news personally. Krist apparently did most of the talking, but it was left to Kurt, after the final farewell hugs, to voice their joint feeling: 'I feel like I just killed somebody.'

The departing drummer, who could also play violin, bass and guitar, had begun to have songwriting aspirations – clearly a no-no in a band that was in that respect a dictatorship. (Kurt had taunted Channing for liking 'elfin music ... you just kind of shudder because it's so stupid and dorky.') That said, his temporary replacement Peters had played on 'Sliver' and, by Kurt's account, helped write it: 'I'm really glad he did, because I love that song!' He also described Peters as 'rhythmically competent', but the fit between them 'wasn't quite perfect.'

Peters had been about to leave for a tour with Mudhoney, and the trio happened to be at Reciprocal Studios where Tad were recording in July 1990. 'Half an hour after they finished we went in there, used their equipment and recorded the song ('Sliver').' Krist was delighted at the spontaneity. 'We jumped right in there and recorded it ... the song gelled together.'

Something else that worked against Peters as a permanent drummer was his preference for a small kit. This didn't sit well with the other two noisemakers, who actually bought him a large but disreputable kit to replace his own: he kept only the bass drum. The writing was on the wall. Besides, as Krist said, 'If he was going to join our band that would be the end of Mudhoney – and we didn't want to be responsible for that.'

The first meeting between Cobain and Grohl, Nirvana's latest and likely short-lived drummer, was less than auspicious – and the same would apply to their second. The pair had first clapped eyes on one another at a party in Olympia where Kurt's then-girlfriend, Tobi Vail, had been one of the entertainments. Dave obviously felt her set contained little of value as he cut it short with a tape of the band Primus, which he brought in from his car. Unfortunately, he compounded the error by boasting to Cobain about it when the pair talked on the phone later. Kurt had not taken to the members of Scream he saw at the party, calling them 'real rocker dudes, assholes.'

Several months then elapsed before Grohl and Cobain met again, this time in Seattle, at the Sea-Tac venue where Scream were appearing. The gregarious Grohl gave Kurt an apple, but his offer was declined because 'It will make my teeth bleed!' Kurt chipped in that they'd been looking for someone to sing harmonies for some while, explaining that Chad Channing's style was too jazzy: 'He'd switch to a heavier thing with us, but still he couldn't do it natural.'

Dave, averred Krist, 'plays some damn fine drums.' Producer Butch Vig, a drummer himself, discerned problems when the band entered the studios to demo *Nevermind*: 'I could tell that Kurt wasn't too pleased with Chad's drumming because he kept going and getting behind the kit showing him how to play things.'

As mentioned, Grohl also had the advantage of being able and willing to open his mouth and contribute on the singing front. 'I think one of the reasons they wanted me was that I sang backup vocals,' he later said, 'but I don't remember them saying "You're in the band."'

Dave began his life with Nirvana as a house guest of Krist and Shelli Novoselic in Tacoma. He then moved in with Kurt at his Olympia flat for some eight months, a period when he worked hard to bring the turtle-loving guitarist out of his shell. Even so, there were times when 'we would sit in this tiny shoebox apartment for eight hours at a time without saying a word.' Other times they'd waste away the days shooting a BB gun in the backyard or heading downtown to see a cheap 99-cent movie.

Kurt's mood was not improved by his break-up with girlfriend Tobi Vail, his silent periods becoming more and more prolonged. Dave was worried about his flatmate until Kurt broke the silence on the drive home from a rehearsal to explain that he wasn't always this quiet and that he would soon recover from the split. He had certainly thrown himself into rehearsals, and the band's habit of playing from ten at night to one in the morning every day for months would pay off in terms of their musical tightness and creating songs. Unfortunately, they neglected to keep tapes of many of the latter, and Dave believes that '30 or 40 songs we had written are just gone.'

Dave's bed was the couch and his staple diet corn dogs from a convenience store down the street, which sold them at three for 99 cents. 'I lived on them for a year,' he revealed, while Kurt (whose bedroom lay en route to the bathroom) recalled with feeling that 'It kept him regular, too!' Kurt would write songs and poetry every night before going to sleep, and would retire to his room and scribble for hours and hours before turning out his light.

While Dave Grohl's post-Nirvana writing has been examined for references to his flatmate-cum-bandmate, it would be 2005 before he admitted to any such inspiration. The song, 'Friend of a Friend' from the *In Your Honour* double album, was written during the period before the band made it, and referred to someone who needed a 'quiet room / with a lock to keep him in' and who had never been in love 'but knows just what love is'. The lyric even contains the phrase 'he says nevermind'.

Grohl marked the song's release by recalling those cold, lonely days in conversation with *Independent* journalist Craig McLean. 'God it was quiet. I had nothing better to do than think with a guitar in my lap. And it was a dark, rainy winter. The sun would come up at 8.30 in the morning, and go down at two in the afternoon, and those were the hours I slept. I didn't see daylight for months. It was fucking depressing. Of any song that I've ever written, 'Friend of a Friend' is most blatantly about my time in Nirvana. I wrote the song about Krist and Kurt and me. I don't even think I ever played it for them. It was just one of those things. And, we needed one more song for the [*In Your Honour*] acoustic record.'

The first gig of what would become the definitive Nirvana line-up took place on 11 October 1990 at the tiny North Shore Surf Club in Olympia. 'The venue was down the street from where Kurt and I lived,' Grohl recalls. 'We sound-checked and I went to get something to eat. When I got back there was a line around the block. I called my mother and said, "Mother, there's at least 200 people in line!" I was amazed. With Scream, the band usually outnumbered the audience.'

Grohl, a man whose pre-gig nerves are legendary in the rock biz, was no less nervous about things when he finally got on stage. 'I didn't know anyone – no one in the audience, no one in the band. I was completely on my own. That was the only thing that mattered, that hour on stage. That's what I was focused on.' They kept blowing the power, but the audience response made up for any frustration.

And after it Kurt confirmed that he was pleased with the performance of someone he'd termed 'a baby Dale Crover ... with a few years' practice he may even give him a run for his money. He's the drummer of our dreams.' The newcomer showed his commitment by breaking his snare drum, a trophy Kurt then proudly displayed to the sold-out audience. Little wonder he recounted in his journal that 'This new kid on the block can't dance as good as your MTV favorites, but he beats the drums like he's beating the shit out of their heads!'

Musically, Dave was into the super-heavy likes of DRI, Corrosion of Conformity, Motörhead and Slayer, influences that came out over a decade later in his Probot project. Kurt and Krist shared his passion for innovative, extreme Swiss heavy metal group Celtic Frost, but other tastes in common went further back. 'No one realises that the people who made *Nevermind* were totally into Flipper and the Butthole Surfers,' Dave says. 'That was the music we grew up with and it didn't necessarily surface in Nirvana's music but the spirit was there. We all grew up listening to the same stuff. It was one of the first conversations I had with Kurt. From Celtic Frost to Neil Young to Public Enemy, we all loved the same music.'

But there was frustration in the fact that everybody moved slowly – too slowly for Dave. 'When I joined the band,' Grohl says, 'I came from a hardcore band that toured as much as possible, six to eight months a year, because we didn't want to come home and get day jobs. When I joined Nirvana, there was no touring for the first eight months. All we did was rehearse and write songs. I thought, "What have I joined?"'

Actually, that wasn't quite true. Dave ventured back to Europe for the second time as a working musician just a month after joining Nirvana when the band teamed up with L7 for a UK tour. The day before they arrived, no one yet knew what name was to be written on the work permit. Maybe they planned to write the name of the band's fourth drummer in a year in pencil in case yet another change took place.

Not only would Dave and his great good humour confound such negative thoughts, he also made his first recording with the band, courtesy of Radio 1's legendary John Peel inviting them to record a 'session'. This took place at the BBC's Maida Vale studios, where 'D7', 'Molly's Lips', 'Son of a Gun' and 'Turnaround' were committed to tape.

At this point, Dave was understandably still feeling his way into the set, and Kurt was reportedly witnessed coaching him through the songs before the final takes. Even so, the results were good enough for the versions of 'Molly's Lips' and 'Son of a Gun' to be issued on the *Incesticide* compilation.

Typically perhaps, the two tracks just mentioned were not even Nirvana songs but cover versions of numbers by little-known Scottish quartet the Vaselines. Formed in Edinburgh in 1987 by singers/guitarists Eugene Kelly and Frances McKee, they were much influenced by the Velvet Underground. The band split the same week their sole studio LP, 1989's 'Dum Dum', was released via Rough Trade, although the following year the original lineup briefly reunited to open for Nirvana in Edinburgh. As well as 'Molly's Lips' and 'Son of a Gun', Nirvana would perform 'Jesus Doesn't Want Me for a Sunbeam' on their 1994 *MTV Unplugged* appearance, while, even before that, Nirvana-inspired interest in the band would result in a 1992 Sub Pop compilation of their official recordings.

It might have been thought the choice of another band's songs would add to Dave's frustration – but as he admitted later, the versions Nirvana recorded sounded nothing like the originals at all. 'Having never heard any of the records until we came out of the studio, I had no choice but to drum and sing the backing vocals my way rather than theirs. But the Vaselines themselves said that they enjoyed what we'd done to their material and that was quite a thrill. I'd like more covers in our live set, but Kurt has problems remembering the words to most of them.'

The pioneering Peel had a deserved reputation for giving air time to ground-breaking bands, having single-handedly broken the Ramones back in 1976 before punk took off in Britain. He had already aired a session by the Chad Channing line-up in late 1989, and this session, broadcast in early November, was the second of four BBC recordings they made – three for John Peel, one for Mark Goodier.

Though they were supposedly promoting a single, 'Sliver', recorded before Dave had joined the ranks, its absence from the Peel Session was some indication of the importance that task was accorded. It was the rapport Nirvana struck up with the UK music press that would prove of greater significance in the months and years to come. Ironically, the local tour manager, one Alex Macleod, had handled Scream's European tour: though he and Dave didn't hit it off on that occasion, they managed to co-exist reasonably happily.

Dave recalls going to see the Pixies at Brixton Academy while he was in London. 'They opened with 'Debaser'. It was the first time a song had made me so happy that I started crying ... it lit some sort of fuse in me.' Kurt's fuse was obviously a short one, as Nirvana's appearance at a London Sub Pop showcase in a slightly more compact venue saw four guitars trashed in just half an hour. By all accounts it was a triumphant performance, *Melody Maker* offering alternative descriptions of the band, as either 'Hüsker Dü tuning up', or 'The Kinks with a headache.'

The Sub Pop label was still staggering under the weight of cash-flow problems, so with Nirvana gathering press attention like flies round waste matter a change of label was clearly on the cards. The UK shows were attended by many A&R men eager to run the rule over one of the hottest unsigned bands in the world.

Now defunct music weekly *Melody Maker*, who turned out to be Nirvana's staunchest supporters in the UK, were quick to send a journalist to their London hotel before a date at the Astoria in Charing Cross Road. Unusually it wasn't Everett True, Kurt's pal and a former musician who had introduced the Seattle scene to a UK audience, but someone known as Push. He listened intently while Kurt expounded on the abilities of the band's latest recruit.

'It wasn't that we were unhappy with Dan [Peters'] drumming,' he explained. 'It was just that Dave has qualities which match our needs a little closer. He takes care of backing vocals, for a start. We were blown away by him when we saw him playing with this band Scream a few months ago and Krist and I agreed we'd ask him to join Nirvana if ever we had the chance; ironically that chance came just weeks after we got Danny in.'

Dave was quite careful at this stage to speak only when he was spoken to, and not to presume too much of his new position; given the band's record of keeping drummers, he was perhaps sensible. Even in 2003, he'd claim that 'The only surviving member of Nirvana is Krist Novoselic,' reasoning that the bassist was the only one of the two of them who had been at every gig the band ever played.

Once returned from Britain, the courting of Nirvana by the major record companies became quite an amusing scenario. A few years before, Guns N'Roses had spun out this aspect of their musical life to ridiculous extremes, as they couldn't afford to feed themselves; Nirvana reacted similarly. Kurt happily chowed down on the expensive food provided to the detriment of the conversation, while Krist was inclined to get a little merry.

Dave, who guiltily felt the band were 'getting away with something', simply enquired after the A&R men's backgrounds in an attempt to ingratiate himself. 'Every one of them had worked at Tower Records,' he laughed. But guilt at eating into their expense accounts was quickly replaced by humour when he recycled their business cards to 'lounge bands all over Tacoma' who had the erroneous impression he was the individual on the card. One can only guess at some of the subsequent conversations after Dave had invited the hapless musicians to 'give me a call'.

One of the band's most assiduous suitors was David Geffen, the man behind the mega-platinum success of bands from the Eagles to Guns N'Roses. Having started a new imprint, DGC, to corner the alternative rock market, he needed to find a third world-beater to rank with his previous successes and start the label off with a bang. They already had Sonic Youth, but Nirvana were potentially even bigger.

The 'transfer fee' of $75,000 not only helped Sub Pop out of a potential cash crisis – two record sleeve designs had attracted unwelcome legal action which was tying up their time and resources – but they retained the promise of future income in the shape of royalties on the next two albums and a logo on the cover.

The deal satisfied Kurt on two counts: his loyalty to Sub Pop might not have let him sever the ties so conclusively (indeed, Mudhoney stayed with the label for another album), yet he could now get his music to a far larger potential listenership. He may not have liked Guns N'Roses – the two groups famously came to blows backstage at the 1992 MTV Video Music Awards – but he was undoubtedly impressed by the size of their audiences.

Yet he wasn't going to turn his back on deserving musical causes – not by a long way. A final 'thank you' to Sub Pop came in the shape of a 7-inch single, a live 'Molly's Lips', as well as a contribution to an eponymous compilation by the Olympia indie label Kill Rock Stars.

Signing with Geffen in January 1991, the band members were to be put on a wage until the advance of $287,000 came through. Yet because they'd fallen in with Sonic Youth's management company, Gold Mountain, who had plenty of savvy, their contract favoured a higher royalty rate instead of the maximum possible advance – a tactic that would prove a far-sighted one.

You'd think that Dave would have been able to supplement corn dogs with a more balanced diet, but the truth was the group were dirt poor and had to pawn their belongings to get by. Dave recalls going downtown to sell T-shirts to the Positively Fourth Street record store – success on the mission meant he could give corn dogs a miss in favour of the more luxurious Hungry Man Dinner! But when Dave went down to Los Angeles to hang out with friends L7 at a Rock For Choice benefit gig (he had started a relationship with their bass player, Jennifer Finch), he didn't have enough money to get back and had to ask Krist to wire him some.

That was when he first learned that Kurt had started experimenting with hard drugs – the heroin habit that would cause him so much trouble and contribute to his fatal unhappiness. Dave couldn't believe what he was hearing down the phone and the subject came up again when he returned. Kurt said he hadn't enjoyed it and wouldn't do it again; Dave believed him. His analogy was that of a kid putting a firework up a cat's backside 'for the hell of it', to see what happened. Krist, too, felt Kurt was 'playing with dynamite' and openly preached against the habit. If he wanted an escape from his existence, things were about to change ... couldn't he see that?

Something else that was about to change was Kurt's love life. Dave was the go-between in the early stages of Kurt's romance with Courtney Love, as she was a friend of Jennifer Finch. (The pair had briefly been in a band together with Kat

Bjelland of Babes In Toyland fame called Sugar Baby Doll.)
Dave had talked to her on the phone and enjoyed the
experience, so when Courtney revealed she had a crush on
Kurt – whom she'd met when Nirvana opened for the Dharma
Bums in Portland, Oregon in 1988 – he could reveal that it was
reciprocated.

Courtney, who thought Kurt was 'passionate and cute, but I
couldn't tell if he was smart, or had any integrity,' gave Dave a
heart-shaped box (later immortalised in song) to pass on to his
friend, so that when the pair met in person at a Butthole
Surfers show in June 1991 the stage was set for romance.
Having just come out of a relationship, however, Kurt decided
that he would concentrate his energies on the forthcoming
album, so they would not meet again until the Reading
Festival in August.

Kurt told gay magazine *The Advocate* in 1993 that Krist and
Dave liked Courtney before he did. 'During that time I knew
that I liked her a lot, but I wouldn't admit it. She and Dave
were really good friends – I shouldn't say this, but they
almost wanted to get together for a time. When we were on
tour in Europe some of our shows collided with Hole shows,
and Courtney would hang out on the bus with us, and Krist
and Courtney were really good friends. And it hasn't changed
at all.'

The sessions for *Nevermind*, for which Dave had specially
purchased a loud brass snare drum nicknamed 'the
Terminator', took place in May and June 1991 at Sound City
Studios in Van Nuys, California. Recording was a relaxed
affair. Krist recalls that they 'slept every day, then lay on the
couch and played pinball,' while, according to Kurt, 'We
downed a lot of hypodermic cough syrup and Jack Daniels,
and just lounged in the recreation area of the studio for days
on end, writing down a few lyrics here and there.'

In truth, the words were 'an accumulation of two years of poetry – I picked out good lines, cut up things.' As well as the obvious 'Teen Spirit', 'Polly', 'Lithium' and the bittersweet 'Come As You Are' were three more highlights, while a surprise track – 'Endless, Nameless', hidden ten minutes after the last listed track on all but the initial batch of copies pressed – featured Kurt smashing his axe, just like on stage. Interestingly, it was assumed by the band and the record company that 'Come As You Are' had the best chance of crossing over into the mass market.

As it transpired, 'Teen Spirit' did the job and 'Come As You Are' was the follow-up. But behind the scenes, Kurt's health was causing concern. He suffered perennial stomach pains, never properly diagnosed, which would eventually prevent Nirvana from touring in support of *Nevermind* (then at Number One). The band's behaviour generally was so erratic they even got kicked out of the album launch party held in a Seattle club, which degenerated into a food fight.

Producer Butch Vig had just completed the Smashing Pumpkins' *Gish* and was selected ahead of Don Dixon and Scott Litt, both of whom had produced REM, and David Briggs, who helmed several classic Neil Young albums. Vig, who'd later perform as a drummer himself with the band Garbage, had seen Nirvana before but never with new member Dave Grohl. He was soon convinced.

The summer of 1991 found Nirvana on tour with Sonic Youth, giving Dave his first taste of European festivals. And he enjoyed the experience, largely due to his label mates. 'Every day we were fortunate enough to see Sonic Youth run through all their best songs – at the time, 'Kool Thing', 'Schizophrenia'. It was a virtual greatest hits, every day, out in the rain. I loved it. I think the very first one was that Pukkelpop thing in Belgium. We went on at 11 o'clock in the morning; the Ramones headlined. It was great.'

Dave wasn't much of a drinker and paid little heed to the bottles of Glenfiddich and vodka supplied at every show – and usually accounted for by Krist and Kurt respectively. But the performance of 'Polly', for which his services were not required, gave him the chance to acquaint himself with a bottle of the finest red, should he so desire.

Nirvana arrived at the Reading Festival on 23 August to play the opening (Friday) night as the 'next big thing' – signed by David Geffen and about to be part of a multi-million dollar marketing campaign, yet with their forthcoming album still unheard. They could have been shot down in flames, but returned westwards with the cheers of public and critics alike ringing in their ears. Kurt's final act was to leap into Dave's drum kit, dislocating his shoulder. Plans were immediately made to rebook them, and they would duly return to headline the following year.

If popularity was a double-edged sword for Kurt Cobain, it was his bandmate Krist Novoselic who put his finger on the problem. 'We've always treated people with that mentality with a little bit of contempt and cynicism,' he said of the 'Guns N'Roses kids' who, Kurt now saw with dismay, were getting into their music. 'To have them screaming for us ... why are they screaming? What do they see in us? They're exactly the same kind of people who wanted to kick our ass in high school.' He was understandably appalled, too, to learn that a group of so-called fans had carried out a gang rape while singing 'Polly', his story of a girl hitch-hiker who was brutally assaulted.

But you can't pick and choose your audience, particularly when it grows with such unexpected speed. Anton Brookes of Bad Moon, Nirvana's UK press agents, recalls the period when US audiences 'got' Nirvana as their 1991 tour with Pearl Jam and the Red Hot Chili Peppers: 'When they played 'Teen

Spirit' there was a euphoric roar when they got to the quiet verses, and that had never happened before in the smaller venues. They'd gone to another level.'

During the recording of *Nevermind*, Dave apparently hit the drums so hard that the heads had to be replaced after every second song. Comparisons between the final recordings and the demos cut at Smart studios with Chad Channing show remarkably little difference but for the force with which the parts are played. Dave admits his predecessor came up with some 'really cool stuff', even if he wasn't the most solid or consistent sticksman.

Producer Butch Vig agreed with Cobain and Novoselic that the band had found their ideal drummer: 'Grohl is incredibly loud and rock solid. One of the best drummers I've ever worked with.' Referring to Sound City studios in Van Nuys, California, where *Nevermind* was recorded, Vig said: 'I'm a drummer so I'm very particular about drum sounds. The studio had a great big tracking room, which would help us get a good live drum sound.'

Dave's aim was certainly not perfection, the struggle for which he rates as 'the biggest problem with recording today. So much music lacks character, charisma and personality because people are too concerned with making things as glossy and glittery as they can get. For example, Pro Tools and digital editing have almost destroyed the things that I loved about drummers from the 1960s and 1970s. The legendary drummers – whether you're talking about Buddy Rich, Gene Krupa, John Bonham, or Keith Moon – were famous for having their own feel, which meant they weren't perfect metronomes. It was nice to hear John Bonham's laziness or Keith Moon's sloppy aggression – or even their drunken drum fills. That stuff sounded cool ... Perfect metronomic time really detracts from the overall feel of a song.'

The explosive drumming on 'Smells Like Teen Spirit' was driven by an argument between Grohl and Cobain. According to Vig, 'For some reason Kurt really got on Dave's case and pissed him off.' Grohl's resultant angry flailing powered the track. Cobain, a bit of a drummer himself, had definite ideas as to what he wanted, and this could prove a stumbling block to progress. 'If you ever looked at his jaw, he would be moving his jaw back and forth just like he was playing the drums with his teeth,' Dave observed to *Rolling Stone* magazine's David Fricke. 'He heard in his head what he wanted from a rhythm and that's a hard thing to articulate.'

Dave's all-or-nothing approach caused a problem with the recording of the almost folky 'Something in the Way', the most recently written song on the album and its official closer. Bass and drums were added to Cobain's gentle acoustic guitar and vocal performance, but Dave, in producer Vig's words, had constantly to be reminded to 'play wimpy'. Said Vig: 'It almost killed him to tap his way through.'

About a week before *Nevermind* was officially released, Nirvana played a show supporting the album at the Beehive, a small record store in their hometown of Seattle. When the Red Hot Chili Peppers had played an in-store performance there, about 150 people showed up. But the buzz on the first major label release from Nirvana was so strong that fans were lining up at 2.00 pm for a 7.00 pm show. By 4.00 pm, about 300 kids had somehow packed into the tiny store and another 200 were milling about outside.

After fortifying themselves with a few locally-brewed Ranier beers, Dave, Kurt and Krist headed into the Beehive and, by all accounts, gave an unexpectedly amazing performance. Even through a crude record store sound system and with a microphone that kept slipping from the stand, Nirvana put forth a show that was ferocious and passionate.

In early shows, Cobain's delivery had been a grab bag, swinging between a British rocker and a drunken Elvis, but now he had found his true voice and it was a killer, able to deliver raspy and bloodcurdling screams in a thrashing rocker or drop to more intimate tones in a ballad without going off-key. Needless to say, Dave's powerhouse drumming nailed everything down perfectly.

The arrival of *Nevermind* in September 1991 hit the rock world with the force of a hurricane. *Vox* magazine was typical in stating that, on this showing alone, Nirvana were 'the first truly inspired band of the 1990s.' The reason? 'An album that looks set to catapult the Seattle trio into the big time without alienating their hard-core following.' *Q* magazine described *Nevermind* as a 'guitar-heavy blend of bubblegum punk' and praised Cobain's 'skilful intermingling of Stooges-style brute yobbism (grinding guitars and yelping vocals), American punk and late 1970s art-rock'.

The biggest advocate of Nirvana and the Seattle scene was, surprisingly enough, a British journalist. Everett True of *Melody Maker* had been flown across to see Nirvana at the University of Washington in February 1989 ('they were CRAP') and was instrumental in making sure that Britain was 'the first country to pick up on the Sub Pop revolution.' He also claims to be the man who introduced Kurt Cobain to Courtney Love. He even planned to write a book with Kurt 'but thought I'd leave it until he became less famous ... oops!'

True it was who immediately fingered 'Teen Spirit' as 'single of the year, in case you were wondering how to fill in those readers' polls' when he reviewed it for *Melody Maker* in September 1991. Unlike when he gave the same honour to 'Love Buzz' many months before, it was the first of many ecstatic reviews for a single and album in which Nirvana 'hammered melody to fury', as Seattle writer Grant Alden put it. It also ensured that they eclipsed Mudhoney, whom the critics (including True) had unanimously considered the Seattle band most likely to succeed.

Some journalists figured Nirvana were the figureheads of grunge, while others felt that with *Nevermind* they transcended the genre. Fashion-wise, the retail business seized on the Cobain 'non-image', and plaid workshirts, striped jumpers and shredded jeans were suddenly flooding the high streets as a new 'grunge look'. As Cobain tried to subvert this trend with granddad cardigans and even cross-dressing, so he seemed to attract more column inches as the 'celebrity du jour'.

For Dave Grohl, still toting his shoulder-length hair, it was one big laugh. 'We were scamming the world. How on earth could anyone think that we deserved to be this huge band ... Have you seen us live? It was funny. All of that – MTV, magazines, critics' choice – was all irrelevant. All that was important was the three of us playing music. And I don't think we wrote one bad song. Everything we did when we were together was fucking great.'

Despite the change of label, Dave thought the new album 'would be like another successful independent record vibe. I didn't think it would be that much different to *Bleach* – just a progression.' Events suggested he got that one all wrong. *Nevermind* enjoyed a truly meteoric rise, entering the US charts on its September 1991 release at a more than respectable Number 144. The next week saw it move up to 109, then 65 and into the all-important Top 50 at 35. Three weeks later, it was poised at Number Four, its progress boosted by MTV's heavy rotation of first single 'Smells Like Teen Spirit', a track of which alt.country star Ryan Adams memorably said: 'If you're in a bar and it comes on, if you don't air guitar by accident, you're thinking about it.'

Nevermind intrigued even before you heard it: the cover picture of a naked baby in a swimming pool, about to make a grab for a dollar bill dangling on a fish-hook, offered a mind-blowing image of corrupted innocence. (Ironically a minor furore broke out when it was pointed out the baby's penis could be seen – band and record company rejected a 'tastefully airbrushed' alternative.) *Melody Maker*'s reviewer Simon Reynolds saw the message as follows: 'A naked infant, swimming through uterine waters, is lured to the surface by a dollar bill on a fish-hook. Nirvana say: don't do it, kid! Leave your blissful brine for this corrupt world, and it'll be the first, and worst, mistake of your life.' Having only enjoyed an initial pressing of between 40 and 50,000, *Nevermind* was reckoned to have sold 10.5 million by early 2004, making the cover image even more ironic that was intended.

The end of October saw *Nevermind* certified gold. In January 1992 it reached the top of the US chart (the three million mark was reached as it hit Number One), and it would alternate with country star Garth Brooks for several weeks thereafter. As if all this wasn't enough, latecomers were now busily and hungrily rediscovering Nirvana's Sub Pop past: *Bleach* was now selling at the rapid rate of 70,000 copies a month.

Nevermind acquired its title, said Kurt, 'because most people would just as soon forget or say 'never mind' than take a can of spray paint or start a band. People just don't do things very often any more. I'm kinda disturbed about it.' So this was a call to arms, a rejection of complacency.

Nevermind won critical praise commensurate with its sales, which were boosted by three more major hit singles after 'Teen Spirit', cleverly spread throughout 1992 to give a boost to the album at times when sales might have declined. 'Come As You Are' was released in March, 'Lithium' later that summer and 'In Bloom' in December.

Just as Nirvana had followed heroes Sonic Youth to Geffen, so a flock of indie bands followed the band's example and signed to majors; the Melvins, Butthole Surfers, Shonen Knife and Daniel Johnston were just four to make the transition. 'No one had expected Nirvana to take off, not even Geffen,' Mark Arm of Mudhoney explains. 'The label smelled money and signed anything they thought would make them more...'

In Britain, DJs Mark Goodier and John Peel were first to air *Nevermind* but Geffen's radio pluggers were keen to get 'Teen Spirit' on daytime radio. Both single and album reached Number Seven, despite Nirvana playing unexceptional UK dates and cancelling others. The 'Lithium' single preceded their second Reading festival appearance in August 1992, the album having gone platinum the previous month when its 300,000th UK copy was sold. On the other side of the coin, many 'traditional' rock bands saw Nirvana's success as a potential death knell. 'When I first heard *Nevermind* I thought, fuck, there goes my career' said Billy Duffy of the Cult.

With the extensive roadwork success demanded, there was going to be a problem for Nirvana to find the time and inspiration to produce a follow-up of the same majestic proportions. And Kurt was never going to produce a carbon copy of *Nevermind* anyway. 'I would hate to keep rewriting this formula for ever,' he confessed. 'I've mastered this. It's over as far as I'm concerned ... I can probably write a couple more albums like this ... but be less and less happy every time.'

It was left to Krist Novoselic to pose the crucial post-*Nevermind* question: 'Where do we go from here – are we going to be the Led Zeppelin of the 1990s or are we just going to fall apart?' The answer was both, but the impact of Nirvana and their classic album is still being felt in so many ways.

The six-week autumn 1991 tour of the States promoting *Nevermind*, which began north of the border at Toronto's Opera House on 20 September, would go down in rock history as one of the legendary tours everyone wished they had witnessed personally. 'Playing those songs was almost meditation,' Grohl recalls. 'You would lose yourself, although you were still in control. There was a conscious effort to please ourselves – and then maybe everyone else.'

The final gig was a homecoming soirée in Seattle on Hallowe'en, at the Paramount Theatre, with Mudhoney and Bikini Kill. By that time they were public property, though at least one surviving participant remembers surprisingly little. 'It's so hard to remember everything,' Grohl admits. 'I wish I'd kept a journal. I wish I'd taken pictures. I felt as confused then as I do now about the whole thing.'

The set list remained unchanged throughout, kicking off with 'Aneurysm', the US B-side of 'Teen Spirit', and ending with 1989 EP track 'Blew', which often signaled what Novoselic called 'a freak-out at the end where things would get smashed up.' The Metro in Chicago saw Dave and Kurt totally destroy the former's battered drum kit in an attempt to persuade the record company to buy him a new one. 'There was no music,' Grohl says. 'The audience watched for 15 minutes as Kurt and I were bouncing the shells, trying to splinter them, trying to get rid of this set and handing it to the audience.' But this was unusual. 'As much as we had a love of bands that just made noise, like Flipper and Scratch Acid, we also felt obligated to perform. Kurt never wanted things to sound bad.'

On stage, the trio were an unstoppable team. Off it, however, Dave didn't hang out with his band mates the way he had with the Stahls in Scream. 'Franz and Pete were like my brothers,' he says. 'We spent all our time together, in the van going to gigs, sleeping on friends' floors. In Nirvana, we didn't hang out. We'd pull into town on the tour bus, do interviews, play in front of thousands of people, do more interviews, go to the hotel, and watch TV until we fell asleep.'

Courtney Love has claimed that Kurt hated Dave, that 'he liked him for the first year but then he tuned into an asshole.' Grohl, for his part, has never claimed the pair were best mates. Clearly the relationship between Kurt and Courtney had distanced the pair, while he admits he got frustrated at Kurt's increasing unreliability due to drug use. Yet he points to the music as evidence to the contrary, claiming that 'Everything else is secondary. Ultimately the music is all you have to listen to. You can pick up a cheap biography and get the inside scoop, but...'

Dave knew they'd made it when, on 11 January 1992, exactly 15 months after his first Nirvana gig, he played in front of the cameras of *Saturday Night Live*. The US television institution had not only been a part of his life but had been a small-town boy's first exposure to punk. He had fond recollections of seeing Devo and the B-52's on the show, so to be playing on it 12 years later was 'crazy ... I felt like I was going to faint. Number One on the chart that week, too...'

The sledgehammer opening track, 'Smells Like Teen Spirit', had been released a fortnight earlier than the album from which it came and was already opening up the world's singles chart like a particularly ferocious chainsaw. The guitar riff, played solo first of all before being repeated as the band crash in behind it, had just about the same effect. What exactly the words meant, though, was anybody's guess: the title, it was suggested, was inspired by a spray-painted graffiti carried out by Kathleen Hanna, lead singer of the band Bikini Kill. 'Kurt Smells Like Teen Sprit' indeed exists on a wall back in Olympia, which the singer had moved to in 1987. Cobain initially took this as an admiring reference to his rebellious nature, claiming to be unaware that 'Teen Spirit' was the brand name of an underarm deodorant aimed at teenage American girls.

Cobain was given to making contradictory statements about the song. These include: 'I was trying to write the ultimate pop song.' 'It was a scam, a time-marker. What I was into was making money and abusing people's trust.' 'The entire song is just making fun of having a revolution. But it's a nice thought.' It's always been the case, though, that Nirvana lyrics have been taken, line by line, from other writings. Like REM's, they have the ability to mean whatever you want them to mean. What's certain is that *Nevermind* contained many of the ingredients of teen rebellion – as incendiary an album as, say the Sex Pistols' *Never Mind the Bollocks* nearly 15 years earlier. 'When we went to make this record,' Krist later told *Rolling Stone* magazine, 'I had such a feeling of us versus them.'

Yet despite the impact of 'Teen Spirit' and 'Come As You Are' this was more – much more – than a two-song album. 'Lithium', the final US single to be lifted from the album, was a loud crowd-pleaser of the type fans loved but Kurt himself would come to loathe, while the attractive 'In Bloom' was chosen as a single in Britain in December. While he'd grow increasingly frustrated with the rock anthem aspect of Nirvana's output, Kurt was never unhappy about the fact that his songs were singles material. 'All my favourite songs are pop songs,' he once insisted. 'Pop just means simple, and that's what punk rock has been forever until it turned into hardcore.'

If Grohl's playing with Nirvana inspired and defined a generation of drummers, it's the raw simplicity of *Nevermind* he's understandably most proud of. 'Our intention was to do something so straightforward that it was almost childlike; simple rhythms and simple patterns – the most direct songwriting. It's bare bones, simple drumming and I think the fact that it is so stripped down and so easy to nod your head to is why people still listen to it. My goal in Nirvana was to make air drummers out of a generation of people that had no idea how to play the drums. The idea was to get people swinging along to those flams, and cranking it up and playing along in their cars – having never held a pair of drum sticks in their lives.

'The albums that turned me on to drumming as a kid had basic rhythms you know, like the Beatles or AC/DC, or even the drums on disco records. I could hear the kick and I could hear the snare, and it was so simple it made me want to pick up sticks because I thought I could do it. Then of course I turned into a metal head and it was all about how fast I could play! But at first, it was that simple rhythm that got me. All the drumming that I've done since *Nevermind*, I don't think that I've gone in that direction again, and I'm really proud of having been a simple drummer.'

When *Nevermind* leapfrogged over both Guns N'Roses' *Use Your Illusions*, U2's *Achtung Baby* and Michael Jackson's *Dangerous* to top the American album chart, it was clear that in just a few short months Nirvana had made an indelible mark on rock music as we know it. But behind the scenes, there were problems. A British band called Nirvana from the 1960s were unhappy that a new act should have come along and 'stolen' their name: another, Los Angeles-based band of the same name also showed up and demanded money to yield their moniker: they got $50,000.

Even when *Nevermind* hit Number One in America, Kurt never forgot his roots. 'Stay Away' from the album saw him slipping his favourite Aberdeen graffiti, 'God is gay', into the lyric. And the above-mentioned appearance on top-rated US television show *Saturday Night Live*, performing 'Teen Spirit', saw many references to their earliest days. Krist and Dave both wore Melvins T-shirts in a tribute to the group without which this trio would have remained in the imagination, and when the guests came out to wave goodbye under the closing credits Kurt and Krist decided to kiss each other. You can only imagine the reactions of the two 'faggot-hating' rednecks in Aberdeen.

That sense of humour was still evident when Nirvana flew to Australia in February 1992. A photo shot for their *Rolling Stone* cover story saw Kurt don a home-made T-shirt proclaiming 'Corporate Magazines Still Suck'. But February 1992 was also the month the stakes were raised when he flew on to Hawaii to marry Courtney Love. (They were married by a female non-denominational minister.) Celebrity marriages have always been easy targets for spiteful writers, but the Cobain-Love alliance would inspire some of the most vitriolic comment ever made about a rock star and his family.

The Beatles, Kurt and Dave's earliest musical influence, were the biggest band rock has ever seen. Yet even the flak Paul McCartney took for including wife Linda in his post-Beatles group Wings, or the press treatment of Yoko Ono once she'd married John Lennon, pale besides the big guns that opened up on Kurt and Courtney. When Courtney's band Hole was signed (also by DGC) for a huge sum, one industry figure was quoted by *Newsweek* as sniffing that 'sleeping with Kurt Cobain is worth a million dollars.'

Success affects different people in different ways. For Grohl, the end result of Nirvana's runaway popularity was 'a dose of humility, the realisation that we're as normal and fucked-up as everyone else.' He admitted, though, that having girl fans bang on the window of their car as they made their way into and out of festivals was hard to deal with. And the timetable for a member of a successful band was no less unsettling: 'Wake up, do a sound-check, play, travel, barely eat. You don't have time to have real lives.' With that in mind, as of July 1992 he had no plans to join his bandmates and get married. 'I can't imagine marrying anybody, especially now. Why the fuck would anybody want to get married in the middle of such an insane situation? It's crazy!'

He saw his future as encompassing a return to school when real life intervened 'in a year or two.' Graphic arts and commercial design, his favoured subjects, no longer 'yanked my crank', but he still felt that completing his education would help him get on in life. Nirvana was just a passing phase, if a breathtaking one.

Like Cobain, Grohl had misgivings about the band's massive success and the bandwagon-jumping fans already lampooned on 'In Bloom'. 'We didn't expect the record to go this well. We knew it was against the grain. I mean the first thing that started freaking me out was playing shows and seeing sort of remedial redneck logger guys in the front row. I had never expected that kind of audience.'

After a show in Belfast, Grohl expressed uneasiness with fan worship to *Select* magazine: 'Tonight was insane. All those people thrusting little pieces of paper in our face. For what? To prove that they stuck a piece of paper in our face and we had a pen at the time? I don't understand that. We are not the resurrection of Christ. We are another fuckin' band. It's no big deal. Nirvana is not a big deal.' He'd expound further to Michael Azerrad in Nirvana's official biography, explaining that he began to develop claustrophobia as everything went out of control. 'It felt as though it couldn't be stopped, or we didn't know where it was taking us and we were just sort of along for the ride.'

More importantly for Dave, he also developed a fear of flying, which, added to a newly acquired claustrophobia and his 'traditional' stage fright, didn't help his mood. Always a hurdle to be overcome before showtime, his fear now was that hundreds of people would be inconvenienced by his inability to play. And with everything going on around the tour, each performance was a test of mental strength for the drummer. He admits to having become 'sick of playing' – a first for this likeable character – so it was a relief when the tour was abandoned in December 1991 just before the Scandinavian leg.

This was littered with early-morning flights designed to bookend Dave's day with the performances in the evening. So the relief was palpable when Nirvana took the stage at the Trans-Musicale Festival in Rennes to play what was their final gig. Grohl celebrated by taking lead vocals on the opening song, a cover of the Who's 'Baba O'Riley'. But, once home, he admitted it took only three days for withdrawal symptoms to set in. No matter how stressful the situation, it seemed his love of music would win through.

The success of 'Smells Like Teen Spirit' opened so many new avenues to Nirvana that it was unsurprising the song came in for some heavy-duty analysis. But from where he was sitting, Dave couldn't go along with the critics' deep and meaningful interpretations. When you'd seen Kurt scribbling five minutes before the vocal needed to be laid down, it was hard to see the words as anything more than a series of rhymes designed to fill up the time allotted. The drummer ascribed its success in equal measure to the 'funny and clever title ... something a friend had written on the wall' and the band's video performance 'at the pep rally from Hell.' As for a message, he flatly didn't think there was one.

Musically, he pointed to a 'weird lull, a void' that had seen precious little quality rock hit the US charts in the year before the album's release. The time was right for a band to come along and unite the 'stoners, skaters and derelict kids' who saw

Nirvana as kindred spirits and who latched onto Kurt's 'catchy, simple' songs.

Dave added to those songs with some inspired stickwork – notably the cymbals at the end of 'Come As You Are' and the snare-drum roll that marks the transition to the chorus in 'In Bloom'. Even road manager Alex Macleod pinpointed Grohl as 'rock solid the whole time' and 'a good influence' on his fellow band mates. Barrett Jones was serving as his drum tech at this time, so he at least had a friendly face to confide in as things went wrong.

The autumn/winter 1991 European tour to promote *Nevermind* had created stress fractures in Nirvana's structure that would never fully heal. Much of this was due to the presence of Courtney Love, who was touring Europe with Hole at the same time. She would even cancel concerts to hang out with Kurt, and the action was so intense that his room-mate Dave was forced to seek sanctuary with road manager Macleod – by all accounts hardly his favourite person.

Dave and Krist's response to Kurt's escalating drug problem was described by the singer as 'passive-aggressive'. In other words, they wouldn't confront their colleague but just give off 'bad vibes'. The whole thing was 'something not to be talked about'. So much so, in fact, that the rhythm section did not see or hear from Kurt between *Saturday Night Live* and the filming of the 'Come As You Are' video. They had heard from another source that he was in rehab, but beyond that they knew nothing.

Next on the agenda was an Australian tour which, Dave recalls, he knew from the off was not the best thing for Kurt to be doing. An additional problem was that he was suffering stomach pains that doctors assumed were the symptoms of coming off heroin. Hence he was prescribed methadone but, because it was known Down Under as Physeptone, he was

4

THE ZEPPELIN EXPLODES

The relationship between Kurt and his two band mates had been on a downward spiral since his wedding to Courtney on the island of Hawaii in late February 1992. Dave had been present when the pair tied the knot, but Krist's wife Shelli had been un-invited after the 'happy' couple suspected her of gossiping about Kurt's drug habits. Naturally, hubby declined to attend without her.

The next step in the unravelling relationship came when Kurt insisted on the song publishing being renegotiated. The agreement had been for each member of the band to enjoy a third each of the band's income, a logical move given the trio's initial penury before the Geffen money started coming through, but as sole lyric writer Kurt believed he should have 100 per cent of the moneys accruing from the words. When it came to the music, he was prepared to offer 25 per cent, to be split between his rhythm section. This equated to a total of 6.75 per cent per song – not exactly a generous offer, but one he insisted was non-negotiable. 'Betrayed, bullied and humiliated' was one critic's summation of the feelings of Grohl and Novoselic, who had been dismayed to find that the agreement would be backdated to include *Nevermind*.

The pace of life was now slowing noticeably. Nirvana had played constantly for some three years, and neither Kurt (who was now an expectant father) nor Krist were keen on continuing indefinitely. Dave, being Dave and still a single man, was get-ting antsy and wanted to tour. But the row about royalties had all but split the band, and things were now on the slide.

A two-week summer tour of Europe in 1992 saw the band's Gold Mountain management send out 'minders' to ensure Kurt behaved himself. This isolated Kurt and Courtney even more, and not long after their return to the States Kurt booked into rehab. Meanwhile, Courtney's band Hole had been signed for a reported sum of a million dollars, even more than Nirvana had got. This made her the obvious target for unflattering press, a profile in *Vanity Fair* magazine causing her and Kurt considerable grief by portraying her as, among other things, someone who had used drugs during pregnancy. This in turn led to social services taking an interest in the case and forced them to fight for custody of Frances Bean, born in August 1992.

Despite the fact that Courtney claimed she stopped using drugs when she knew she was pregnant, there was nothing to stop magazines calling her a 'junkie mum' and suggesting all sorts of things about the likely state of the child. In point of fact, Frances Bean Cobain arrived a happy, healthy and extremely normal child. Yet the innuendo continued, fuelled by Axl Rose's reported on-stage remarks about Courtney that set up the backstage clash at the MTV awards.

A British tour in June 1992 was the scene for high drama when, after a gig at the King's Hall in Belfast, Kurt collapsed with convulsions. He was placed in a wheelchair and taken to an ambulance with stomach pains that he later revealed were so terrible he had to go to hospital to get a strong enough painkiller. He was hospitalised again that August, adding fuel to the fire of constant 'Nirvana To Split' headlines. And just to add to the agony, he'd returned home in July to find that notebooks containing lyrics he intended to use on the new album had been irreparably damaged in a flood at his home.

In the midst of all this, the band crossed the Atlantic to make their contracted appearance at the Reading Festival on 30 August, Kurt being wheeled on stage in a medical gown to mock reports of his physical incapacitation. Having played the Festival in 1991 as relative unknowns, the band's return just 12 months later was as conquering heroes. The reason of course was the success of 'Teen Spirit', which had soared to the heady heights of Number Seven in the UK charts. It was no coincidence that Abba tribute merchants Bjorn Again, booked as one of the support acts in a postmodern ironic fashion, 'Abba-ised' it in their well received set. Its writer, however, did more than Abba-ise it, he positively deconstructed it. The lyrics were messed up and the guitar break mangled 'like he was fighting his own fame,' as one commentator put it.

Dave rates the show his single greatest moment with Nirvana. 'There had been so many rumours that the band was breaking up, that Kurt was in rehab, that we were self-destructing. We stepped onstage in front of 60,000 people without rehearsing and played one of the greatest shows that we ever had. It proved that the three of us had a chemistry that went beyond a rehearsal room or a magazine cover.'

As the music (and more general) press rounded on the Cobains, so Dave and Krist circled wagons and fell in behind their band mate. The prospect of an unauthorised biography by British writers Victoria Clarke (long-time partner of Pogues mainman Shane MacGowan) and Britt Collins was also causing much agitation, lawyers' letters and (allegedly) threatening phone calls resulting.

With Cobain still in bad shape, the gigs Nirvana did play were contracted with money in mind. But an October 1992 trip to South America was no holiday, and Dave for one was dismayed at the lack of intimacy that conjured memories of the Monsters of Rock tour he'd seen Van Halen and Metallica play four years or so before. 'We played football stadiums and I felt this big [making gesture with thumb and forefinger]. You just think, "What the fuck are we doing? What is this about?"' That said, Nirvana were under-rehearsed and treated their vast audiences in cavalier fashion, Kurt teasing with the riff to 'Teen Spirit' but frequently not playing the song itself.

The year of 1992 ended with the release of *Incesticide,* a collection of B-sides, radio sessions and oddities which satisfied their record label's wish to put something out for the Christmas market. The album features all four of Nirvana's drummers to have recorded with the band and demonstrates not only the quantum leap in clout when Grohl took over at the kit but also how crucial he was to the band's success. Dave appears on 'Been a Son', 'Turnaround', 'Molly's Lips', 'Son of a Gun', '(New Wave) Polly' and 'Aneurysm', all from sessions recorded for BBC Radio 1's John Peel in October 1990 (shortly after Dave's arrival in the ranks) and Mark Goodier at the end of 1991.

Another purpose of this album was to act as the carrier of an open letter from Kurt, which revealed his personal unhappiness at the situation he found himself in. The sleeve note wasn't to make final copies of the album for what were described as 'time and printing constraints', even though he'd insisted they be included, so it remains both unknown to and unread by the general public. Kurt's targets were many and various: firstly Lynn Hirschberg, a writer whose article for US style magazine *Vanity Fair* had portrayed the Cobains in a light they considered unfavourable. From specifics, Kurt then asked anyone who 'in any way hate homosexuals, people of a different colour, or women' to 'leave us the fuck alone! Don't come to our shows and don't buy our records.'

Dave was forthright when interviewed by Michael Azerrad for *Come As You Are: The Story of Nirvana*. Commissioned in an attempt to tell the story from the band's side and first published in October 1993 when Kurt was still alive, it lived up to the hype of being 'by far the most intimate look ever at one of the most significant pop-music groups to emerge in years.' The drummer admitted that, for the first year or so he was in the band, it was a waste of time him turning up to interviews because Krist 'had a lot to say … Kurt had the beyond-clever snaps of wit … and I was like a paperweight.' He admitted that, even by this time, he didn't feel an indispensable third of the band. 'I don't feel like a new guy any more,' he commented, adding that 'I don't really know if I feel vital to the band.' The other two, he explained, had a shared sense of humour that rather excluded him. If all went wrong, he explained, 'They could always get Dale [Crover].'

The problem seems to have been that Dave received little if any praise or reassurance from Nirvana's remaining duo. Yet he also admitted that there was musical chemistry that went beyond words, creating arrangements and bridges for the songs with little or no discussion. 'Anybody could do what I do … but there is a chemistry that clicks sometimes.' The band members saw little of each other 'off duty'; the eight months spent sharing every waking hour with Kurt had seen to that, let alone marriage to Courtney, which now monopolised his non-musical attention.

Dave also found the level of fame he was having to deal with difficult to stomach, and would 'go home at night and clean the house' after his Nirvana duties had been discharged. Nor did he want to do interviews, partly through laziness and partly because 'I play drums, and that's about it.' Who wanted to know what he had to say? That would of course change through time, but for now he was happy to live the simplest of lives. Besides, he told Azerrad, 'there's so much that goes on with Kurt and Courtney that I can't keep up with.' Certainly, the press's attempts to do just that meant the pair became something of a publicity magnet. And Grohl didn't mind that one bit.

In April 1993 Nirvana played a concert at San Francisco's Cow Palace to raise awareness of and generate aid for rape survivors in Bosnia-Herzegovina. L7, the Breeders and Disposable Heroes of Hiphoprisy were also on the bill. This wasn't to be a year of great live activity, however, with expectation levels for their as-yet-unwritten new album hitting hysterical levels. The record, *In Utero*, was finally released on 21 September.

Having only enjoyed an initial pressing of some 40,000, *Nevermind* had sold nine million by early 1994. Kurt was never going to produce a carbon copy – and announced just that by forsaking producer Butch Vig in favour of Steve Albini. The controversial former Big Black frontman was always going to be a producer who set out to fulfil his own vision, and would therefore be a counterweight to record-company pressure. It was even suggested at one point that Kurt wanted to use an eight-track machine to record on: most modern studios feature 48. 'They want to do a very raw, very dirty album,' confirmed a record-company spokesman.

Their producer had made his name producing the Pixies, Breeders and the Wedding Present. Dave: 'When we talked to him [Albini] before recording, he made a point about "Are your songs prepared? Are you going to come into the studio and fuck about for two weeks? Are you going to write in the studio?" We said "No no no." We set up and recorded.'

Steve Albini found Dave the easiest Nirvana member to work with. He lauded his 'rock solid' drums, and told Michael Azerrad that watching Grohl play drums was 'probably the highlight of my appreciation of the band.' Dave was also a 'pleasant, very goofy guy to be around.' After doing his homework before the sessions, listening to the band's previous recordings, Albini commented: 'Dave Grohl is an absolute monster of a drummer, it's so hard to imagine a record with him drumming on that wouldn't be at least fun to listen to.' Grohl joined in the mutual appreciation. 'I happened to love Steve Albini,' he told Q magazine. 'He really prides himself on being the biggest dick you ever met in your life and he does a good job of it. He's also an incredibly intelligent producer.'

Dave's playing certainly benefited from Albini's tactic of placing a large number of microphones around the room to make the most of the natural reverb – the result being a sound miles away from the previous album's studio-enhanced sheen. The secret, he explained to Azerrad, was the combination of 'a good drummer ... and a kit that sounds good acoustically.' This was the simple yet effective approach that ensured *In Utero* was sonically light years away from its platinum predecessor.

Dave was struck by the fact that, while *Nevermind* songs had a verse and chorus that were typically repeated, the new album boasted far more lyrics, indicating that Cobain had a lot more to get off his chest. The singer had progressed, opined Grohl, from 'teen angst to rock-star angst ... Kurt feels he's backed up against a wall and he's just going to scream his way out.' The album's original title, 'I Hate Myself and Want to Die', was changed, but the tenor of the songs remained desperate.

The powers that be – Geffen, Gold Mountain – had not wanted the band to record with Albini. Understandably, they would have preferred 'Nevermind Part 2', which would have been guaranteed multi-platinum status. Faced with this wall of disapproval, the band themselves started to doubt the production, which did not have a defined bass sound and buried the vocals far lower in the mix than Butch Vig had.

But in the end they realised they would be criticised whatever they did. In a last-minute compromise, two tracks, 'Heart Shaped Box' and 'All Apologies', were remixed with REM producer Scott Litt, some vocal boosting and bass definition being added to the final mix. Though the band weren't satisfied with the way *In Utero* turned out, they didn't want to be seen to cave in to external pressures; this was a low-profile compromise. The album sleeve carries the credit 'recorded by Steve Albini' in preference to the more usual 'produced by'.

Recording took place at Pachyderm Studios in Cannon Falls, Minnesota and was completed for a total cost of $24,000. Albini took a flat fee of just $100,000, even though a royalty would have earned him far more. Recording sessions started on Valentine's Day 1993 and basic tracks and overdubs were completed in a week, after which Albini spent a few days mixing the songs. Kurt later described it in Azerrad's *Come As You Are* as "the easiest recording [Nirvana had] ever done.'

Like his band mates, Grohl heaped praise on the sonic quality of the finished product. 'This album sounds like Nirvana! *Nevermind*'s only flaw was that it had no flaws. Play it alongside our live tapes and it's a sharp, thin thing compared to this big boom, this rumble, this khhhhhsss. *In Utero* is boom and rumble, man!'

The album's heavily confessional tone struck a chord in listeners and reviewers alike. 'Serve the Servants' was a thunderous and typical opener, its power and intensity lightened by an unexpected hint of melody at the edges: *Melody Maker* perceptively likened it to mid-period Beatles, something that must have delighted the Lennon fan on guitar. That was an influence several picked up on: 'His voice really is uncannily like John Lennon's,' *Melody Maker* insisted, 'how he drags it over his lyrics and lets it catch along the way.'

The classic Nirvana line-up
of Cobain, Grohl and
Novoselic that changed
the face of rock music.

Unusually it was Dave and Krist who courted (the headlines) at the MTV Awards in 1993.

While the cover design of *Nevermind* was a masterstroke, this subsequent
photo shoot was arguably less inspired.

Nirvana's refusal to play the corporate rock game extended to looking grumpy
in photos. Thankfully Dave grew out of it...

Nirvana outgrew club venues at a stroke, but the rollercoaster of fame moved too fast for Dave Grohl's liking.

A pre-haircut Dave in his new Foos frontman role at Brixton Academy, London, in late 1995.

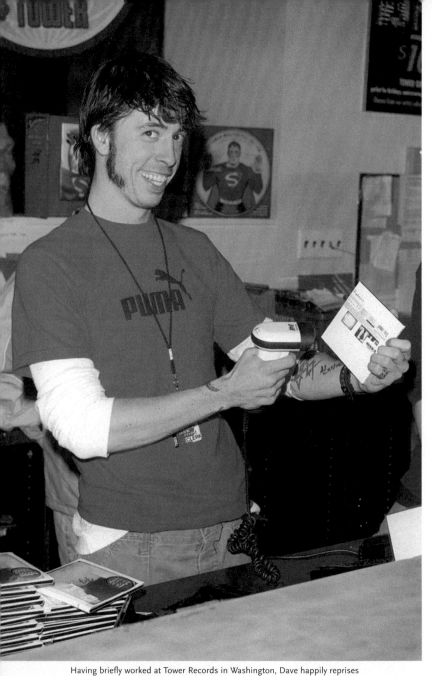

Having briefly worked at Tower Records in Washington, Dave happily reprises his former job in New York for promotional purposes.

Top: Foo Fighters appeared on BBC-TV's *Later... With Jools Holland* in November 1999, where they played 'Learn To Fly' and 'Generator'.

Bottom: Live at Las Vegas' House of Blues with Gibson SG in October 2000.

On stage at the V Festival, August 2001, where the Foos played between David Gray and the Chili Peppers.

At least four of the songs – 'Dumb', 'Pennyroyal Tea', 'Radio Friendly Unit Shifter', and 'All Apologies' – were written three years earlier, suggesting Kurt was having trouble creating new music. Even so, only one track – 'Scentless Apprentice', credited to Cobain/Grohl/Novoselic – contained input from anyone else, though a secret track called 'Gallons of Rubbing Alcohol Flow Through the Strip' was also a group composition. A jam recorded in Rio de Janeiro in January 1993, it was included on UK and Australian copies of *In Utero* and starts about 20 minutes after the end of 'All Apologies'.

Tragic Seattle-born actress Frances Farmer, who had posthumously supplied Courtney Love with her wedding dress, was namechecked in 'Frances Farmer Will Have Her Revenge On Seattle', while 'Very Ape' and 'Tourrets' were pure blasts of punk energy. Yet the two tracks that caught the attention in a 'Teen Spirit' style were 'Scentless Apprentice', with its blistering flamethrower guitar riff, and 'Rape Me' – described by one reviewer as 'the simple cry of anyone who ever hurt' but guaranteed to cause controversy and receive minimal radio exposure.

Dave had contributed the main guitar riff to 'Scentless Apprentice', and even though Kurt observed in a late 1993 MTV interview that he had initially thought the riff was 'kind of boneheaded', he was happy with how the song developed and was hopeful Novoselic and Grohl would contribute more to the band's songwriting. (A demo of the song on the Nirvana box set *With the Lights Out* illustrates its development.) 'Rape Me', meanwhile, was always going to bring Nirvana and their record company into conflict. Singapore's government-sponsored Controller of Undesirable Publications considered the album unacceptable for containing the track. Predictably, Nirvana refused to remove it.

It was actually an anti-rape song, when the 'moral majority' could be persuaded to look past the deliberately inflammatory title. Kurt's wish to release this as a single (it eventually came out as the B-side of 'All Apologies') caused palpitations in a music business where Nirvana were neck and neck with Guns N'Roses as the most unpredictable act in rock.

But for a clue to Kurt's state of mind, look at the album's previous two working titles: the bored-out-of my-skull 'Verse-Chorus-Verse' and the self-explanatory 'I Hate Myself And I Want To Die'. It seemed he saw himself as having turned into something he despised.

Then the album sleeve, with its photo montage of foetuses, earned an immediate ban from major US record retailers Wal-Mart. Perhaps the only real surprise was that the album had such an inoffensive title, since everything the band had done – from the infamous 'Crack Smokin', Fudge Packin', Satan Worshipping, Motherfuckers' T-shirts to the 'Corporate Rock Whores' slogan that helped make their name – had been as in-your-face and upfront as you can get. Acceptable to Sub Pop, but not a label with an image (and the Eagles) to uphold.

While sales of *Nevermind* had been amply assisted by the presence of a best-selling single in 'Teen Spirit', no such track existed on the follow-up long-player. Even so, *In Utero* proved the album of 1993 just as certainly as *Nevermind* was the album of 1992. (It was released in late 1991, but let's not split hairs.) *In Utero* made Number One in Britain (where it went gold) and the United States (five times platinum), was third in *Rolling Stone*'s review of the year's albums and went Top Ten in Sweden, Australia, New Zealand, Portugal, Finland, Norway, Holland and Austria.

The 'Heart Shaped Box' single, which reached Number Five in Britain, was notable in giving Dave his first solo Nirvana writing credit in the shape of a B-side titled 'Marigold'. Initially called 'Color Pictures of a Marigold', Kurt had overheard him working on the song and felt it had promise. The two jammed on it and it was recorded during the sessions for *In Utero*. A small but significant milestone for Grohl.

Dave felt there were 'three potential responses to this record: a) this is Nirvana's pretentious noise, we want to destroy our career record; b) this is brilliant, now we can see *Nevermind* was obviously not a true representation of this band; and c) we don't like Nirvana anyway and this one sucks twice as bad!'

The touring with Nirvana, when it happened, was punishing. And Dave was not going to be the man to pull out when things got tough. 'I remember in Nirvana getting sick, I'd slept in a draught or something. Anyway I woke up coughing and wheezing, but I just took some medication and kept going,' he recalls. 'A few days later I was getting worse and I saw a doctor and I was like, "I'm getting better, right?" and he said, "Nope, you've got the Walking Pneumonia, your lungs are filled with fluid."' But he kept going nonetheless, relying on his inbuilt work ethic to see him though. So it wasn't surprising that he took a dim view of his band mate's 'self-harm', especially when this caused gigs to be cancelled.

In summer 1993 Dave had taken a break from the madness to travel the world with his soon to be wife Jennifer Youngblood. They'd taken time to have a holiday in Italy and ride motorbikes across America, before Dave enjoyed a fortnight's reunion with his former band Scream: 'Humping our own gear into CBGB's and sleeping on friends' floors restored my faith.'

On 18 October 1993, Nirvana started a three-month tour of North America. This saw Kurt introducing new musicians, notably a second guitar in Pat Smear from the Germs, and also strings. 'Having Pat on stage has freed me to spend more time connecting with the audience,' explained Kurt, before hastily adding that he didn't see himself 'ever becoming Mick Jagger.'

Dave was very much in favour of this development. 'For the longest time, we had looked for a second guitar player in

Nirvana,' says Grohl. 'We thought it would be great to get Steve Turner from Mudhoney or Buzz [Osborne] from the Melvins or Eugene [Kelly] from Eugenius. We were rehearsing one day, and Kurt came in and said, "Pat Smear from the Germs is going to be our second guitar player." Krist and I had never met him, and I just imagined this bloated, tattooed, bitter old mess. And he came to rehearsal, and it was so incredibly refreshing that it made everything instantly great.

'We couldn't have found anyone more perfect for Nirvana than Pat,' he continued. 'He showed up and he had the same effects pedals as Kurt had, and Kurt had really obscure, old, extremely hard-to-find pedals. He had this façade, he played all sloppy. But when we were mixing the album, he showed us how to play 'Blackbird', one of the most intricate Beatles songs.'

Grohl would, of course, later recruit the newcomer into his Foo Fighters line-up. For the record, Krist Novoselic was also a Pat Smear fan: 'He's got a lot of spirit and spunk, and that rubs off on the band,' he said.

Another new face, cello player Mori Goldstone, gave this impression of his employer: 'He sort of had a depressive streak, but he basically seemed optimistic and had ideas for the future. I think,' he concluded significantly, 'I think he was pretty overwhelmed in general by his fame.'

A lasting memento of this tour would be provided by *MTV Unplugged*, recorded on the nights of 18 and 19 November 1993 at Sony Studios in New York for broadcast by the cable television giant. Established artists like Eric Clapton, Rod Stewart and Neil Young had found career-reviving success by appearing on 'Unplugged' releases and issuing the results on compact disc. Yet the results had not been far from the kind of music they were already known for. It was a different matter entirely for Nirvana to shed the power-chords and sonic attack that was an integral trademark of their sound and come out with acoustic guitars and cellos, but it all tied in with Kurt's quest to remain fresh and unpredictable.

The show, which would be aired on 16 December 1993, saw Nirvana tackle songs from a variety of sources: one from *Bleach*, four from *Nevermind* and three from *In Utero*. The remaining six were cover versions: three songs by seminal Phoenix punk band the Meat Puppets, plus one apiece by David Bowie ('The Man Who Sold the World'), the Vaselines and blues singer Leadbelly ('Where Did You Sleep Last Night?', a song Kurt had played back in Aberdeen days).

'Dumb' and 'Polly' were the tracks that came with strings attached, while the bleak, moving 'Pennyroyal Tea' was performed by Cobain alone. The studio version had been planned as Nirvana's next single from *In Utero* but didn't make it. This performance added that lost lustre and restored it to its rightful prominence.

The Meat Puppets' Chris and Curt Kirkwood had actually been flown in at Nirvana's expense to play on their three songs in a kind of showcase: it was almost as if Kurt wanted to give them a leg up. And unusually for these sessions, where groups are given the chance to re-record any songs they are not happy with, Nirvana breezed through the set with no retakes whatsoever. The only down side was that few genuine fans had managed to get tickets for the event at the Sony Music Studios on Manhattan's West 54th Street. Kurt made a point of signing autographs for those who had.

The audio from the show was released in October 1994, months after Kurt Cobain's death, as *Unplugged in New York*, and predictably headed for the top of the charts. It's impossible to say how it would have been received had it been released in any other circumstances. Certainly, it seemed very much as if Kurt was 'cleansing his palate' before embarking on some new direction – with or without Nirvana, it was impossible to say.

The way his future music might have gone is unclear. He seemed to want to regress, perhaps in the hope of shedding the 'undesirable' fans he'd attracted and restoring Nirvana to cult status. *In Utero* had been Cobain's attempt to get back to basics – exemplified by the decision to replace Butch Vig by Steve Albini in the producer's chair – and the album veered more into noise, power, and less into the pop of *Nevermind*.

You couldn't help wondering if he was actually seeking to lose the fans who'd homed in on a hit band and return to his hardcore following. And therein lay the paradox. The music he was producing was as compelling as anything from the punk era and beyond. On the other hand, he wasn't comfortable sharing that message with the masses. 'We're not proud of the fact that there are a bunch of Guns N'Roses kids into our music,' he'd declared when *Nevermind* shot them into the spotlight. 'We don't feel comfortable playing larger venues.' Not that he now had much choice in the matter.

When he prepared to shoot *MTV Unplugged in New York*, Kurt made one request of producer Alex Coletti – that 'If there's any shots of 'em smiling, can you put them in? My wife says I don't smile enough on TV.' At the end of set opener 'Come As You Are', he gave what Coletti called 'the most sinister smile,' which duly made the final cut. Maybe, just maybe, he was finally enjoying live performance.

What would turn out to be Nirvana's final recording date occurred in January 1994 when they convened at Bob Lang Studios in North Seattle. Unfortunately, Dave and Krist spent two of the arranged three days waiting for Kurt to show. This frustrated Dave, but gave him the chance to commit some of his own music to tape, notably 'Exhausted' and 'Big Me'.

On the third day, Kurt arrived, and several new songs were attempted. One, 'You Know You're Right', was completed to a point that it could be included on the 'Nirvana' compilation album, released eight years later. But this was the final cut. The out-of-control train that was Nirvana was about to hit the buffers.

5

MEMENTO MORI

With Kurt's life out of control, Nirvana's future in
early 1994 looked similarly unpredictable. But still
the band and the bandwagon rolled on as they
headed for a European tour in February that was scheduled to
be their longest to date. Early shows in France were well
received, and the caravan progressed through Portugal, Spain
and Switzerland to Italy.

The end of 1993 had found Dave taking time out from the
circus and getting involved with *Backbeat*, a film based on the
early days of the Beatles in Hamburg and specifically the life
of their original bassist Stuart Sutcliffe. Rather than try to
replicate the sound in precise detail, the filmmakers recruited
an alternative music supergroup to pay a more approximate
but spirited homage. It consisted of Dave on drums throughout, the Afghan Whigs' Greg Dulli on vocals, noted producer
Don Fleming on guitar and vocals, REM's Mike Mills on bass
and vocals, Sonic Youth's Thurston Moore on guitar and Soul
Asylum's Dave Pirner on lead vocals.

This line-up had convened at Ocean Way Studios,
Hollywood to rock 'n' roll their way through such Fab Four
standards as 'Twist and Shout', 'Slow Down', 'Bad Boy' and
'Long Tall Sally', though it was notable that the Lennon-
McCartney compositions that made the Beatles' name were
conspicuous by their absence – not surprising, as they had yet
to be written at the time the film was set. Britain enjoyed

singles 'Money (That's What I Want)', 'Rock and Roll Music' and 'Please Mr Postman'. Confusingly, two albums were released with the similar title *Backbeat: Music from the Original Motion Picture Soundtrack*, the other featuring jazz instrumentals. Grohl's version had scenes from the movie as its cover, the other a painting by Stuart Sutcliffe.

The events that followed Grohl's return to the fray were sufficient to script any number of movies. In the early hours of 4 March, Cobain, in a coma, was rushed to Rome's Umberto Prima Hospital having overdosed on a mixture of champagne, Roipnol and Clorariohydrate. He emerged from the coma the following day and was discharged several days later, but it had given partner Courtney Love a scare. 'I woke up at six in the morning or something, and I reached for him ... I know it sounds glib, but I really thought he was dead,' she said. She also admitted that 'We're going to go back to the therapist when it all calms down.'

Three dates into his final tour, Kurt had called Courtney in tears after he'd walked through the audience in Madrid and been given the thumbs-up by kids smoking heroin off tin foil. 'He did not want to be a junkie icon,' Love told journalist David Fricke – but it was too late. His audience now thought of him as much as Kurt Cobain the drug user as Kurt Cobain the singer, songwriter and musician. And even the reassuring presence of Courtney by his side couldn't change that.

His empathy with the fans appeared to have well and truly evaporated. Cobain's diaries railed at fans whom he accused of stealing his notebooks. 'The most violating thing I've felt this year is not the media exaggerations or the catty gossip but the rape of my personal thoughts,' he said. 'Ripped out of pages from my stay in hospitals and airplane rides, hotel stays etc. I feel compelled to say "Fuck you" ... to those who have absolutely no regard for me as a person. You have raped me harder than you'll ever know.'

Yet even he seemed to concede that there was an element of hypocrisy in this, coming from someone who seemed to revel in obsessive self-hatred. 'For every one opinionated, pissy, self-appointed rock judge-curmudgeon, there's a thousand screaming teenagers. Hope I die before I turn into Pete Townshend.' He would get his wish.

Following an alleged suicide attempt on 18 March, a less confrontational version of an 'intervention' meeting was attended by friends and colleague of Cobain, including Grohl, following concerns about his increased heroin use. The aim was to persuade Kurt to face his problems.

Sadly, just under a month later, on Friday 9 April 1994, came the news that shook the world. Reports started coming in that a visiting electrician had found a body at the Cobains' Seattle home. Medical examiners confirmed that Kurt's body had been identified; he had 'died of a gunshot wound to the head, and at this time, the wound appears to be self-inflicted.' Notwithstanding this verdict, conspiracy theories that Cobain had been murdered soon began to spring up, with everyone from Courtney Love to Geffen Records as the masterminds behind it.

Not since the death of John Lennon in 1980 had a generation been faced with such an event. And the reaction was surprisingly similar. Thousands turned up to hear Courtney read his alleged suicide note at a vigil (inevitably, it soon appeared as a T-shirt print), while even grunge arch rivals Pearl Jam sent expressions of sympathy. The rock world had lost more than a leading light – it had lost the spokesman who'd put the thoughts, hopes and fears of a generation into words and music.

Kurt's suicide meant the cancellation of the band's remaining European dates, including what would have been the band's first UK tour since 1991, which had already been rescheduled following the incident in Rome. Unused tickets became instant collectors' items.

Prophets are without honour in their own country – at least while they're still alive – and it was proposed that a statue of Kurt should be erected in an Aberdeen park. Krist Novoselic threatened to smash it down, arguing that Kurt wouldn't have approved, so the statue – by sculptor Randi Hubbard – was offered for sale to the highest bidder, the proceeds to go towards a scholarship fund set up by his old school.

After the dust had settled, Geffen Records released the televised acoustic set in November 1994 and to no one's surprise it topped charts worldwide. Grohl and Novoselic paid an undisclosed sum to free themselves from any further obligation to the label, and announced future plans: Grohl, switching from drums to guitar, was aiming to relaunch his career with a new group, Foo Fighters, while his surviving companion planned to write a book about the whole Nirvana experience.

Death, of course, made a martyr of Nirvana's main man, and it took Dave Grohl to pop the balloon: 'It's changed the way I look at musicians that passed [away] before Kurt,' he said when, on the tenth anniversary of his death, the familiar Cobain visage could be seen on the front of hundreds of magazines, music-related and otherwise. 'Ian Curtis of Joy Division, Jimi Hendrix, John Bonham of Zeppelin – you have to consider these people as human beings who had bad habits and were very real. It's funny that a person can become an image...'

For Dave, there had always been an inevitability about the ending. 'I always had the feeling that we could only be so good for so long. I couldn't see myself being 45 years old playing 'Smells Like Teen Spirit'. But nobody really knew what was going to happen. That's one of the reasons why it was so exciting, 'cos even in the last year of Nirvana things were pretty unpredictable – in both bad and good ways. It's something I'll never long for again 'cos when you've had something so good, why would you want it again? It'll never be as good as the first time. Success is more of a personal thing now. I set myself goals and try to do different things. Like being a singer and playing guitar. When I feel too comfortable with that maybe I'll go and play the clarinet.'

For now, though, he found himself relentlessly chased by the media. 'The day after your friend dies and *American Journal* wants to talk to you and [prominent television journalist/anchorperson] Diane Sawyer wants to do an interview ... It made me so fucking angry. It made me so angry that nothing was sacred any more. No one could just stop, not even for a day or a year or the rest of our lives, and just shut the fuck up. So I decided that I was just going to be the person to shut the fuck up.'

Grohl dropped from view, re-immersing himself in his family and spending time with his mother in Washington DC. 'Krist and I kept in touch, and we would get together and talk, make sure we were each doing OK,' he said of his band mate. 'Eventually, very slowly, things got back to a more normal pace. Everything changed, and it's going to take a long time to get used to that.'

But there was to be no shortage of demand for Nirvana product. The CD of *MTV Unplugged in New York* topped the *Billboard* Pop Albums chart for a week in November, while the band won a Grammy Award in 1996 for Best Alternative Music Performance. Ironically, one of the competitors was (first LP) *Foo Fighters*. The year 1996 also saw the release of a live Nirvana LP, *From the Muddy Banks of the Wishkah*, in September, containing concert performances culled from the whole of the band's live career, 1989 to 1994. This too topped the *Billboard* album chart for a week and reached Number Three in the UK. While two songs, early versions of 'Polly' and 'Breed', pre-dated Grohl's time with the band, there was much here for him to be proud of.

Krist Novoselic had been involved in its compilation, Dave being occupied with other matters. It was rumoured that Dave had intended to put together a similar disc to accompany *MTV Unplugged in New York*, but was too emotionally stressed to consider the project so soon after Kurt's death.

If *Muddy Banks* filled a gap in presenting Nirvana live – 'plugged' and in their element – there would be a long gap before a box set, *With the Lights Out*, was cleared for release. This was largely due to wranglings between Krist and Dave on the one side and Courtney Love on the other. All kinds of unsavoury quotes were traded over the matter, and it seemed as if Grohl and Novoselic would be denied their wish for 'closure'. That was in 2001, the time of *Nevermind*'s tenth anniversary.

Grohl and Novoselic claimed Love 'couldn't care less about Nirvana fans. She is using Nirvana's music as a bargaining chip to increase leverage for her personal gain, without any regard for the Nirvana legacy.' For her part, Love maintained Cobain was by far the driving force in Nirvana's success, and that Grohl and Novoselic were little more than hired hands.

The sticking point appeared to be 'You Know You're Right', the track the trio had recorded in early 1994 during the one fruitful day in a three-day session. (As it had never been released before, all parties had to agree to its appearance.) In the event, this appeared as an enticement to buy on a self-titled Nirvana compilation of otherwise well-known material, released in October 2002, which went on to sell over one and a half million copies in the United States alone. 'You Know

You're Right' became a single with a video that topped the MTV Countdown.

But if the success of that album was financially rewarding, the box set was the project that mattered to fans and musicians alike. The peace treaty with Love had seen the set's track list extended to include the best material from the boxes of cassettes Cobain hoarded between 1987 and 1994. (A compilation entitled *Sliver: The Best of the Box* followed.) Meanwhile, Novoselic revisited his Nirvana past in the long-promised book *Of Grunge & Government: Let's Fix This Broken Democracy!*, which also addressed his longstanding interest in political activism.

The final three-CD set, released in November 2004, not only included previously unreleased tracks but also a bonus DVD of footage of the band. As the Geffen Records press release confirmed, 81 tracks were included in the set, 68 of them never previously issued, while the DVD shows previously unseen footage of the band at rehearsals, in the studio and during live shows. Sleeve notes by Thurston Moore completed the package.

'We were looking forward to releasing unheard Nirvana material for our personal sense of closure,' Grohl and Novoselic had said before the lawsuit with Courtney was settled. 'As the cycle of life moves forward, we are each living our own lives and moving on to new things. We only wanted to go on with the assurance of knowing that all of Nirvana's music is where it really belongs; in the hearts and minds of millions of people in the world.'

Grohl's first live performance after Cobain's death came on 12 July 1994 in the company of Krist Novoselic and a ten-year-old guitarist, Simon Timony. He had released a four-song EP which he'd sent to Kurt and the gift had been mentioned in the sleeve notes to the out-takes album *Incesticide*. His then stepfather's band Half Japanese had opened for Nirvana in the autumn of 1993 (Jad Fair has been described as 'Kurt Cobain's favourite singer'), which gave the band and the infant prodigy the opportunity to meet, and Simon had even got on stage with Nirvana that November at the Roseland Ballroom.

The reason for the performance was a festival being held in Olympia by local label Yoyo, and Simon Timony's band Stinky Puffs, which also included his mother on drums, had asked Krist if he would like to sit in. Dave had arrived as a spectator and was persuaded to set up another kit and join in. 'Come on with us ... this'll be good for you,' his former band mate urged. And though Dave insisted 'I'm gonna fuck it up – I don't even know your music,' he agreed. The assembled press made a bigger deal of the event that it probably deserved, though the set, which was recorded and released the following year as a mini-album boasting the unlikely title *A Little Smelly Bit of the Stinky Puffs*, contained a song the youngster had dedicated to his dead muse, 'I Love You Anyway'.

Nirvana's musical legacy, of course, just wouldn't go away. In February 1998, readers of *Q* magazine voted *Nevermind* fifth greatest album of all time, while *In Utero* came in at 63. A year later, the February 1999 issue cited 'Smells Like Teen Spirit' as the readers' choice for best single of all time. Nirvana's popularity appeared not only to be enduring but increasing; the evidence came in January 2003 when *Q* readers voted *Nevermind* as greatest album of all time, with *In Utero* up to 11th place. The same magazine then nominated the band's legendary appearance at the Reading Festival in 1992 as one of *the* gigs of the 1990s. The list goes on and on...

Grohl is well aware he will never escape his past, and that his obituary will likely be headed 'Nirvana drummer...' Likewise, he will never have a last word to say on the subject, as the questions will keep on coming. But this will do for now.

'It was incredibly funny. Because there we were, these three people playing music in someone's garage, and all of a sudden we made a record and everyone looked at us like we were the rebirth of rock 'n' roll. And I thought, "What the fuck are you talking about? We're just a band." They looked at us as if we were spokesmen for a generation. It was so strange. I didn't feel any different from the people who came to see us play. And people were looking at us and looking at Kurt especially to tell them what to do. That was when it stopped being quite so hilarious and just became scary. I'd never want to be a spokesperson for anything in case I said the wrong thing.'

It was time for Dave Grohl to step out from behind the drums and sing his own words...

6

STRIKING OUT

'**N**one of these songs are about Kurt. I wouldn't even embarrass him like that.'

The forthright words of the former drummer with Nirvana, now guitarist, singer and frontman of his own band, Foo Fighters, laid to rest the first part of his musical journey and marked a new beginning. He was addressing the audience from the stage of London's King's College on his band's eagerly awaited UK debut in June 1995.

The point was well made. There was a link to Dave's glorious past in blond-cropped guitarist Pat Smear, who had been added to Nirvana's stage line-up in their closing months to beef up their sound. His presence at Dave's shoulder emphasised that there was clearly no embarrassment about his early days. And it would be crazy to feel that the bidding war, in which the world's labels behaved like frenzied sharks in the contest to sign up the new four-piece, would have been anywhere near as intense had the magical seven-letter N-word not been involved.

Yet the band one writer would memorably describe as possessing 'a unique adrenalised thrill that comes only from the shotgun marriage of speed, volume and the sweetest melodies on earth' was, on first hearing, well worth consideration on its own merits. Grohl was running as fast as he could to get the project off the ground, while simultaneously distancing him and them from past events and formations.

'When we started this group, I just wanted to make it seem real and in no way contrived. You know, this pretentious sort of "rising from the ashes of despair" thing. It was like: "Fuck that, man."'

Anonymity is something only craved by those who have lost it. For Dave Grohl, releasing a solo record called *Foo Fighters* had been an attempt to suggest a band project at a time when he had yet to recruit the musicians he would line up with under that name. Likewise, the invention of a new 'pseudo indie-label' imprint, Roswell, might encourage the purchaser to believe he was in possession of something almost home-made, and certainly not a product of the major label system. 'I wanted to get an independent distributor to send it out into the world,' Grohl somewhat naïvely claimed, 'maybe 10,000 or 20,000 copies, so that people would think, "God, who is this band Foo Fighters? I've never heard of them before." I just wanted it to be this real anonymous release.'

This was, of course, nothing more than wishful thinking. The ever-eager press had been waiting for either of the surviving members of Nirvana to make their move, and it was clear that millions would watch the drummer's next venture, whatever and whoever it should involve. Yet expectations were not that high in some quarters, with one former publicist confessing that he had felt Dave would merely 'go out and play the big clubs while he counted his *In Utero* royalties.' Certainly, while the past notoriety of Grohl and Pat Smear would count for something in the short term, a band fronted by a drummer was unlikely to make it to the post-Nirvana big league inhabited by the likes of U2 and Red Hot Chili Peppers.

Not that Foo Fighters was the start of the story of 'Dave Grohl, Songwriter'. As has previously been mentioned, the song Kurt overheard Grohl working on in the drummer's initial months with Nirvana in Seattle, 'Color Pictures of a Marigold', had been recorded during the sessions for *In Utero* and released as a B-side on the 'Heart Shaped Box' single, titled simply 'Marigold'. It was the only Nirvana song to feature Dave on lead vocals.

And he was able to take full advantage of the fact that he'd stockpiled material while not in a position to use it. Of the debut disc's dozen songs, only four – 'This is a Call', 'I'll Stick Around', 'Ecstatic' and 'Wattershed' – had been written since the demise of his former band. His aim in making a record of his own was to get 'everything as together as possible, having everything be tight and in sync.' With seven days to record 15 songs, 'there wasn't too much time spent sitting on a chair thinking.'

But let's rewind a minute – because anyone who thought Dave Grohl's first 'solo' release was the *Foo Fighters* album was wrong. If they could dive into their record collection and locate a cassette copy of *Pocketwatch* by a band called Late!, then a close inspection of the small print would confirm that they were in possession of a rare and significant artefact that had strong connections with the Foos' release.

The ten-song tape-only release on the Arlington-based Simple Machines label was the product of two sessions some six months apart in 1990 and '91, cut in different studios. Grohl, who played and sang everything except some backing vocals supplied by producer Barrett Jones, was credited as the fictitious Alex 'Vanilla' McCloud.

The first session had taken place in Laundry Room Studios two days before Christmas 1990 – mere weeks, remember, after he had joined Nirvana – and yielded such tracks as 'Hell's Garden', 'Petrol CB' and 'Friend of a Friend'. Renamed 'Winnebago', 'Steel Forces' would become the B-side of Foo Fighters' debut single in re-recorded form, while 'Milk' would become 'Alone+Easy Target' , a track on the debut Foos LP. Last but far from least, 'Friend of a Friend' would be re-recorded for 2005's *In Your Honour.*

Simple Machines' Jenny Toomey heard these early efforts and, impressed, hassled Dave for a tape. 'About six months later he gave me one when I was visiting Olympia. My label was releasing a series of cassettes that focused on music that was unfinished, imperfect, or unfinished and perfect by bands that no longer played [gigs], like Geek, My New Boyfriend and Saturnine. It made perfect sense for Dave to add his solo tape to the list and he said yes.'

The tape's final track listing read as follows: 'Pokey the Little Puppy', 'Petrol CB', 'Friend of a Friend', 'Throwing Needles', 'Just Another Story About Skeeter Thompson', 'Color Pictures of a Marigold' ('Heart Shaped Box' B-side), 'Hell's Garden', 'Winnebago', 'Bruce' and 'Milk'. The recording date quoted for the other tracks was 27 July 1991, which ties in with Jenny Toomey's recollections, but Barrett Jones claims that the tape was the product of several different sessions.

The tapes released by Simple Machines were duplicated from the second-generation copy Grohl gave Toomey – 'but it's been a sort of thorn in our side,' she told *Goldmine*'s Gillian G Gaar in 1997. 'Each mention of the cassette in *Rolling Stone* or wherever translates to piles of mail, and for the most part these kids have never bought anything through the mail from an independent record company. So when they haven't received their tape in two weeks they write us nasty notes about how we've stolen their $5 and their mothers are going to sue us ... But the one strange redeeming quality of the tape is the tape itself. Almost every time I listen to it – even now, at this point of definite saturation – I still think it's a great record. It has a depth and vulnerability and crunch that you don't find on a Foo Fighters record.' Toomey believed it benefited from lacking the 'formula that goes through [the new record] ... He plays these noisy, Melvins-like songs with his sneaky, sinewy melodies and this great voice coming over it. And his melodies are just heartbreaking.'

An upgraded CD version of *Pocketwatch* was mooted, in which the existing tracks would be supplemented by bonus cuts, but as Foo Fighters took off this was quietly dropped. According to Toomey, Grohl 'went back and forth with the idea and then it fell off the face of the earth. Which I can understand and appreciate, but his modesty is killing us! I know he also thinks it's cooler to have it this way.'

The cassette is no longer available, though the songs still exist on-line for those prepared to look for them. The material has also cropped up in various permutations on a number of bootlegs: titles such as *Dave Grohl Demos*, *Fighting the N Factor*, *Pocketwatch Demos*, *Reading '95 & Unreleased Demos* and *Up Against!* exist, many of them also containing live Foo Fighters material from a later period.

Encouraged by what he had achieved off his own bat, Grohl had continued to demo tracks of his own when Nirvana were off the road, and by the band's demise had gathered some 30 or 40 unreleased songs (although he'd only rate 15 as being of recordable quality). He seriously considered a regular job or a college course in the six months following Kurt's death, admitting that 'I was as confused as I'd ever been. I was always going to be 'that guy from Kurt Cobain's band', and I wasn't even sure if I wanted to make music any more. But eventually the desire finally came back and I realised I was going to do what I'd really wanted to do since I'd written my first ever song – book myself into a studio for a week, choose the best stuff I'd ever written and really concentrate on them.'

A seven-day studio session took place in Bob Lang's studios in October 1994 and the 15 songs recorded would form the basis of the first Foo Fighters album. The music invariably came first, to such an extent that Barrett Jones had to bully him into taking time out and writing lyrics so songs could be finished. 'I was in the corner with a pad of paper trying to find something to rhyme with Ritalin!' said Grohl, who estimated coming up with a singable lyric took up around half the total session time.

Job done, Dave then made his first mistake of the week. 'The trip to the tape-to-tape duplication lab downtown to run off 100 copies. My second mistake was my generosity: that tape spread like a virus, and before I knew it I had an answering machine full of record company jive. I'd give tapes to everybody,' Grohl continued. 'Kids would come up and say "Nirvana was my favourite band" and I'd say, "Well ... here, have this."'

Without any pre-release promotion or advertising whatsoever, Foo Fighters' debut album had become a hot property and, even two months before the album's official release date, radio stations in Los Angeles and Seattle began airing unfinished tracks. 'There's really not much you can do,' Grohl eventually conceded. 'If you don't want anyone to come to your shows then don't make a record, don't be in a band. Stay in the basement.'

Like so many fine albums, *Foo Fighters* was committed to tape with great speed, a week being all that was needed to complete releasable versions of the 12 songs. Greg Dulli of the Afghan Whigs (with whom Grohl had previously worked on the *Backbeat* soundtrack) was an interested observer who confessed himself 'completely fascinated' by the process. 'He'd do a whole song in about 40 minutes. He could do it because he has perfect time. He'd lay down a drumbeat and work off that. He'd play drums, run over and play bass, then put two guitar layers over the top and sing it.' Dulli is the only other musician featured on the album, playing a guitar part on 'X-'.

The result stunned *Metal Hammer* reviewer Pippa Laing, whose five-star review said it all, with an inevitable nod to Nirvana: 'Grohl has transferred from drum stool to mic and guitar with astounding ease. His vocals have the same winsome quality as Cobain's, but, and here's the crux, Grohl's achieve a far wider range, never grating.' *The Rough Guide to Rock* similarly rates it 'a brilliantly paced and infectiously catchy debut. Distortion, melody and attitude merge to make this an essential release.'

But press interest and analysis, piqued by the pre-release 'leaks' that had caused Capitol to call up radio stations and order them to 'cease and desist' playing unfinished versions of tracks, remained intense. It was somehow assumed that Dave's first solo musical statement would reflect recent events, and every line of every song was perused with this in mind. Grohl, who insisted 'By no means am I a lyricist' and regarded most of the first album as meaningless rhymes, later revised his opinion. He admitted that 'a lot of times the things you write down [on the] spur of the moment are most revealing. Now I look at them and some of them seem actually to have meaning.'

The final line of 'Weenie Beenie' – 'One shot, nothing' – was just one supposed reference to Kurt's suicide, even though the song was written around 1991. The obligatory round of post-release interviews took this further, and Dave admitted that 'It really pissed me off. If I was to meet someone knowing that a good friend of theirs had died, the last thing I'm going to do is ask them right off the bat: "How do you feel?"'

While he admitted that 'No one has ever said anything to my face like "You were a fucking asshole for doing this,"' Dave sensed a tinge of resentment in certain quarters. 'I'm sure that the thing I was supposed to do was become this brooding, reclusive dropout of society and that's it. Nirvana's done, I'm done, that's the end of my life. Fuck that.'

He also revealed he missed Nirvana 'with all my heart. I listen to live bootlegs all the time because I miss it so much. I miss Kurt. I dream about him all the time. I have great dreams about him and I have sad, heart-wrenching, fucked-up dreams about him. I miss it all a lot. But if you're dealt a fucking hand then you deal with it. And I'm not about to just drop out and stop living. If there's anything I've learned over the last three years,' he concluded, 'it's that you've got one life and you'd better live it as much as you can. I'm not going to sit back and be some fucking pitiful mess because that's what everybody wants me to do.'

The first album was released on Independence Day, 4 July 1995. (Coincidentally or not, Independence Day 1947 was the day of the incident at Roswell that gave Grohl's record label its name.) The original plan had been to press a limited run of a few thousand with no indication as to Grohl's involvement. When news got out, Capitol Records won the bidding war, but the label name and logo remained. Dave realised that, had he not had a past, Foo Fighters would 'have been just some other band, and I'll be the first to admit that. But to denounce that or say I really wish I hadn't been in Nirvana would be a fucking lie.'

Its maker didn't rate *Foo Fighters* that highly, considering it 'an excuse to get in the van and run around the world for a year. It was never intended to be a solo project.' When it was suggested it possessed the same vibe, feel and level of excitement in its grooves as *Nevermind*, his comment was telling: 'I know what you're saying, but it's just ... well, let's say I hope not.'

Inevitably and depressingly, initial press interest in *Foo Fighters* was mixed with morbid curiosity about the previous year's events. *Rolling Stone* had a writer who apparently spent four days without success trying to set up an interview, his editorial brief being to make it Kurt-centred. His request was refused. 'People forget there's still a lot of pain there,' Dave's publicist explained. And Dave agreed: 'He was a nice guy [the *Rolling Stone* reporter], but he just kept saying to me, "I'm on the line here, I've gotta ask you about Kurt and that stuff," and I kept on saying to him, "Well, I won't talk about it. I mean … it's very uncomfortable, that stuff."'

The artwork included a picture of Dave holding a kid's toy ray-gun – an XZ38 Disintegrator Pistol from the 1950s. The intention was to tie in with the record's name and tongue-in-cheek sci-fi image. The photo, taken by Dave's first wife Jennifer, was used in all innocence. 'To me it's just a toy,' he told *Rolling Stone* magazine. 'It has nothing to do with anything. I love kitschy 1940s and 1950s space toys. I thought it would be a nice, plain cover – nothing fancy. Then I thought I'd catch so much flak, but everybody said it would be okay, I made sure everybody knew it was just a toy. People have read so much into it. Give me a fucking break!'

The album kicks off in joyous fashion with 'This is a Call', the first single (backed by out-takes 'Winnebago' and 'Podunk') and a song its writer described as 'a little wave to all the people I ever played music with, people I've been friends with, all my relationships, my family. It's a hello, and in a way a thank you.' It was also quite a contrast to the rather negative 'I'll Stick Around', which some said was about Courtney Love.

Even had it not followed the Nirvana 'soft verse/loud chorus' blueprint, the song, with its line 'I don't owe you anything', was always destined to be something of a talking point. 'I realised people might think it was about Kurt,' says Grohl, 'but it would fucking break my heart to think that people are under that impression. That was my biggest fear.

Besides that, anything else is trivial and stupid. And I knew while I was recording it that it was probably the strongest song I've ever written, because it was the one song that I actually meant and felt emotionally.'

'Big Me', written with wife Jennifer in mind, deals with life and love in rather more flippant fashion. Dave: 'Girl meets boy, boy falls in love, girl tells him to fuck off!' Grohl's least favourite song was, surprisingly, one of the last to be written: on the plus side, 'Oh, George' sounds quite confessional and was a throwback to his first recordings. By contrast, 'Alone+Easy Target' and 'Good Grief' are guitar-driven anthems pointing the way to the Foos' group future.

'Floaty' has some of the relentless feel Dave so admired in Led Zeppelin, though he was still self-conscious about his voice and used effects on this track to disguise it somewhat. Double-tracking was also used elsewhere to beef things up a little. 'For All the Cows' was commercial enough to be considered as a future single, while 'X-Static' found Dave's vocal playing second fiddle (if that's possible) to Greg Dulli's guitar. 'Watershed' was 'inspired by my love of hardcore and old school punk rock', said Dave – the two t's in the title refer to punk pioneer Mike Watt of Minutemen/fIREHOSE fame. The album plays out on the melancholy, minor-key 'Exhausted', which fades from hearing in understated style. 'It's sad but it makes you feel good,' said its creator hopefully. And the feelgood factor of the album was undoubtedly the key to its success.

Lyrically, *Foo Fighters* lacks substance – a charge Dave was happy to confess to a couple of years later. 'The lyrics are so dumb, so bad … for the most part it was nonsense.' He reserved his biggest belly laugh for 'This is a Call'. '"Fingernails and … Minicine"? Minicine is a fucking acne medicine!'

Reviews didn't come better than *New Musical Express*'s nine out of ten. 'Hurtling, memorable songs, satisfyingly crunchy guitars, and an unambiguously joyful spirit .... Grohl sounds blazingly optimistic ... [a] talented man at last gaining the confidence and wherewithal to seize control of his own artistic destiny ... a massively important record.' Unusually, the *NME*'s 'inky' rival *Melody Maker* agreed. 'Bloody Essential!' it screamed, deeming it 'a play-loud summer blast ... so blissfully on-the-money it's almost as perfect as the Young Gods, were the Swiss maestros weaned on Hüsker Dü and Anastasia Screamed. We're talking that breathtaking, that joyously gone.'

Rolling Stone's four-star assessment was also upbeat, if more measured. 'Like Nirvana's best work, these songs sagely embrace alternative rock's essential contradiction – this is popular music devised by an alienated few.' *Spin* rated it 'flawed yet worthy' and a 1996 Grammy nomination for Best Alternative Music Performance duly followed. As noted earlier, it would miss out, ironically, to Nirvana's *MTV Unplugged*.

No matter how proud or otherwise he was with the result of his efforts, Dave Grohl now needed a line-up to promote it. Everyone he selected for his new band came with a history. 'But it just means that everybody knows what they are doing. After playing music for so long and being in different situations, you learn to deal with everything, whether it's being fucked up or being away.'

Bassist Nate Mendel (born Nathan Gregor Mendel in Seattle on 2 December 1968) was the first to be recruited, and would prove as much of a fixture in Foo Fighters ranks as Krist Novoselic was in Nirvana – though physically a sight less imposing. (There had been rumours that Krist would indeed be a Foo Fighter, but these never panned out. Besides, he was turning his attention more and more towards politics.) Mendel's career in music since forming his first band at age

14 had been spent as a four-stringer: while he felt playing the guitar 'looked way cool', the fact that his friend Jason Cobb was already more than just proficient pointed him to the lesser-stringed alternative. 'As soon as I picked up that bass,' he said, 'I went on a 20-year detour into punk. I'm still on it.' A friend had told him the bass was the easiest instrument to play, which sealed the deal.

Home was a small town on the east side of Washington State where the youth were supposed to make their own amusement. It was, he later confessed with typical wry understatement, 'not one of the most cosmopolitan places you can imagine.' The town simply wasn't on the rock 'n' roll route map, and the only bands that came were booked by the kids. They tended to be of the punk persuasion, and it was when Scream, featuring one Dave Grohl on drums, came to town in 1986 or '87 that the two first met.

Nate was certainly a major cog in the promotional wheel, 'learning how to book bands and venues and learning how to promote.' Music was 'so much fun and integral to your life.' He particularly appreciated Scream because they were on a reggae label and one of the better hardcore bands around. This compliment came despite a face-off with fellow bass player Skeeter Thompson as they queued for the men's room: 'He looked like an angry bastard,' says Nate, who admitted 'I thought he was going to kill me.'

Anyone who was anyone would eventually escape the confines of a town whose sole purpose was as a dormitory for a military base where nuclear devices were tested. And Nate Mendel was no budding Homer Simpson. His means to a different end was a college course in Seattle, from which he graduated with a degree in history and journalism, but he modestly claims the course was 'just a cover for my other reason [for moving] – which was to form a band.' He was by no means a beginner, that first band, the provocatively named Product of Rape, being followed by the suitably named Diddly Squat. Around this time he had the song title 'Free' tattooed on his back, so certain was he it would be a hit; it wasn't, but the tattoo remains.

Nate's first Seattle exposure came as a member of Christ on a Crutch, who toured for a few years and even released singles before finishing in 1993. Next stop was the 'straight-edge' outfit Brotherhood, whose 'great songs' could only satisfy him for a trifling six months before punk called once more. No sooner had Chewbacca Kaboom introduced him to drummer William Goldsmith than they had changed name to Sunny Day Real Estate and picked up an album deal with the same Sub Pop label that launched Nirvana. Despite the fact that 1994's *Diary* album was the label's second bestseller after *Bleach*, they continued setting up their own gigs, using the street smarts Nate had picked up when promoting in his home town.

Nate's 'in' had been guitarist Dan Hoerner, while singer Jeremy Enigk was a pal of Goldsmith's from their previous band, Reason For Hate. The music was described by some critics as 'emocore', and tours with Soul Coughing and Shudder To Think were well received. The band fostered an eccentric image by such tactics as naming their songs after numbers, and declining to speak to the press or even be photographed. A second album, simply titled *Sunny Day Real Estate* but also known as 'The Pink Album' for obvious reasons, emerged in 1995. But the career of Sunny Day Real Estate hit the buffers when their frontman found religion, so Nate and William Goldsmith found themselves on the job market.

Nate's girlfriend, whom he married in October 1995, was a friend of Jennifer Youngblood, alias Dave's better half, so invitations to Sunny Day Real Estate shows were reciprocated by Thanksgiving dinner chez Grohl. The first meeting with

Dave, in a bowling alley on the aforementioned feast day, led to events unlikely to be forgotten by either of them.

They repaired to Dave and Jennifer's house, which had recently been plagued by strange happenings like burglar alarms going off or feelings that there was someone else in the room with them. When the Thanksgiving festivities degenerated into a ouija board session, the spirits spelled out the fact that a baby had been murdered in the house. Later it was confirmed that a Native American infant had indeed been killed there. 'We never found out who was behind it,' said Dave, who claimed he threw the ouija board onto the fire.

Auditioning for an ex-member of Nirvana might have daunted some individuals – but not Nate. They'd impacted on his world, as they had with anyone between 12 and 32, but he'd considered what they were doing – certainly up to and including the release of *Bleach* – a step backward from his own career in which he was not only playing gigs but organising them. Nirvana were more part of the bar-band scene, playing to older people – the United States having a drinking age of 21, not 18 as in Britain and Europe.

Nate was also, he now recognises, in a bit of a stylistic straitjacket as part of a hardcore scene 'which had an in-built contradiction. It was supposed to be about individualism but really it was very restrictive. I was hearing this record *Bleach* everywhere and this grunge stuff coming through, but I didn't really rate it … until I realised that basically it was just a really good record.' He was equally impressed by Dave. 'He really went out of his way to make people forget he was in this really huge band, which I thought was really cool, really admirable.' For his part, Dave appreciated his new band mate for his frankness, directness and politeness: 'He was a very nice guy.'

Drummer William Goldsmith (born 4 July 1972 in Seattle) came as a package with Nate Mendel from Sunny Day Real

Estate. He'd admired Christ on a Crutch, Nate's former band, but admits it took him a year to get to know him, 'cos he's pretty quiet. Now he's like my brother. After Sunny Day Real Estate we knew we didn't want to play with anyone else.'

They made a powerful rhythm section and Goldsmith, who was influenced by the classic but ill-fated British duo of Led Zeppelin's John Bonham and the Who's Keith Moon, undoubtedly knew how to hit things so they stayed hit. He'd been drumming since fifth grade at school, though his willingness to improvise and add to the written part had seen him slung out of the school orchestra. Subsequent bands, such as the 11-man Screaming Hormones, made little or no impact, and the four years prior to joining Sunny Day predecessors Chewbacca Kaboom were spent quietly learning up music theory. Not something you can envisage Moony or Bonzo doing...

After the band split in 1995, Goldsmith was the only member who elected to stay in Washington DC. He admitted later that it was a low point in his life: 'This was all I had pretty much been doing. I had finally focused on one band and now it was over ... I was just thinking, "What the hell am I going to do?"'

But help was at hand in the person of Dave Grohl, who had witnessed the power of William Goldsmith at first hand at a venue called the Party Hall, a centre of Seattle punkdom, and rated him 'the good drummer of the scene'. His concern was not to find someone who would replicate the drums on the tape, 'but someone who had really good energy. There's not very many of them ... and when I saw Will play I was really amazed.' Rock photographer Steve Gullick, who accompanied reporter Everett True as he covered the scene for *Melody Maker*, remarked that the only two drummers he'd ever seen hit the skins harder were two Daves – the Melvins' Dale Crover and Mr Grohl.

The latter believed he had found 'a fucking awesome drummer' in Goldsmith, one possessing 'the kind of intensity that I would expect ... I sometimes say I'm the least charismatic member of the band – I spend every day with William!' Yet if he needed to be cheered up, it would be Goldsmith he'd head to for a cuddle. The bonding between the FFs' two Gs, Grohl and Goldsmith, took place in the latter's Washington DC basement. 'After the second or third time we had the songs down,' said an impressed Grohl.

Unfortunately, William was the victim of a freak accident during their second rehearsal that sent him to hospital after a drumstick splintered and 'spun up and stuck into my head between my eye and my nose.' It was too dark to see the extent of the injury, though blood was spurting everywhere. 'Dave just laughed and said, "You're bleeding a little bit. Come into the light." I did and he screamed, "Don't look in the mirror!"'

There was then the matter of a second guitarist to be considered. It was never likely that Dave would handle lead guitar and vocal duties on his own, so a foil had to be selected – probably the most crucial decision in his assembly of a band so far. He recalled Nirvana's search for a similar musician in which the Melvins' Buzz Osbourne, Mudhoney's Steve Turner and Eugene Kelly, late of Nirvana favourites the Vaselines and Eugenius, had been the reported front runners. In the end, the finger of fate pointed at Pat Smear, a man who, apart from his musical skills, was at the other end of the visual spectrum from both Cobain and Grohl.

Born Georg Ruthenberg, Smear (later described by an awestruck Grohl as 'the coolest guy in the world') certainly lacked nothing in terms of an exotic lineage – and at 6'1", this boxing fan presented an imposing figure. His Cherokee Indian mother and German father had got together in Los

Angeles, where he was born on 5 August 1959. His youth had been nothing if not dramatic, a spell with a religious sect being followed by another as a pupil at the Innovative Program School, an educational establishment in Santa Monica which majored on 'problem children'. As it turned out, he had soon-to-be famous classmates in the shape of Sonic Youth's Kim Gordon and Black Flag's Kira Roessler.

Another significant alumnus was Darby Crash, then trading under his given name of Jan Paul Beahm and described by one impressed critic as 'a disturbed high school dropout ... a combination of Johnny Rotten and Sid Vicious rolled into one obnoxious blast of phlegm, and fury.' Together he and Smear formed the Germs, whose 1979 album *GI* was hailed as a cult classic. Produced by Runaway Joan Jett, it bridged the gap between New York New Wave and Los Angeles hardcore. An all-female rhythm section of Lorna Doom (bass) and future Go-Gos' singer Belinda Carlisle (drums, soon replaced by a succession of sticks people) completed a line-up that seemed set to go places. Unfortunately Crash's fatal heroin overdose in December 1980 ended such thoughts – and, by departing this world the day before John Lennon, he ensured his demise was noted by relatively few outside the band's circle. Out-takes and live recordings have since surfaced, but few if any capture the essence of a band whose influence can be seen today in the likes of Green Day.

Smear more than played his part in building the legend. Indeed, in a scene where it was considered not the done thing to own more than one guitar, he would show up with no instrument at all, borrowing one from the support act once they'd finished their set. He broke his rule for the band's farewell tour, when he purchased an obscure Swedish guitar, a red Hagstrom, for just over $100, in the process beginning a love affair with the brand.

The Germs' music certainly made an impression on Dave Grohl and Kurt Cobain. But Smear diversified, starring in Penelope Spheeris' rock-doc *The Decline of Western Civilisation* (one of Dave's all-time favourite films) and going on to appear in *Blade Runner*. A re-entry into the rock 'n' roll world appeared possible when the Red Hot Chili Peppers shortlisted him as a replacement for guitarist John Frusciante when he quit the band in May 1992. But Nirvana nipped in to secure his services when it was felt a second guitarist was required. So he found himself playing a part in that band's latter days, riding the same tour bus as Kurt while the rhythm section travelled in the other.

For Pat Smear, Kurt Cobain's death was a replay of the Darby Crash demise nearly a decade and a half earlier, and it appeared to hit him just as hard. He spent a good deal of time, quite possibly a year, in front of a television with a remote control in his hand. 'I didn't know if I ever wanted to be in a band any more, ' he confessed in a rare interview. It took Grohl a certain amount of courage to risk rejection by handing him his tape when they met in a club, but Smear took it home and 'flipped'. He hadn't known what to expect, but was so impressed he went right back to the club – but begging for a job was out of the question. 'I didn't want to ask to join the band. I waited for him to ask me.'

According to Dave, he gave Pat the tape 'as a friend, but he said he really liked it, especially 'For All the Cows', so I asked him to join.' The invitation duly issued and accepted, Pat was the first linchpin in Dave Grohl's return to the stage. By choosing someone he had played with before, albeit mostly seen the back of, he was limiting the risk and splitting the pressure. It also helped establish Foo Fighters as a band in its own right rather than the one-man show the eponymous first album had been.

Yet Dave had had his doubts as to the sincerity of Smear's acceptance. 'Until he said he was getting his guitars ready for the [first] tours I swear to God I thought he was too cool for us,' he insisted. For the first couple of weeks I thought he was just being nice and wasn't 100 per cent into it.' The fact that he preferred to play barefoot and insisted on a case of Perrier water on the tour rider were just two more jigsaw pieces that went to make up the picture of a fascinating individual.

Smear was an essential element of Foo Fighters because of his proficiency as an editor in Grohl's songwriting process and his ability to provide comic relief in the van. When Grohl was asked to assess each of his current band members, he rated Pat 'definitely the star of the show, the focal point of the band, and everyone looks up to him. William makes things exciting. He's like everyone's little brother, and we love him and take care of him. Nate is like the foundation. He's the solid, level-headed, intellectual type.'

The Foos would prove to be a band that, from the off, was able to travel the world in five-star luxury on a first-class ticket. In contrast to the wranglings over money in Nirvana, Grohl confirmed his nice-guy status by sharing the royalties from the first album among the band, notwithstanding that they had not played on it.

The first Foo Fighters world tour lasted some 18 months and gelled the four disparate characters into a slick, well-oiled working unit. But meeting his public inevitably stirred unhappy memories for Dave, who would look out from the stage at many gigs to be confronted by hundreds of Kurt Cobain images staring from the front of, more often than not, unofficial T-shirts. 'The commercial exploitation of it all is horrible,' he admitted, adding that he felt the lack of respect shown by these market traders was 'unbelievable ... You're dealing with a human being. Some people use the name Kurt Cobain like he was a fucking plastic doll – he was a human being with a mind, a heart and a soul. It's just too bizarre to have something like that happen to someone you've known.'

He recognised, however, that only 'maybe 30 per cent' of the people who came to his new band's early shows had bought the *Foo Fighters* disc. The remaining 70 per cent 'were coming just to see someone from Nirvana in person. I think also a lot of people came down to see if we could pull it off, to see if it was as good.' Comparisons, he admitted, were inevitable.

The very first Foo Fighters broadcast took place at the behest of Pearl Jam's Eddie Vedder, who booked them for his *Self Pollution Radio Show* on 8 January 1995. Two tracks were played from some early band demos, though they were played at that time under Dave's own name. His friendship with Vedder led to him guesting with his band on three Australian dates a couple of months later. He jumped up to play on three covers: The Dead Boys' 'Sonic Reducer', 'Against the 70s' by Mike Watt and 'Rockin' in the Free World', a Neil Young song.

The Foos' transition to the live stage was carefully planned, with no great fanfare or flashbomb. An informal 'keg party' in Seattle in February was the venue for a performance to family and friends, while the public caught a first glimpse with an unannounced slot in support of an unknown band called the Unseen. Intended as a break from mixing the album, it happened at a club in Arcata, California, in late February. The Foos were determined to enjoy the event in their own way, creating their own merchandise by stencilling their logo over charity-shop-purchased T-shirts by the unhip likes of the Hooters. Their set over, they had a drink or three and made merry to the headliners' set of bar-band covers.

Krist Novoselic was at a benefit gig at Seattle's 150-capacity Velvet Elvis Art Lounge in early March 1995, the second of two curtain-raisers after one in Portland, where demand to see them exceeded the available space by a factor of three. Krist watched intently but did not participate as the band unveiled new songs like 'This is a Call' (the first single), 'I'll Stick Around', 'Big Me', Good Grief', 'Winnebago' and 'Ecstatic'. After further wood-shedding dates at Silverlake and Albuquerque, the Foos then embarked on their first low-key US tour, opening for Dave's good friend Mike Watt on 20 dates that stretched from late April to mid-May.

Watt was the man credited with helping put US punk guitar-rock on the map in the 1980s as one third of the Minutemen. Without Watt's seminal first band, there might have been no charted way forward for the likes of the Chili Peppers or even Nirvana. But the Minutemen – who toured incessantly in the early 1980s, often with Black Flag, and released records on the SST label that would catch the ear of Kurt Cobain and many more US punks – finished abruptly in 1985 when guitarist D Boon was killed in a car accident.

Watt and drummer George Hurley were dragged from their depression by Ed Crawford, a young guitarist from Ohio whom they backed for the next seven and a half years as fIREHOSE. That ended in 1994, and Watt was newly solo and pushing his album *Ball-Hog or Tugboat?* when Grohl's band joined forces with him. Dave had played drums on two tracks on the album, 'Big Train' and 'Against the 70's'; Krist Novoselic played Farfisa organ on the latter, with Eddie Vedder contributing guitar and/or vocals. Pat Smear also popped up elsewhere. But it was in introducing Dave to the live arena that Watt (who was saluted in song via the first-album track 'Wattershed') would be his greatest favour.

'It was so incredibly refreshing to go out and do something where you're frightened, really scared to do it,' Dave later recalled of his debut as a frontman. 'Every once in a while, in the middle of a set, my stomach would turn and I'd have a little panic attack. I don't have the charisma of Bono or Steven Tyler or whoever, and by no means do I want to be considered Front Guy. That's like my worst nightmare.'

Another problem cropped up when audience members insisted on calling out for Nirvana numbers. 'I was afraid I was never gonna shake it off,' said Grohl, who had originally thought they were joking when they shouted for such songs as 'Heart Shaped Box.' Fortunately this was to be just a temporary annoyance.

April 1995 saw Dave bring it all back home with a show at the Black Cat in Washington. When the club opened in late 1993, Grohl invested in a 20 per cent stake, saying simply 'It's something I wanted to do,' even though the club at this point was merely a 'break-even proposition.' The manager, fellow punk drummer Dante Ferrando, had wanted 'investors who were in it for the right reasons. People who knew that a rock club is not a great investment and want to do it anyway so that the music gets heard. Dave was an obvious person to approach of all the people I knew who might have money to invest and who might be interested in Washington having another good live music club.'

Following a temporary derailment when Goldsmith popped his left elbow out of joint while hurdling a concrete post in a parking lot, they took the show on the road again – this time headlining. Determined to keep things low-key, Foo Fighters stuck to playing medium-sized venues in the company of Shudder to Think and Wool, the post-Scream project headed by the brothers Stahl. They broke off to make a debut TV performance courtesy of David Letterman, where the current single 'This is a Call' was duly plugged.

Although strictly speaking a new band, it was madness to let the Foos make their Reading Festival bow in the summer of

1995 on the *Melody Maker* stage. Even allowing for Nirvana's history with the event – was that show really only three years earlier? – demand to see Dave's current band meant an inevitable crush, cases of heat exhaustion, and a set that ended abruptly after 20 minutes to the disappointment of all. How ironic that their second single, released just days later, was 'I'll Stick Around'.

Reading's organisers had tried without success to get the Foos to give up their headlining second stage status to play the main stage. This they duly did the following year. The one saving grace about shortening the set to a mere four numbers was avoiding injuries to those who'd scaled the tent poles to get a clear view of their heroes. Stagediving from such altitudes wouldn't have been advisable.

The Reading show had been preceded by the Foos' UK debut, the previously mentioned deliberately low-key effort at King's College London on 3 June. They were technically support act to Teenage Fanclub, but there was little doubt who the majority of the crowd were there to see. The album was still days away from release, so it was to be expected that a fair few Nirvana T-shirts peopled the refectory where a higher than usual preponderance of music business people were curiously awaiting the next chapter. The set they heard was basically the album, plus unreleased 'Butterflies' and future B-sides 'Winnebago' and 'Podunk', delivered by a band Dave later admitted were 'like baby does [deer] in the headlights.'

The gig had been the record company's idea, Dave told *Raw* magazine. 'They said, "Why don't you come over and do one show in London to legitimise yourselves as a band?" I thought it sounded kind of stupid to fly over on Wednesday, play on Friday and fly out again on Sunday. But then I started thinking that if we went over and played a good show it would probably be fun. At that time we were sort of waiting for the English press to tear us to shreds. Because they usually do. Sometimes they love you at first and then they knock you down. But it was actually really fun and I was glad that the few people who were there got to see us play.'

There were those who considered the timing a little disrespectful – notably *Melody Maker*'s Everett True, the man who'd put Seattle and Nirvana on the map as far as British music fans were concerned. He penned a scathing review of the King's College show and later admitted to having 'a large element of resentment ... almost like "How dare Dave get on with his life?"' 'I know what you mean,' Grohl responded when the pair met again towards the end of 1995. 'I had almost a year of sitting on my ass and doing nothing and I realised I had to get out and do something now or else sit on my ass forever.'

Dave considered that the majority of fans were happy that he was playing in another band: 'At first it was kind of difficult for people to see Foo Fighters as a band in its own right, cos when we played shows before the album came out people were just coming to see us because I used to be in Nirvana. To see the progression from that to the way it is now has been really nice.'

He explained there were certain things he still wouldn't discuss. 'I'm not gonna sit around and discuss Kurt's suicide cos that's personal. It's mainly out of respect. You don't do that, especially when a person isn't around to defend himself any more. It's like talking behind somebody's back. With my family and friends I'll talk about it as much as I want. There are a lot of people who are very protective of me, wanting to make sure nobody makes me angry. But I'm not Michael Jackson. I'm a pretty normal person. I appreciate people want to take care of me but I'm a big boy now. I'm 26 years old. I think I can take care of myself now.'

The first single, 'This is a Call', had done particularly well in Britain, where it headed into the chart on the first day of July, peaking at Number Five and remaining their biggest UK hit in that format for seven years until equalled by the Grammy-winning 'All My Life'. Next up was 'I'll Stick Around', which was backed by two otherwise unavailable tracks. The Velvet Underground-sounding 'How I Miss You' featured Dave's sister Lisa plunking bass, while 'Ozone' was an obscurity aimed at fellow Kiss fans, being a cover of a solo track by their guitarist Ace Frehley.

It became the Foos' second UK chart entry at Number 18, and was promoted in Europe by further August festival appearances in Holland and Belgium. After a month on home soil, they were back out again in October, kicking off a European tour in Sweden. As they worked their way through Scandinavia, reports suggested that the first new songs written with the band (as opposed to Grohl solo) were finding their way into the set, along with a cover version of the Gary Numan/Tubeway Army electro-pop classic 'Down in the Park'. The song being a decade and a half old, there were probably many fans who were unaware of the original. A studio version would later appear on the soundtrack album of the *X-Files* film.

Foo Fighters' first full British tour in November 1995 sold out well in advance, and a relaxed Grohl was determined to enjoy the moment. 'I figure you're the guys who couldn't get into the tent at Reading,' he wisecracked to the crowd at Brixton Academy – and the audience loved it. Fans at Wolverhampton, Glasgow and Leeds had played 'spot the new song', the likes of 'Up in Arms' and 'My Hero' enjoying their first live airings.

Little wonder, then, that Dave was already looking forward to the next record. 'We've got eight or nine new songs and we've been really trying to experiment – using a different tempo, new chords and different moods. Avoiding monotony is a big challenge and the next album will see us recording together for the first time. That's something to look forward to.' He felt that there was still a fair amount of scepticism about. 'Some people want to see our next album be a fucking mess, but we're glad about that because it's just another obstacle that we have to overcome. You know, there's a lot more to this band than this fool who played drums for Nirvana.'

The end of 1995 saw Foo Fighters heading eastwards, after launching the third single from the album, 'For All the Cows', on US TV's *Saturday Night Live*. Australia, Japan and Hawaii all proved happy hunting grounds, a New Year's Eve gig in Sydney cementing a bond between the band and that city. Unfortunately, William Goldsmith had to miss a gig in Singapore through ill health, but Foo Fighters returned to the States in good spirits.

A year and two million sales on from the debut album, Grohl would reflect on Foo Fighters' status: 'I guess everyone will always see this as being my band. The press hate to put four faces on the cover of a magazine. They just need one, and that's a fucking shame. When it comes down to the real shit – which is the four of us in one dirty little practice room – then it's just the four of us.'

He didn't feel the band had the personalities to be 'a sensation like Oasis or Alanis Morissette. The music we write, sure it's poppy and has some hooks and melodies, but I just don't think it's the kind of thing that eight million 12-year-olds are ever going to be able to palate.'

It was now time for Foo Fighters to consider their first recording as a band, but frustratingly the year had been booked out with live dates and an early-in-the-year recording session would only yield one track, 'Enough Space', that would make it onto the next album. Instead the ensemble launched their next US tour in March 1996 by inviting members of the press to a bleak, concrete-walled rehearsal room on the Seattle outskirts. There they were ceremonially handed protective earplugs by Pat Smear. 'This is the loudest fucking practice room I've ever been in,' he smiled, before turning up the volume knob on his guitar and proceeding to suit actions to words.

The 32-date tour wended its way from Denver to Los Angeles, where they played a free show at the legendary Whiskey A Go Go. Annoyingly for the other band members, the new single release was yet another first-album track, 'Big Me', but at least they were featured on the bonus tracks which were taken from a BBC Radio 1 session from the previous November.

The European festival circuit called that summer, two months of concentrated live performance that caught them at something of a peak. Their critically acclaimed set at the UK's Phoenix Festival ended a run that took in Poland, Norway, Belgium, Ireland and France. A smattering of club shows took their two-month tally to an astonishing 40-plus. Also active that summer were the re-formed Sex Pistols, who were cashing in on the 20th anniversary of 'Anarchy in the UK' with a 'Filthy Lucre' tour, much to ex-punk Dave's delight. Other artists with whom they rubbed shoulders included metal-rave synthesists the Prodigy and legendary glam-rocker David Bowie: relationships would be formed that would bring collaborations in the months and years to come.

The end of the touring in August 1996 saw Dave faced with a dilemma. 'I just wanted to stay home for a while,' he admitted – but he couldn't resist the chance to score a Hollywood movie when it was offered to him. The clinching factor was that he could write the (mostly instrumental) music for *Touch* without having to leave home, so he took on the task after a week's vacation. As with his first album, he once again performed virtually every note save for a few guest spots by the likes of John Doe of X.

He also drafted in Veruca Salt's Louise Post to appear on a number of tracks, and the pair were the subject of relationship rumours, wife Jennifer Youngblood having now departed the scene. The rumours were intensified by the pair's duet on a steamy track called 'Saints in Love', while another, 'Touch', was compared with Cocteau Twins. Many felt a disc of Dave and Louise together would be a highly marketable proposition, but it was not to be.

Directed by Paul Schrader, *Touch* starred Bridget Fonda and Christopher Walken and was based on an Elmore Leonard novel about an unscrupulous faith healer. It wasn't critically well received, one reviewer suggesting that while Paul Schrader had 'done some interesting work in the past as both a director (*Light Sleeper*) and a writer (*Taxi Driver*), here, he has gone off track.' The soundtrack album that was released on Roswell/Capitol in March 1997 as *Music from the Motion Picture Touch* (and somewhat formally credited to David Grohl) is, however, well worth investigation, attracting such praise as 'Who would have thought that a drummer would turn out to be grunge's Renaissance man?' from the *Sunday Times*. It's all the more amazing when you consider it was completed in two weeks without any visual inspiration.

By early October, Grohl and his fellow Foos were ready to begin pre-production on the new album at Barrett Jones' 24-track studio. Simultaneously, the month also saw the release of yet another of Nirvana's back pages in the shape of *From the Muddy Banks of the Wishkah*, a collection of live performances stemming mainly from the autumn 1991 US tour that brought them to prominence. Rated 'a gloriously electrifying aural photo-book of a truly legendary rock 'n' roll band' in *New Musical Express*, the release made it clear that Dave Grohl hadn't yet, and indeed might never, escape the shadow of his former band.

CHOPPING AND CHANGING

G rohl has often said that he prefers to avoid confrontation. Hence departures from the Foos' ranks over the years have been less than clear-cut, causing complications when a short sharp break might have been advisable. The decision to dispense with original drummer William Goldsmith, made public in early 1997, was the first such event.

The sacking was not only traumatic for the musician concerned and the man who made the decision, it also impacted on Goldsmith's long-time band mate Nate Mendel. The pair had been recruited 'as a piece' from Sunny Day Real Estate, and were as close as brothers.

'Dave wasn't used to dealing with situations like that,' the bass player later opined diplomatically. 'I think now, given his experience, he would deal with that differently. He was learning to be a leader. It put a lot of strain on mine and William's relationship. But things are different now, we're talking again.' In an interview with *Kerrang!* magazine, Mendel suggested his long-time rhythm partner had been (over?) fond of partying. 'He took care of it for everybody. He'd get drunk, smash windows, wind up on someone's floor across town...' Given Dave's 'born again' attitude to drink and drugs, perhaps this was not the wisest behaviour.

That said, and perhaps mindful of the dictatorial nature of the Nirvana experience, Grohl was bending over backwards to bring democracy to Foo Fighters. So much so, indeed, that ten of the 13 songs on second album *The Colour and the Shape*, the first to be recorded by the four-piece band, were credited to the group as a whole. The other three were noted as having been written by Smear and Grohl.

Gil Norton, a producer who had many respected credits, oversaw the recording; perhaps most notable among his previous accomplishments was the Pixies' *Doolittle*. Dave particularly admired 'his knack for making a really fucked-up sound sound really ... divine. He can sort of polish a really messy guitar sound so that it's still a messy guitar sound, but it's really clear and distinct. The clarity on all those records is really great. You can hear everything. It's so good.'

The pair had met in New York to listen to some tapes of the band rehearsing. Dave admitted his experience of producers was minimal, so he didn't know what to expect. But he was not disappointed. 'We sat down and started listening to them and within two seconds he started making suggestions. He got through the verse and the chorus of one song and he said, 'Oh, you know what you should do? You should take that guitar line and the chorus and bridge it...' It was exactly what I imagined a producer should do.'

In the studio, his new friend turned into 'a fucking whip-cracker. He has to do things ten times because that next take might sound a little better.' This exacerbated differences between band members and ramped up niggling tensions. But in terms of lyrics, Grohl's admitted weakness, pressure proved a positive. With just four weeks to write lyrics for 13 songs, he came up trumps. The former reluctant lyric writer found plenty of inspiration in recent events. The end of his marriage was the major factor that fed his muse, leading one critic to remark that 'The album seethed with pain, anger and regret, and featured some excellent songs to boot.' Grohl himself, a notably private person, reflected that the album had been recorded in the midst of 'an awful time'.

'It's strange, the way it's all fallen into place,' he later mused. 'It seems like it was intended to be this thematic, conceptual thing. It wasn't, but when I look at it now ... I was joking that the cover should be just a picture of a therapist's couch. It's just weird. The way it's worked out is just really weird. And it's liberating. The lyrics are like my therapist's notepad. Completely bizarre. I can really say if people start asking about the last six months of my life, I can honestly say, "Go read the lyrics." I'm not even saying "Go try to figure it out from the lyrics," just read them. It's right there.'

Leaving aside the personal nature of his song words, he felt that the bar had been raised now he had a band to translate his ideas into music, obliging him to raise his game on the lyrics front. 'If you have a song like 'February Stars' where the music seems so powerful and compelling,' he revealed, 'you want to match that with [words] that really hit home.' In general, he concluded, 'I wanted the lyrics to be far more personal and revealing.' They were.

The first album's lyrics had been obscure for a good reason. 'They were nonsense,' he stated, only partly in jest. 'A few songs meant a lot, but for the most part I just needed a vocal track. In no way do I consider myself a clever lyricist, or even a lyricist. I can't even write fucking postcards. How am I going to write songs that really grab someone? The first album, *Foo Fighters*, I was just so afraid of anyone understanding anything I had to say – but I had no choice for this record. It's a question of what is more difficult – writing something you genuinely feel, or to mask something. I think it's more difficult to write something that means nothing. They're about last winter, the winter of my discontent.' Gil Norton, he explained, was the catalyst, refusing to let Grohl break for dinner until he'd written some lyrics: 'Every time I wrote a bad line I'd get 40 lashes.'

Production wise, he didn't want to make the record a lo-fi basement project, Grohl says. 'I'm sort of tired of these bands who write really amazing pop songs and record them on an 8-track for the sake of recording their album on an 8-track; people who think that's the punk rock purist thing to do. That would be the wrong thing for this band. For these songs.' With four or five guitar parts going on at once, he explained, 'I'd rather have this sound like a Queen record than, say, a ... Rapeman [Steve Albini's band] record.'

Musically, he conceded that 'I could never have made an album like this on my own.' When he was a one-man band, he explained, 'I could hear the song in my head before it was finished. And when it was finally mixed I knew exactly what it was going to sound like. This time it was such a mystery.'

The guitar chemistry between Grohl and Pat Smear seemed to have gelled from the off. Dave pointed out that when he was up high on the guitar fretboard, Pat would be 'way down here', but for the most part the newcomer was left to his own devices – as long as the result passed the acid test. On one song, Dave actually plucked up the courage to ask him to play a different chord. 'I was so scared. It's so scary saying "Maybe you should try this..." I sat there thinking about it for five minutes. "How am I going to ask him to do this? How am I going to say that's not the right chord?"'

The first recording session for the album at Bear Creek Studios in Woodinville, WA, had taken place before Christmas, but with Gil Norton a notoriously hard taskmaster there had been many takes for each song – unlike previous albums, when accuracy had often been sacrificed for spontaneity. An album's worth of material was laid down, but the atmosphere was not satisfactory.

The new year of 1997 had brought a welcome distraction for Dave in a guest appearance at David Bowie's 50th birthday party. 'He looks totally fucking amazing! He's 50 years old, he could practically be my parent,' said a star-struck Grohl. His appearance on 'Hallo Spaceboy' saw him drumming on a stage for almost the first time since Nirvana, discounting his low-key appearances with Mike Watt. When *Melody Maker* asked him how it felt drumming again, Dave's four-word answer was 'It hurt. Really bad!' He then added: 'I was laughing at William so bad, cos he was looking like he'd just seen a ghost.' Prophetic words?

Having paid his respects to the Thin White Duke (Dave would later make a cameo appearance, playing guitar this time, on Bowie's next album, *Heathen*), the Foos' main man returned to the task in hand. While William took a break from the band to be with his family in Seattle, the focus moved to Grandmaster Studios in Hollywood. This was handy for Dave, who had moved to the West Coast after his marriage break-up.

William was apparently waiting for a call to rejoin his band mates to record his drum tracks when he was told he was out of the band – a certain D Grohl played on every track. The split was announced on 4 March, the official statement reading as follows: 'We are all very sad that William is leaving. It's like losing a family member. Plus he's such an amazing drummer. It is my sincerest hope that he will continue to rock the universe in all his future endeavours.'

The Capitol Records press release accompanying the album's May appearance was at pains to put the record straight – or at least still any ripples. 'Rumours that Goldsmith was ousted or left due to Grohl's alleged recording over his tracks have proven unfounded, as Goldsmith has left on completely amicable terms. "The idea that I just scrapped his tracks and did them over is just wrong," Grohl explains. "We re-did entire songs. The LA recordings are different versions. Completely different. We basically re-did a lot of the record. William just felt that he didn't want to go back out on the road again for such a long time. I don't know if he'd ever gotten used to the idea of being in a band that would play a festival in front of 60,000 people or a headlining show for 4000. Let alone doing things like that for a year and a half. I think William felt like he'd be more comfortable living a more stable, grounded life."'

There was, it seems, no animosity on Goldsmith's part, just a certain world-weariness. 'I just wasn't happy. It got on my nerves as far as expectations of my drumming went. I guess a lot of people wanted me to be Dave, and I would rather be me.' His contributions would remain on the tracks 'Doll' and 'Up in Arms'.

Melody Maker's Victoria Segal, talking to Grohl not long after Goldsmith's allegedly acrimonious departure, found him, in her words, 'hiding behind the old musical differences/other goals barrier. Dave doesn't like to be rude.' Mind you, she was also not encouraged when she claimed there was 'a cohesion on this record that the debut LP didn't have. A specific dominant mood. "Hmm. I don't know what that would be." Well, a battered romanticism: "If you walk out on me / I'm walking after you", "It's true the two of us are back as one again" – they're the lyrics that stand out. "Interesting."' The Grohls' marriage split was not then public knowledge, and he was clearly not in the mood to encourage speculation.

Dave's ability to slip in behind the skins as if he'd never been away may have something to do with the fact that he had never quite quit the drumming mindset. 'When I play the guitar I look at it like a drum kit,' he explained. 'The lower strings are kicks and snares, and the higher strings cymbals. Sometimes a guitar riff can be a kick and snare pattern – the lead riff in 'Everlong' is like playing the drums and then you've got a chorus with strings ringing out over everything else, like washing on cymbals. I approach everything that way – even lyrics and vocals are a lot like playing the drums.'

Back in 1996, Dave had perfected 'a cookie-cutter answer' to the question of what the new album was going to be like, 'cos I'm gonna get it so much. It's gonna be such a natural progression. You look at the first LP and it was basically a studio album, recorded by one person, so you don't have the dynamics of four different personalities, you don't have the contribution of three other amazing musicians. So this album will probably take advantage of the live aspect of recording rather than sounding so studio-ish.' Even so, there was just one first-take recording on the completed album.

That pat answer, he concluded, had 'a nice professional vibe. I could almost con myself into thinking I know what the fuck I'm doing.' When the time came to be more explicit, the songs on *The Colour and the Shape* were, according to Grohl, 'about everything that's happened to me in the last 18 months.' He felt it was important to do something that was unexpected: 'We had to grow and mature. There is a song called 'The Colour and the Shape' that we were going to put on the record that was almost like another 'Weenie Beanie' sort of song, just another screaming, fast, hardcore song, but we decided not to put it on, because it was a step backwards, we've done that already.'

His relationship with producer Norton improved over time, to the extent that he proclaimed, 'I learned more from Gil than anyone else. That recording session was a lesson in patience. We wanted to make a tight, hard-rock record, and I always thought my guitar playing was pretty tight, but Gil taught me the meaning of 'spot-on'. He tuned my ear a little bit, so now I can tell when a guitar part is really, really on. Doing 30 takes in a row, trying to get things perfectly in sync. That was work, man! I had never experienced that level of precision before. It was a great lesson.'

First single from *The Colour and the Shape* was 'Monkey Wrench', a song Dave described as sung by someone who realises he is 'the source of all of the problems in a relationship and you love the other person so much you want to free them of the problem...' He really put a lot of passion into the vocal, auguring well for the album, which followed a week after the single in May 1997.

It was preceded by 'Doll', a track retained from the William Goldsmith sessions and a song of regret that sets the tone for what would be a really confessional album.

'Hey, Johnny Park!' takes Dave back to his carefree childhood when his best friend of that name lived across the street. 'We were like brothers from the age of five to 12,' he explained, 'but I haven't heard from him since I was about 14.' Whether this version of Friends Reunited actually put them back in contact is unknown, but the song had one foot in heavy metal musical territory. 'My Poor Brain' is the cry of someone who just can't take the pressure, and the musical temperature was ratcheted up several notches. Grohl's shorthand of 'Jackson Five to Black Sabbath ...sling it all in there' only goes part of the way.

'Wind Up', with lyrics tellingly described by Dave as 'The story of the relationship between the journalist and the musician', seems to hark back musically to Grohl's youthful, hardcore days. It contrasts markedly with next track 'Up in Arms', a pure and simple power-pop song with a theme of reconciliation. Another huge rocker, 'My Hero', tells how

Grohl's youthful heroes were 'ordinary people – people you can rely on.' Hockey player Jim Craig was an obvious candidate here. Next, as if to avoid establishing a mood, comes 'See You', Dave's favourite song and one he claimed nobody wanted to put on the record. Any resemblance to 'Crazy Little Thing Called Love' by Queen is purely intentional.

'Enough Space' was inspired by a movie called *Arizona Dream*, one of Dave's favourite films, while 'February Stars' is a song that starts out slowly before building to a huge riff monster. 'A song about hanging on by the tips of your fingers hoping you don't slip and fall,' said Grohl, giving a rare insight into his personal life, was always destined to be a single and a live favourite, while 'Walking After You', 'an emotional, sappy song about getting dumped', almost has a touch of the Lou Reeds about it. It was the odd song out on the album and a throwback to *Foo Fighters* in that it had been recorded as a solo effort at the studio of Washington's WGNS radio station during a two-week break to assess the work in progress. It was the only demo-style track to make it on to the record, and Grohl acknowledged that 'It was the moment. I'll never be able to capture that again.' The song also appeared on British television, making the soundtrack to BBC2's cult drama *This Life*, but, as recounted later, it would make an altogether more prestigious return in a large-screen situation.

Final track 'New Way Home' embodies the realisation that Dave had come through the negative experience of separation with renewed hope for the future: 'At the end of the day, you realise that you're not scared any more and you're gonna make it.'

Given that the first album had been mined four deep for singles, it was no surprise that a similar number would emerge from its successor. 'Monkey Wrench' had been the first in April 1997 to be followed three months later by 'Everlong'.

More time would elapse before the appearance of 'My Hero' (January 1998) and, belatedly, a new version of 'Walking After You' in June. The album reached Number Three in the UK and Number Ten in the US. In 2005 it remained Foo Fighters' biggest US long-player, with 1.9 million units sold.

Reviews tended to be middling. *Rolling Stone*, who gave it three stars out of five, described it as 'a big, radio-ready, modern-rock sound ... gives the impression that Grohl is working out some romantic issues – there are lots of relationship tunes both about breaking up and about a new love...' *Spin*'s six out of ten rating reflected 'a simple rock guy in a simple rock band who occasionally manages to write some really good songs. He'll probably never come up with a godhead masterpiece, but then again, he already played drums on one.' *Entertainment Weekly* was keener. 'The band heard on *The Colour and the Shape* is not a ragtag slacker unit but a bunch of confident, powerful pros – brawny, metallic, able to shift gears and tempos on a dime ... In fact, the album often feels like the new-wave metal Metallica should have but didn't concoct with *Load*.'

Though Dave told *Kerrang!* magazine he still hated his voice, he admitted that it now 'sounds good on record. It works in the studio. And I feel a lot more comfortable singing now because I've had it blaring out at me from monitors for the last year.' As with *Foo Fighters*, however, Gil Norton had not been averse to a touch of automatic double-tracking in places to give the vocal a bit of added substance.

Grohl had nothing but the highest praise for his colleagues' efforts, especially four-stringer Mendel, whose work, he felt, enhanced the whole. 'Nate's an amazing bass player,' he enthused. 'He's so good at finding a sub-melody. I come up with a riff and I want to find a perfect vocal melody, something that's unpredictable, clever, and not so similar to anything else.

I'll think I've found that perfect melody and I'll be singing along, thinking, "This is so great, it goes so well with the chord progression," and then Nate starts doing this bass thing that just blows the vocal melody away. He's just got such a great sense of melody.'

By the final stretch, the band was bouncing between recording and mixing in the space of the same day. 'I had resigned [myself] to the idea that I was going to be in the studio for the rest of my life,' says Grohl. 'By this time, it was the middle of February. Four months of being in the studio. And the one day that I had off while we were in LA, I went to another studio to go fuck around. I just couldn't be out of the studio. After the record was finally done, it took me two weeks to get used to the idea, the feeling of not being in the studio.'

Maybe he just needed somewhere to call home because, from the previous November to May, he hadn't had anywhere permanent to live and had been pursuing an itinerant lifestyle. 'I was sleeping on friends' floors, then I'd go to a hotel for a week, then back to my friend's floor. It was probably a good idea to find somewhere to live, to have some kind of foundation before we go on the road. So I had four days to find a house. I got all my stuff from Seattle and drove to LA and found this house, but I'm never here! My neighbours must think I'm in prison.' Loneliness, however, wasn't an issue. 'I'm currently single. But I'm also currently not speaking about my personal life to anybody. I don't get lonely. I have a wonderful circle of friends and how could you possibly get lonely surrounded by 15 people every day for a year?'

If the departure of William Goldsmith hadn't been premeditated, no time was wasted in introducing his replacement. The chosen one was Taylor Hawkins, formerly the man stroking the rhythmic fires behind the angsty Alanis Morissette, a fast-rising young Canadian singer.

Hawkins and Grohl first met in late 1996 at a festival in Seville headlined by Neil Young. At that point Hawkins, a major Nirvana fan, had ascended rock's greasy pole to the point that he was playing behind the former child star Morissette, whose first grown-up album, the confessional *Jagged Little Pill*, would top 16 million US sales by 1998 (28 million worldwide) and win her numerous industry awards. At that time, then, Alanis was bigger than the Foos – but while Taylor admired her songwriting, saying 'I thought she was really clever, especially since at the time there weren't many people like her around,' he remained an out-and-out rocker at heart. He was such a Nirvana fan he was convinced Grohl would think him 'a dork' when they met. But he was surprised to find that his future boss and best friend was 'really complimentary, just a really nice cat.'

So when the invitation to change horses came via a phone call, he didn't think twice. 'The Alanis tour was hard work,' he'd later explain. 'There was a definite feel of this won't last forever – get the money.' His gut feeling proved right as, daunted by the scale of her sudden success, Morissette would take a step back from the merry-go-round of fame and take three years to follow up *Pill*.

Grohl, for his part, explains that he had in fact been seeking advice from Hawkins rather than seeking to poach him. 'I called him in LA to ask if he knew any [available] drummers, thinking that he wouldn't want to join my band in a million years. When he said "Yeah, me," I jumped at it.' Taylor takes up the story. 'After I said I was interested, Dave said: "You're with Alanis Morissette, who's sold 30 million [sic] records: why would you want to be in our little band?" And I said, "Because I love your music. And I want to be in a band that plays rock!"' He felt his current position was being 'part of this machine supporting someone else'; clearly he saw more potential in the Foos than merely being Dave Grohl's backing band.

The route from an Anglo-centric Californian kid impressed by the music of Queen and The Police to Foo Fighters drummer had taken Taylor down many a byway and backwater. The first indication that he would make a living hitting things was at age ten, when he went round to a neighbour's and was taught his first rhythms on 'a little crappy drum kit' after the members of the band had given up and gone outside to play ball. He'd always envisaged himself as a guitar hero – 'playing the drums was for idiots!' – but he picked up the rudiments remarkably quickly and within a week was playing along to his favourite records. 'And then my life just became drums, drums, drums.'

His childhood had been incomplete because there was nothing at which he considered himself 'special'. Now he could make up for lost time – and did. A Jane's Addiction-style band called Sylvia was his first adult 'paying' gig, but it was when he traded Sylvia for Sass – Canadian singer-songwriter Sass Jordan – that things really began to take off. 'This guy told me she needed a drummer because she was going to tour Europe. So straight away I was, like, "Yes!" Going to Europe sounded good to me.' Even better than that, he found himself sharing a stage with the mighty Aerosmith.

But that was as far as Taylor saw himself going: 'I thought I'd be able to say I'd been on tour when I was older and working in a music store selling drum kits.' Until, that is, his fairy godfather stepped in again. 'He told me there was this other lady from Canada trying to put a band together ... He sent me the record, and it wasn't the Police, but I was being paid to play the drums.' This was, of course, Alanis Morissette, who, in a short space of time, became 'the biggest thing since sliced bread. That's when we went over to Europe playing a festival and that's where I met Dave and the Foo Fighters.'

But wouldn't working with the greatest drummer in post-punk music threaten to bring different stresses and strains? Not according to Hawkins, who claims 'it wasn't a problem for me so much as other people.' His big advantage was being able to play a tour (in support of *The Colour and the Shape*) before having to come to grips with recording. He could adjust from the music he had been playing, get in tune with the Foos' rather different approach and be fully prepared to take on the task that had seemingly damaged the confidence of William Goldsmith.

Because, as the band's main writer, there was little doubt that Dave Grohl would have a style of drumming in mind for each and every song. Taylor put his dilemma in a nutshell: 'Do I play like you? Do I play like me? Do I play like us?' After a period of adjustment it all settled down. 'He knows where he wants them to go because they're his songs, but then he also gives me leeway to add. It's more of a collaboration – and that's how it should be.'

From Grohl's viewpoint, 'Taylor is a way better drummer than I will ever be,' and he denies that he is 'some sort of fucking drumming institution or something'. Having interviewers question Taylor as to what it's like playing drums for Dave Grohl 'makes no sense.' Grohl was just happy to have someone behind the kit who's 'capable of anything under the sun.'

Taylor Hawkins' life as a Foo Fighter began in Santa Monica's Alligator Lounge, before the band's second album had hit the record racks. The secret gig basically showcased the new album material, with a few standards from *Foo Fighters* tagged on as crowd-pleasers.

It was gratifying for Grohl that his peers, as well as the public, appeared to be listening to what he was doing as well.

While touring *The Colour and the Shape*, Grohl was asked by rap giant Puff Daddy to remix his track 'It's All About the Benjamins'. It seemed the man who'd recently adopted a beard and a more severe haircut was the acceptable face of rock. The track in question had already been remixed by Tommy Stinson (of the Replacements) but Puff Daddy wanted it to be 'more rock'. 'I laid down some drums, some distorted bass and some effects,' said Grohl, 'but in the end it was too 'rock' for his liking, so he remixed my remix with Tommy's remix!'

After the Alligator Lounge warm-up, the band headed for Britain. And, in a curious re-creation of Dave's first Radio 1 session for Nirvana when he'd cut Vaselines cover versions, he took his own band, coincidentally with a new drummer, into the self-same Maida Vale studios to essay a set of songs by other people. These included Killing Joke's 'Requiem', Prince's 'Drive Me Wild' (a hit for Vanity 6), 'Baker Street' (Gerry Rafferty) and 'Friend of a Friend'. Of course, in point of fact, the last-named title saw him covering himself, and that only because he couldn't remember all the lyrics to the originally intended 'Carry On Wayward Son' by Kansas.

The first world tour by Foo Fighters kicked off in Britain, too – at the Cambridge Corn Exchange, to be precise. 'Our first night was an absolute nightmare,' Dave revealed to Radio 1's Steve Lamacq later. 'It was actually the first proper show we'd played since the Phoenix Festival, so it was like eight months or something like that. It was just a technical nightmare. My guitar kept cutting out and, I'd never done this before, but halfway through the first song I just threw down my guitar, ripped the mic off the stand and just kind of hit the Henry Rollins pose. It was great though, really fun.'

Not content with the Maida Vale sessions, Radio 1 were at the Manchester Apollo for a live broadcast, live and studio BBC recordings finding their way onto subsequent Foos

singles as bonus tracks. A pair of shows at London's Astoria, a
venue with which Grohl was familiar from Nirvana days,
ended the UK leg, with the *Times* acclaiming it as 'assault rock
'n' roll at its finest.'

While he was less able to augment his voice with studio
trickery in a live situation and was forced to rely on his natural
gifts, Dave revelled in the fact he now had two albums' worth
of material to choose from. 'It's so nice because we have these
13 extra songs and the dynamic of the set is just so much ... it
just works. We have heavier songs; we have more poppy sort
of singalong, bouncy songs and the set list just works its way
from beginning to end now. It just works.'

The highlight of the tour, though, had been at Glasgow's
Barrowlands, in Grohl's view 'one of the greatest places to play.
And it's nice because we have a new drummer, Taylor, and he's
really made his way into the band, within two shows it just
clicked. And now we just rattle through the set, just: 1, 2, 3, 4
and we don't give anyone time to breathe and I've been screaming my brains out for the last four nights. It's a little harsh.'

July 1997 was a memorable month for three gigs in
particular, two small, one large. The first saw Dave bring it all
back home as the Foos steamed into the US leg of the world
tour and stopped off at the 9:30 club in his adopted home city.
'I always shoot myself in the foot when I play in Washington,'
admitted an excited Grohl, 'because I call everyone I know and
tell them to come down and hang out, and I'm so excited to
see everybody. But then of course there's not time to spend
with everyone, and by the time I go on I think, "My God, my
whole soccer team from when I was in fifth grade is here and
I haven't had a chance to talk to them." But that's the way it
goes and I hope people understand.'

The month ended with an unusual 'invite-only' show which
took place within spitting distance of Seattle when EMI

Records North America – Capitol's parent company – celebrated their annual convention in 'beautiful British Columbia'. Since the hottest bands on the label at the time were Radiohead and Foo Fighters, they were invited to perform at the minimal-capacity Rage club to an audience of sales reps, secretaries and sundry label employees bulked up by contest winners supplied by a number of magazines and radio stations. With Radiohead the 'opening act' and their new disc *OK Computer* as hot an item as *The Colour and the Shape*, the Foos were spurred on to an unforgettable performance, sadly witnessed by few.

In between those gigs the Foos paid a flying visit to Japan for a rock festival with the Chili Peppers, Beck and Green Day. The chance to play with the Prodigy – 'the best live band in the world' in Grohl's view – would have been a memorable enough experience for Dave and his band mates, even had it not coincided with a typhoon. And even for a man who'd seen most things in the past decade on the road, this was a new and unforgettable experience. 'The show went on and I'm on the stage, the rain coming in sideways, so hard I can't open my eyes. I'm standing in a puddle, holding an electric guitar, with about 60 million watts of power running through everything, thinking for sure I was about to die. They had to cancel the second day because the stage was sinking into the ground. I totally fucking loved it. It was insane.'

The summer of 1997 had found the Foos in 'polite refusal' mode. Every festival organiser had wised up to the fact that Foo Fighters was no longer just a one-man band, and invitations were laid on the table from every self-respecting outdoor event on the rock calendar. Reading, Donington, Lollapalooza...

Aside from the Japanese debacle detailed above, the sole exception/acceptance went to V97 in Britain, because they were offered another chance to play with the Prodigy. Shows at Chelmsford and Leeds were well received, and the band headed home. Little did fans in Britain or their public in general realise that a second upheaval in the ranks was about to occur. And this time it would be the lead guitar berth that was up for grabs.

The Foos' final public show with Pat Smear took place, appropriately enough, in Seattle, at the Bumbershoot Festival on 28 August. It also unexpectedly threw up the rapturously received prospect of a partial Nirvana reunion when Krist Novoselic took the stage during the encore to busk a version of Led Zeppelin's 'Communication Breakdown' and Prince's 'Purple Rain'. Taylor Hawkins admits he was star-struck and, that, looking around at Pat, Krist and Dave, felt 'I'm in Nirvana right now! That was pretty cool.' The spontaneous moment apparently came about because bassist Nate Mendel was being heckled by someone in the audience and didn't feel like carrying on.

So this time Pat Smear was the man heading for the exit door, and the potential reasons were legion. His distinctive, stuttering guitar had certainly made itself felt on *The Colour and the Shape*. But all was not well beneath the surface. Smear did not apparently respond well to direction and Foo Fighters' upcoming support slot to the Rolling Stones was said to have been anathema to this unreconstructed punk.

Another reported sticking point, which Dave dismissed as 'a bunch of internet crap', turned up on the Yahoo music website. 'A news report this week on radio station 102.1 The Edge confirmed the long-standing rumor that Pat Smear has officially left the Foo Fighters. The report stated that he is leaving mainly to avoid being caught in the middle of the ongoing feud between Foo Fighters leader Dave Grohl and his ex-wife; supposedly the hostility between Mr Grohl and the former Mrs Grohl has escalated since Dave Grohl began dating Veruca Salt's Louise Post, and Smear has chosen to extricate himself from this awkward situation by extricating himself from the band.'

'He doesn't like doing press and he hates flying,' was the combination Dave preferred to proffer. He backed up the departure with a theory. 'When Pat joined Nirvana, all his friends were placing bets as to how long he was going to last. This is the longest he's stayed in a band since the Germs. Pat had never really toured other than with Nirvana. He's never been in a band for more than a year, so his career in Foo Fighters was as long as he'd ever experienced. When Pat left it was understood that we were going to continue. All bands make a pact that if one person leaves they're going to break up but it never really works out that way, particularly when things are going well.'

Other suggestions included the 'fact' that Dave's guitar was always given prominence in the live mix. It was also spread abroad that Pat was to replace Eric Erlandson as guitarist in Courtney Love's group, Hole. This move would have been akin to a footballer transferring to a hated local rival, had it come about. But it didn't.

'Pat decided he wanted to leave a while ago, but he agreed to finish some of the touring. Pat's doing his own thing. It's cool,' insisted Grohl as he reeled under the second departure from the ranks in a matter of months. A clash of commitments was blamed. 'I tried to get him to stay but he's always working. He wanted to do MTV's *House of Style* and maybe his own record. He just wanted to do something else, which I completely understand. I wish I could sometimes have a week to decide what I want to do, but our diary is booked up months in advance.'

Pat indeed continued to receive plenty of post-Foo exposure as the new host of MTV's fashion show *House of Style*, into which he was to inject some 'much-needed life and whimsy.' And his departure in mid-set at the MTV Video Awards was stylish indeed. That this was to be an amicable separation was confirmed as he brought on his replacement, arms aloft. Having thundered through two songs of a brief three-number set, he announced: 'That song was my last with the band. I'd like to introduce Franz Stahl, who will be taking over. Rock on, guys. Foo Fighters!' A lesson learned after the Goldsmith affair?

If Pat Smear had been a connection with Dave's past through his links with Nirvana, then the new recruit would see him delving even further back into his address book. And the name he came up with was somehow inevitable – Franz Stahl, after all, was the man he'd left in the lurch when quitting Scream in 1989 for the Nirvana drum stool.

The demise of Scream soon afterwards hadn't managed to split Franz and brother Peter, who'd formed a band called Wool. (Readers may recall they supported Foo Fighters on their first US tour.) They also released an EP called *Buddspawn* and album *Box Set* (both on London Records) and toured the UK with the likes of Tool, L7 and, in 1993, Rage Against the Machine.

Dave claimed that, had Wool not been in existence, Franz would have been his first choice as Foo Fighters guitarist. 'When we started this band, had Franz and Pete not been in Wool, Franz would have been the guitar player in the band. When Wool broke up, I knew someday I'd be playing with him again, and Pat had other things he wanted to do. We've got a world tour planned, and Pat decided it was the right time to leave.' It was also something of a family reunion, as brother Peter was an integral part of the Foo Fighters road crew while planning the launch of a new band, Goatsnake.

When Franz got the call from Dave he was in Japan playing with one of that country's homegrown punk superstars, Jay from the band Lunacy. 'I drank half a bottle of vodka in celebration,' he recalled, delighted that leaving his phone number with old pal Dave had paid off. What he hadn't realised was that he would return from the Land of the Rising Sun and walk straight into a high-profile TV appearance that would constitute his debut as a Foo Fighter.

Having expected to return to a fortnight of rehearsing, the bombshell was dropped that he was to appear at the MTV Awards. So instead of flying back to Los Angeles as had been planned, he took another flight to New York and, after a scant amount of sleep, found himself in rehearsal for the show. 'It was only one song, but it was still the longest moment of my life.' Nevertheless he was pleased 'to be back again with Dave', likening Taylor's recruitment to 'the spark, the infusion of energy that reminded me of when Dave came over to the basement to audition for Scream.'

The fact the new man was awfully familiar, to the Foos' leader at least, came in handy as his first real live dates constituted something of a baptism of fire. The Foos had been paired with chart-topping UK act the Prodigy for a British tour, and as Dave explained there was much debate as to the compatibility of the two acts. 'We were a little worried about the shows because the Prodigy are supposed to be a dance band. I mean, I consider them to be a rock band. But who knows about the kids?' He needn't have worried. 'The response was awesome ... our bands fitted together just fine.'

Having publicly mourned the loss of Smear, Dave had changed his tune somewhat – or at least modified it, with some relief – by the end of the tour. 'I was really expecting there to be some sort of Pat backlash at the shows, you know "We want Pat" or "Where is Pat?" banners. Cos I was really worried about Franz. I was worried that he was gonna be crushed under the weight of Pat-ism. I was expecting it every night of the tour and it didn't happen once.' Dave also went into print suggesting that there were some songs on *The Colour and the Shape* he didn't play on, and, surprisingly, that the rest of the band 'were under his thumb'.

Whatever the truth, Smear was out and Stahl was in. A basic no-nonsense operator, Stahl had refused to use effects pedals when in Scream, combining the throaty sound of a Gibson Les Paul with a Mesa Boogie amplifier pushed to the levels of distortion. A chorus and wah-wah pedal entered his vocabulary during his two years as a Foo, but otherwise he remained refreshingly unspoilt. He publicly looked forward to 'leaving my mark on tape and playing my own parts', but since events conspired to ensure he took no part in an album recording there was little evidence of his stay.

Maybe the biggest impact of the change was the fact that Pat Smear had offered a big stage presence, taking the responsibility for a visual show away from Dave to an extent. Now, with the less visual Stahl at his shoulder, he had to provide far more of the 'rock pose' quotient, something he found he had to grow into. Maybe he could take acting tips from Winona Ryder, his rumoured girlfriend of the time ... but as ever he kept his off-stage life firmly under wraps.

The Foos' first task of 1998 was to fulfil some Far Eastern dates, but the second of two nights in Tokyo was curtailed when Dave was taken ill mid-set – the first and so far last time this has ever happened in his career. Making their way home via Australia, New Zealand and a date at New York's Roseland Ballroom, the band spent their first few days off the road re-recording the track 'Walking After You' for inclusion on the *X-Files* movie soundtrack.

The session took place at Ocean Way Recording in Hollywood, and the reason the song, originally on *The Colour and the Shape*, was being re-recorded was that Dave had not been too happy with the track he'd originally laid down as a one-man effort and wanted to put 'more emotion' into the vocal. Given that the song was one of the more obvious references to his marriage break-up, it was interesting that Dave hoped it would accompany a scene where agents Mulder and Scully finally 'got it together'. 'It would be amazing to see that happen with a song that meant a lot to me playing in the background,' he said. 'That would be pretty beautiful.'

It apparently took about seven or eight takes to get it right, as Dave tried to get all his emotion into the song. That he succeeded is clear from the fact that you can hear his voice cracking and breaking. As a reward, he got to shoot the 'Walking After You' video on the *X-Files* set – though even this was bittersweet as Dave had briefly appeared in the TV show's Season Three, walking in the FBI building with then-wife Jennifer in an episode entitled *Pusher*. The song was released as a limited edition split single in June 1998, linked with a track by Ween.

If linking with *The X-Files* was a cool move for Dave Grohl, then donating another song, 'A320', to the *Godzilla* soundtrack goes down as a lesser achievement. Produced by Talking Heads' Jerry Harrison, and featuring him on piano alongside Tom Petty's Benmont Tench, it was an underrated track and far too good for a film Grohl himself conceded was 'fuckin' lame. We sat through the whole thing wondering where the hell they were going to put the song – and it wasn't even in the movie! Soundtracks,' he concluded, 'act as a recovery fund if the movie does really poor.'

The Foos had stuck their neck out in June by playing the 1998 Ozzfest at the Milton Keynes Bowl north of London, where the audience, drawn by Ozzy Osbourne and his taste in heavy metal bands, were fairly indifferent to their music. (For the record, the other acts were Pitchshifter, Hed(pe), Coal

Chamber, Pantera, Slayer, Fear Factory, Therapy?, Soulfly and Human Waste Factory.) They were fortunate not to receive the customary plastic-bottle greeting from fans who had endured a day's worth of noise for the privilege of enjoying Ozzy and Black Sabbath.

Ozzfest had been a step too far. But for some fans, supporting the Rolling Stones early the same year was a far more dubious move. The band, too, remember the experience with horror. 'They didn't give us a guest list, they reserved 100 tickets that we could buy for $64 apiece,' Dave later complained. 'So if I wanted my sister or girlfriend to come I had to buy a fucking ticket!' To add insult to expense, the Foos didn't get a dressing room in the venue itself (New York's Madison Square Garden) but had to sit in the car park in a trailer. For a band that was dead set against the superstar syndrome, that was nothing less than 'fucked-up bullshit', and certainly reduced Dave's respect for the wrinkly rockers.

After all the aggravation of playing second fiddle to rock's dinosaur elite, it was a relief for the Foos to get out on their own. And the 1998 show was to contain a number of innovations, not least two drum kits on stage so that Dave and Taylor could do percussive battle. 'We get a lot of Genesis jokes, obviously,' said Grohl, in reference to Phil Collins' use of the tactic.

The Foos had finally ascended to the kind of stature Nirvana enjoyed as a touring band, and were now playing the same venues – something Dave admitted to finding unsettling. 'I never remember the names on the itinerary and then we walk in. Yikes. It's bizarre, especially when you have the same dressing room. Most of the venues that we're playing were venues from the very last Nirvana tour. I haven't found any graffiti on the walls that I left. That would be strange. I guess that really would freak me out.'

When the Foos opened their Canadian tour in June 1998 Dave took two hundred-dollar bills from his back pocket before announcing 'Big Me' as 'a stupid love song'. To illustrate the point, he asked for a boy and a girl volunteer to get up on stage and, for the notes he was brandishing, kiss for the entire length of the song. Somehow they survived ... only to be smilingly told 'Get the fuck off of my stage' as they were presented with their prize. Two years later, Dave was offering money from the stage again. This time, he was counting out the price of admission for a guy who had spent the evening throwing things at him. Having been refunded, he too 'got the fuck off of Dave's stage' – without, we suspect, a farewell kiss.

Talking of money, Dave had not only bought his Mom the house he grew up in but taken her advice on investments. 'The least punk rock thing I've done recently was to invest in a chain of Microtel hotels, because they're nice little hotels! My mother stayed in one of them and thought it was really good. I made quite a bit of money out of it, actually. So that's pretty un-punk rock. But I'm something of an expert on hotels. Hell, I've stayed in enough of them.'

Grohl had been rootless again since the break-up of his marriage, and while he enjoyed busying himself in work (notably a production job with female-fronted punks Verbenas, who'd supported the band in 1997), he found himself questioning the life he was leading. Consulting therapists didn't provide a coherent answer, so he dealt with it by relocating from Los Angeles to the comfortably familiar surroundings of Virginia and buying a house there. He'd never intended to leave Virginia, he explained, 'but I just wound up in Seattle because my services were needed. It's so nice being back. I'm near my family and all my best friends. It just feels like "Okay, life begins again. This is where it all starts."'

He'd had a fantasy about buying a farm until he took a reality check and realised that 'I don't even have time to comb my hair, let alone farm anything. I figured I could grow something that wouldn't take up too much of my time ... like Christmas trees. All I'd need to do would be remember to cut them down each December and sit by a road selling them.'

Having discarded that scenario, and being master of his own destiny, he decided to build a recording studio in the basement of his new house with the help of Seattle sound engineer Adam Kasper. Named Studio 606, this would be where the third Foo Fighters long-player would start to take shape in November 1998. Indeed, it would come out bearing the proud inscription: 'This album was made in Virginia.'

The demo sessions for what would become *There is Nothing Left to Lose* were a test for the studio and the band alike. But any teething troubles were overshadowed by the fact that a musical split was emerging between the three established Foos and relative newcomer Franz Stahl. Despite having put over a year into the band, he naturally favoured a harder-rocking approach which suited the stage act but not, perhaps, the studio.

While with the Fighters, Stahl's enthusiasm had proved contagious. But his departure caused Dave much grief. 'It's a hard thing to talk about, someone as personal as a friend leaving the band,' he told MTV. 'I've known Franz a long time and it's tough to talk about something that was painful for everyone. I was probably sadder than everyone else.' His pal and abiding influence had twice been a major part of his life, firstly with Scream and then the second incarnation of Foo Fighters. His role had been a crucial one in Dave's development both as a musician and specifically as a guitarist.

But there was no doubt that, as the album plan began to develop, it was a three-on-one situation. And Stahl was the outcast. 'I love Franz,' admitted Grohl, 'but the three of us were moving at a pace and doing something we'd never done. Nate and I were making this connection where he was complementing everything I came up with...' By implication, then, Franz wasn't – and it was apparent that was Dave's requirement of a Foo Fighter. Furthermore, Taylor Hawkins, who'd yet to record with the band, was champing at the bit. 'He was so ready to go he was playing like a madman,' Dave smilingly confirmed, 'and our enthusiasm was really huge. It seemed like most of the creative energy was coming from right here.'

The odd man out had to go. Nate recalls 'a lot of hugging going on' as the remaining trio regrouped and planned how to cope as a three-piece. Needless to say, that wasn't a problem for Grohl – after all, he had two more people on board than when he cut *Foo Fighters* as a one-man band. 'We all went through it together and it made us closer,' was bass player Mendel's summation of a traumatic pre-recording time.

Once the nettle was grasped and Franz had quit, things immediately started looking sunnier. It wouldn't be the first album they'd made as a three-piece, and Dave was immediately at ease having made the hard decision. 'I did the record sitting on a couch I've had for eight years,' he explained, 'and it was the most comfortable environment you could ask for. There wasn't anyone around saying, "This should be a single, this should be shorter, this should be poppier..." Maybe I'll take the couch on tour!'

The result, *There is Nothing Left to Lose*, was arguably the first Foo Fighters album to win rave reviews which didn't contain the 'N' word. To put it another way, this was now a band that stood on its own feet, and any comparison with past glories was unnecessary. The cover, too, set it apart – a stark black and white shot of the nape of Dave's neck, where the band's distinctive 'FF' logo had been permanently etched.

Grohl and co-producer Adam Kasper went for a record that emphasised feel over precision – 'something a little more garagey, not well-produced and pristine.' In many ways Grohl was returning to the DIY spirit of the first, eponymous album, having got too cautious and pernickety on his initial recording attempt with a Foo Fighters band.

With the guitar vacancy as yet unfilled, Grohl played all the six-string parts himself, leaving effects pedals in their boxes as Franz Stahl would have and obtaining the overdrive tones the old-fashioned way by cranking up the amplifier volume and letting his guitar sing. 'We focused on not using too many distortion pedals, and went for a cleaner, fatter, more natural overdrive,' he told *Guitar Player* magazine. 'We used a Vox AC30 [a vintage 1960s amplifier] for pretty much everything on the record, tweaking the sound so that it broke up nicely when played loud. Sometimes we'd double a track using an old Pro Co Rat [distrortion pedal], and then hard-pan the parts so that a super-distorted guitar was in the left channel and a grindy guitar was in the right. Then we'd sprinkle in lots of clean guitar overdubs.'

Some of this, he claimed, was due to the fact he had been listening to music in his truck 'because my car speakers are ruined – everything sounds a little bit distorted, and I love it. If I listen to the same album on a good stereo system, it doesn't sound as good to me.'

That glorious distortion was immediately apparent in the intro of opening track 'Stacked Actors'. The verse is delivered in a threatening croon almost reminiscent of Jim Morrison before the shouty chorus comes in, the words pertaining to 'everything that is fake and everything that is plastic and glamorous and unreal.' 'Stacked Actors' certainly boasts the album's most muscular riff – and the lyric was undoubtedly aimed at a certain Mrs Cobain. 'I hope people have never seen me or the band as something that's fake or unreal,' said Grohl. 'We always try to lay it on the line and say we're making music because we love making music – not because we want to be seen as demi-gods.'

Despite the venomous lyrical attack this represented ('I fucking hated Hollywood,' its now ex-resident confirmed, 'hated most of the people we met'), the album was typified and will be best remembered for two tracks extracted as singles: 'Learn to Fly' and 'Breakout', both of which combine rock muscle and pop hooks in a way unheard since the heyday of Cheap Trick. The recording of 'Breakout' apparently elicited complaints from Dave's neighbours, who thought 'someone was getting murdered ... my throat was gone after that, man.' The lyrics were inspired by wordplay on the title and 'taking the piss out of your typical tortured romance love story.'

In its turn, 'Learn to Fly' has become inextricably linked with its Grammy-winning video featuring the unique comic talent that is Jack Black. The lyric suggested an upturn in the personal life of Dave Grohl. He would later, surprisingly, reveal it was one of his least favourite songs on the record, but that may be a reflection of its excessive popularity and exposure.

Mid-tempo and insistent, 'Gimme Stitches' – the story of a dysfunctional, self-destructive relationship that, lyrically, could easily have slotted into album two – is followed by the second single, 'Generator'. Its thrashy, pop-punk feel, reminiscent of the Mancunian band Buzzcocks, made it an obvious choice, but *Metal Hammer* magazine was unconvinced. 'It's one thing writing a song that is formula grunge-lite ('My Poor Brain') or fixed-grin cheerful ('Weenie Beenie'), but using a voice box device previously associated with 70s rock god Peter Frampton? Oi, Grohl – no!!'

The pulsing 'Aurora' is not only one of Dave's favourite songs on the album but one of the best he's ever come up with. 'Lyrically, it's just kind of a big question mark, but the words sound good and it's a nostalgic look back at Seattle and the life I once had. That song actually questions the meaning of life, probably.' He also believed it was probably the heaviest thing he'd ever written. All the more surprising, then, that it was late in making the cut.

That was also the case with track seven, the most recent to be written. The band had finished recording and had a couple days off before mixing, when Dave came up with a riff so good it just had to be included. The result was 'Live-In Skin', a song whose lyric insists the singer has to 'live in a skin that's new'. The acoustic-intro'd 'Next Year', dismissed as 'stupid and weird' by its writer, is in fact one of two tracks (the Beatles-chordy 'Ain't It the Life' the other) to offer melodic West Coast rock in an almost Eagles-like vein. 'And I hate the Eagles!' spat Grohl. Maybe it was the effect of that laid-back Virginia lifestyle.

Though Dave declared 'Headwires' his tribute to the Rolling Stones' 'Tattoo You', it is in reality very Police-ish, with Taylor doing his very best 'Every Breath You Take' backbeat à la Stewart Copeland. The final track is the appropriately titled 'M.I.A.', the acronym for Missing In Action. It was something Dave admitted he would happily do every so often. 'I'm outta here and I'll be back whenever, and please don't call.'

A version of Pink Floyd's 'Have a Cigar', featuring Taylor at the mic, was included as a bonus track on the 'Learn to Fly' single. 'We started doing this weird Jane's Addiction, Jesus Lizard version of it and we'd listen to the music of it, and I'd go into the control room and I'd keep singing it over and over again and Dave's like, "You sing it! You fucking asshole, I don't want to learn the fucking lyrics, you sing it!"' While the Foos rated this the most punk rock thing Pink Floyd ever did, it would remain a bit of fun – though their version, featuring guitar by Brian May, also featured on the *Mission Impossible II* soundtrack.

The drummer's biggest contribution was to bring his own distinctive style to the album. 'He's faster, the guy's hyperactive and an unbelievably powerful drummer who's favouring a rather complicated style,' was Grohl's expert assessment, concluding that, while Goldsmith had been 'a bit too influenced by my style,' Hawkins was influenced by a lot of other drummers.

Yet however pleased he was with his percussionist, Dave has been critical of the album as a whole in the years since its release, suggesting it produced less than the expected quota of concert classics. 'I love *There is Nothing Left to Lose*,' he's said, 'those are some of the best songs we've ever written. But when it comes to playing live, it was those songs in the middle ground that never really worked.'

The one thing the band learned from the album, Nate Mendel concluded, was that 'We've got a style – and that it's not bad! We can deviate from it and make original-sounding songs, but we're not going to radically alter what we do.' He felt the songs they'd come up with represented 'a progression in our ability as a band' and concluded that having a trademark sound was 'nothing to be afraid of.'

A rumoured appearance at the 30th anniversary of the Woodstock Festival failed to take place as the band had the small matter of recruiting a new guitarist to deal with. 'We had never auditioned a guitar player before,' said Grohl. 'The other guitarists that were in the band, Pat Smear and Franz Stahl, were just friends we asked to come play. We had the candidates learn four songs from an audition tape. 'Off the Ground' and 'Everlong' are pretty basic rockers, but 'A320' and

'Aurora' have lots of guitar parts going at the same time, so it was interesting to see which parts each guitarist would choose to play. Some people just learned one of the three parts, and others expected me to play everything. But Chris [Shiflett] learned all of the parts and figured out – without me telling him – which parts worked best in which places, since all the parts can't be played at once. Chris proved that he was good at knowing which spaces to fill and which to leave open – that got him the gig.'

The newcomer impressively boasted the ability to be 'just as dirty and sloppy as Pat, or as precise as Franz. He definitely plays really tight, but because of his hardcore punk rock background, he also knows when things should be messed up. He really gets into it when he plays, and you can tell when something's building to a climax – he kind of goes off.'

Californian Shiflett was born on 6 May 1971 and raised in Santa Barbara – but far from growing up a Beach Boy, as he might have done in the previous decade, he was inspired to pick up a guitar as one of the millions who joined the Kiss Army. 'I've loved Ace Frehley since I was a little kid,' he exclaims, pointing to the influence of his older brothers (one of whom, Scott, later played in 1990s punk band Face To Face) and their record collections in his enlistment. Dave, an avid Kiss fan in his youth, could certainly empathise.

Taking in every glam/metal band to visit town, Shiflett graduated from Dio through Night Ranger and Alkatraz to the Los Angeles live music scene, courtesy of some older friends in cars who drove him in. There he witnessed names like Guns N'Roses, Poison and Faster Pussycat before they signed recording contracts. But closer to home he enjoyed visiting punk rock shows in the local park, because 'they were the only places you could go with your friends and get drunk.'

When he turned 18, Chris' mother insisted he get a job. Worse than that, it was at the probation office where she worked, so he became a book-keeper in the records room there 'for years and years'. It may have seemed that long, but it was to prove a mercifully brief interlude in his quest for a congenial career.

Heading for San Francisco, Chris' first job in the music industry was in the offices of the Fat Wreck Cords label, which put him in a musicians' circle. And though he'd not played for any serious groups – Me First and the Gimme Gimmes, 22 Jacks and the Lost Kittens being his first, failed attempts – he was happy to throw in his lot with No Use for A Name when label boss Fat Mike came into the office and asked if anyone knew of a guitar player who'd like to audition to fill their vacancy. 'It was the first band that I'd joined that had records out and went on tour – a real band!'

Not that Chris had time to enjoy the fact. Auditioning on the Thursday, he was on tour the following week, 'stoked to be on the road playing gigs.' Two albums would follow, too, *Making Friends* and *More Betterness*, both of which are worth hearing. He spent four and a half years with the band, 'and we'd always say we wanted to open up for the Foo Fighters.'

He was on the way up, and his rise would become yet more stratospheric when he heard of another vacancy that needed filling. His place would be taken by Infectious Grooves riffmeister Dave Nassie, but securing his place in the ranks of the Grohl Army didn't prove a shoo-in. No fewer than 35 hopefuls endured days of auditioning before a result was arrived at. After his first audition, he admits he was 'camped out by the phone for the next week. Finally they did call and we played together for a second time.'

After that, Chris went back to their hotel and got drunk with Dave, who promised to call him the next day. 'I sat by my friend's phone all fucking day, and finally, about five o'clock, they called to say it was on. That night I went out and got completely mashed on beer and sushi!' Little wonder Chris was grinning from ear to ear as he was unveiled to the press via a secret show at Los Angeles' legendary Troubadour Club in September 1999.

His first impression of his future employer was that he was a whole lot bigger than his pictures suggested. 'I walked into the room and thought, "Wow, he's big." He's about six foot. I joined the band and we were bundled off on tour a week later. I was just wide-eyed, I jumped in with both feet...' Dave, for his part, admits his first impressions of Shiflett were 'entirely wrong. I thought that he was this mellow, soft-spoken guy. And once he joined the band, he turned into one of the biggest party-ers I've ever seen in my life! I remember when he started out thinking, "My God, are you the same guy who tried out with us three and a half weeks ago? Hey! Wow!"' For his part, Chris admitted it took a while for the initial 'Oh my God, I am in the Foo Fighters' to wear off... 'but they do make it very easy to be part of the team.'

Chris shares with Dave a love of the chunky tones of the Gibson guitar. He came into the band with an SG (the standard solid-body beloved of one of his heroes, AC/DC's Angus Young) and has since augmented this with a Flying V (his main stage guitar), a Les Paul and a Firebird. Recently he's also been seen playing a semi-acoustic 335 guitar most often used by bluesmen.

When Chris joined the ranks he was in the bizarre position of having to promote an album he hadn't played on, in the shape of *There is Nothing Left to Lose*. It would be fully two years before he would be able to participate in the recording process. And Dave Grohl, for one, couldn't wait. 'We have guitar leads on our songs now,' he gleefully announced, before revealing that the newcomer had shown hidden depths early on in his tenure. 'We have this new fast song we were recording in the room down there and I couldn't really hear Shiflett's amp. When I went back and listened, he was shredding this fucking Yngwie [Malmsteen] lead! I was like Oh my God ... I didn't know you could do that!'

The material on the new album had its first outing at a series of secret gigs played under the pseudonym of the Cracked Actors. These ranged from Los Angeles to Toronto to New York's Bowery Ballroom. There was a subtext to these shows, in that the Roswell label's Production and Distribution deal with Capitol Records had ended and Dave was looking for a new record company to be his label partner. RCA won the race, making the Foos labelmates to Elvis Presley and (in his halcyon years) David Bowie. The first single, 'Learn to Fly', was released in October as the band suited actions to words and jetted to Australia for their first promotion work, with the album scheduled for release on 1 November.

If ever there was a gig the Foos should not have taken, it was surely the Vogue-sponsored VH1 fashion awards in December 1999. As someone who professed himself against what one enraged fan described as 'self-congratulatory, image-conscious Hollywood bullshit,' one can only wonder what persuaded Dave to show up – could it be the influence of future wife (and MTV producer) Jordyn Blum? Certainly, Kurt Cobain would not have missed the opportunity to wheel out 'Stacked Actors', Foo Fighters' vitriolic third-album opener. Instead, they performed their latest single 'Learn to Fly'. In 1999, Grohl had proclaimed that 'The whole thing in Hollywood about fame and beauty and the glorification of the celebrity just made me want to go fucking crazy and kill everyone.' This particular engagement left fans wondering what exactly the difference was between Grohl and the likes of Courtney Love selling out.

That said, the band that toured Britain at the end of 1999 was quite simply at the top of its game. Grohl took the stage in Glasgow at the Barrowlands in a black sweatshirt bearing the legend 'Virginia Is For Lovers' – but for music lovers there was only one place to be that night. The cavernous shed that traditionally holds a football crowd-style audience was beloved by many bands, the Foos among them. 'We've played there a few times and the audience is more enthusiastic than most,' Grohl acknowledged, noting that many bands who'd been around for years still preferred to play there rather than at more 'prestigious' Scottish venues.

It was, of course, heading towards the biggest Hogmanay of all time, and if it was still only late November the Glasgow crowd weren't about to start counting. From the opening 'Stacked Actors' to the finale of 'I'll Stick Around' – and encores 'New Way Home' and first UK single 'This is a Call' – the show was full on, pedal-to-the-metal rock with a capital R. There was, of course, the occasional moment of between-song levity, as when Grohl teasingly started strumming local heroes Travis' recent hit 'Why Does It Always Rain On Me' to the delight of the massed ranks of community singers and the bemusement of his band mates.

At the Brixton Academy, Taylor's tour was made when boyhood heroes Brian May and Roger Taylor of Queen joined the band on stage to play 'Now I'm Here'. As all this was going on, the album was gaining commercial and critical acceptance by the bucketload.

Unfortunately, the touring schedule which the newly re-formed foursome was committed to was to rub all this gilt off the gingerbread with a vengeance. For the next step was an Antipodean adventure that left them more than a little the worse for wear. Dave and pals headed Down Under in 2000 to join the likes of the Chili Peppers, Bush and Nine Inch Nails on the Big Day Out tour of mammoth outdoor arenas.

On paper, the choice had been an easy one to make – Australia, where it was summer and a tan was easily obtainable, and Japan where it wasn't and it wasn't. 'But,' explained Dave, 'we went and jumped on a festival bill, which was the beginning of us jumping on a bunch of bigger bills for the next year. When I look back, I think we would probably have had more fun and would have been better off if we had just done our own American tour.'

As it was, they joined the Australian Big Day Out. 'It was a strange place for us to be, and a strange place to start the year,' said Dave. Maybe the only person to be enjoying things 100 per cent was Chris Shiflett, who had yet to get used to not having to share his hotel room with two or three more smelly bodies! All in all, he believed it was 'a lot easier than going to work in McDonald's every day.'

Dave hadn't bargained for the potency of the local brew. Whether it was an excess of the 'amber nectar' we don't know, but the boys in blue certainly noticed a moped being driven by the chief Foo Fighter and thrust him in the slammer for driving under the influence. 'I wasn't even driving dangerously,' he protested – but found himself banned from Australia's highways for three months.

'I was having the time of my life on the Gold Coast, which is like Daytona Beach,' he later confirmed, 'and rented a moped and, rather than take the bus down to the show, since I'm a do-it-yourself guy, I drove my moped up on stage like Rob Halford from Judas Priest. Afterward, I had a few drinks and was driving to my hotel a mile and a half away, and I stumbled upon a sobriety checkpoint. I thought I'd breeze right through, because I didn't think I was drunk and I was on a moped, which is like a bicycle with baseball cards in the spokes. But I blew over the limit and wound up in the pokey. Now every time I go to Australia I get stopped at immigration and have to tell my ridiculous story.'

The one thing Grohl took away from Australia was a friendship he struck up with Nine Inch Nails' Trent Reznor which would lead to a musical collaboration several years later.

Next stop on returning from Down Under was opening a US tour for the Red Hot Chili Peppers. The Foos had been guaranteed headliner status from the off, thanks to Dave's previous form, but had agreed to swallow their pride in exchange for the ability to reach some 15,000 people nightly with their music. What they hadn't banked on was the tour extending and extending, such was the popularity of the Chilis and the public's desire to see them, until it hit the five-month mark.

The first half of this marathon tour had been playing medium-sized indoor venues, where the auditorium had been more or less full by the time the Foos ended their set. 'There were a lot of nights when it felt like our show, not like we were opening for anybody,' Dave later recalled, 'and that was the best feeling.' He went on to explain that the challenge of turning every night into that kind of triumph was one they enjoyed living up to, the reward being 'to play to 15,000 people that had never seen you before.'

But as the summer arrived, so the venues escalated to arenas and outdoor sports stadia. 'You're playing outdoors at 7.30 pm so it's light, it's all-seated and you feel like Steely Dan or something. It's just not conducive to our frenetic, energetic live show!' They also, unbelievably, agreed to do in-store sets and radio stations in the afternoons, further frazzling their nerve-ends.

The schedule of 25 days on, followed by a ten-day break, gave the Foos just enough time to shoot videos and make radio and TV appearances to promote their album before rejoining the fray. The usual pattern for the Foos had been to intersperse each 18-month world tour with spells of three to four weeks off, ensuring that they avoided burn-out, but this was a seemingly never-ending trek.

The circus rolled into Canada with the headliners firing on all cylinders, but their support band feeling too tired to get their music over to the people. The end result was the Foos quitting the road at the end of August, cutting short their European touring commitments after the Reading and Leeds Carling Weekenders on the grounds of 'exhaustion', and returning to base. 'We've always been pretty selfless,' said a repentant Grohl, 'but this year is the first time we've ever really stood up for ourselves.'

A BBC radio session and the *Kerrang!* magazine awards ceremony were among the victims of the decision, but as Dave rightly told that very mag, 'The band's well-being is way more important than anything else.' A six-week spell of enforced rest was called for. The tactic of throwing himself into his work was threatening to make Dave a dull boy, and fortunately he would soon have a new love interest in his life to distract him.

'I don't know if I'm a workaholic by nature,' he commented during that summer of 2000, 'or if I'm forced to be. I like the ethic that we've maintained over the last five years but I'm looking forward to a life that's more stationary.' He'd started finding grey hairs which, given his father didn't go grey until 50, was a sign that 'I'm killing myself on the road!' On the plus side, he acknowledged that the past year spent touring arenas had moved them 'one step closer to the Queen we wanted to be. We're much more comfortable now playing in front of big audiences, be it a festival audience or an enclosed arena.'

There was, too, a musical swing in the air as bands like Limp Bizkit found success by fusing heavy rock with hip-hop. Dave saw this as 'a response to grunge ... but there's a kind of negative energy there.' He warned against the idea that the likes of Marilyn Manson could save rock. 'Marilyn Manson is ... a package, a show, a circus. And then another person comes out and says, "Now that's got so boring, what the world needs is another superhero cartoon character to fix it." When really all it needed was good music.'

Back on the boards after their enforced break, the band's show at the Manchester Apollo on 6 December 2000 would be remembered by all who attended for a series of bizarre incidents involving stage-invading fans. The first got up after Dave and Taylor had opened the show by drum-duelling from each side of the stage. Instead of expelling the invader, Dave let him try on his guitar for size. Unfortunately, this encouraged another audience member to try his luck, but when that individual was manhandled from the stage Dave laid down his axe and jumped into the moshpit to rescue the unfortunate fellow. The lights then came up, but the episode had a happy ending when Dave and his fan reappeared from backstage. As *Kerrang!* put it, 'Watching the Nicest Guy in Rock in righteous fury mode was a sight no one at the Apollo was likely to forget in a hurry.'

The British dates ended a year that had seen the most relentless touring schedule the band had ever pursued. But the new year would be just three days old when the list of Grammy nominations suggested the Foos were about to receive their reward. *There is Nothing Left to Lose* was up for Best Rock Album, while 'Learn to Fly' was nominated both for its video (Best Short Form Music Video) and Best Rock Performance by a Duo or Group.

As with its predecessors, *There is Nothing Left to Lose* was relentlessly milked for singles. The initial blast of 'Learn to

Fly' and 'Stacked Actors' was followed by 'Generator', 'Breakout' and 'Next Year', all offering bonus tracks to tempt those millions who already had the long-player. 'Breakout' won single release after it was included on the soundtrack to the Jim Carrey movie *Me, Myself and Irene*, where it rubbed shoulders with the Offspring, not to mention Ben Folds and Wilco.

Press reviews from the heavier end of the press spectrum had called *There is Nothing Left to Lose* one-dimensional, though *Rolling Stone* had praised Grohl for extending a vocal range that had, they claimed, previously 'consisted of two tones – conversational and catastrophic'. Now there was 'greater emphasis on melody and actual singing'. But when it came to the public's response, the fact that the album went platinum (one million units sold) in just eight weeks suggested that, as ever, President Grohl had their vote.

8

BIG LEAGUE

nyone scanning the Foo Fighters discography will
notice the lengthy gap between albums three and four.
One by One was finally released in October 2002, close
to three years after its predecessor and a full year after it had
been scheduled. Fact is, the band had not only junked an
album's worth of music in the meantime but also sidelined
co-producer/engineer Adam Kasper. Only one track bore his
name, the Brian May feature 'Tired of You'.

Given that many people considered this one of the
highlights of the released album, it will forever remain a
point of debate whether the earlier version would have
measured up or even exceeded the Nick Raskulinecz-
produced final product. The 'lost' album, which may never
now see the light of day, is known among fans as 'the million
dollar demo'. But the seeds of discord had been sown as far
back as 2000 when the Foos had energetically promoted
their third album (and second as a band), *There is Nothing
Left to Lose.*

The US leg of their world tour was opened by Queens of
the Stone Age, an unpretentious, gang-like Californian metal
band who quickly won a place in Dave Grohl's heart. 'They'd
step out in front of a couple of thousand kids that weren't
necessarily too familiar with their music and by the end of the
show they would have them on their knees, bowing, praying
in worship to the gods that are Queens of the Stone Age.

Congratulations guys.'

One notable individual gig of the period was the Bridge School Benefit, organised annually by Neil Young to raise money for a school for handicapped children his son attended. 'That guy has built a life and a body of work and all of his music is completely built on love, honesty and humanity,' said Dave. 'The guy is just the closest thing a rock musician could get to the Pope. Thank God for Neil Young. We love you very much.'

The Queens of the Stone Age invited Dave to drum on their next album, re-igniting his love of the percussive arts. So enthusiastic did he become, in fact, that after the sessions he decided to continue his extracurricular activities and launch a musical homage to the metal that had so shaped his youth. As a first step, he laid down seven tracks in his home studio with the assistance of the then-indispensable Adam Kasper, but felt that his singing would inevitably add a melodic edge that would take it too close to Foo Fighters territory.

In the end, he followed the example of non-singing Black Sabbath guitarist Tony Iommi, whose solo album *Iommi* was graced by no fewer than a dozen guest singers. Invited to supply the vocals to a track called 'Goodbye Lament', Dave decided that he too would call on some diverse talents. And he would call the project Probot (more details of which can be found in Chapter Nine.)

Having recorded the Queens of the Stone Age album and kicked off the Probot project, Dave prepared to hit the road again with the Foos. But, as he has since revealed, it was beginning to feel like a chore. Even the prospect of recording a fourth album lacked the allure it surely deserved. But events were to conspire to put everything on the back burner, for a while at least.

In an eerie echo of the Kurt Cobain tour overdose, Taylor Hawkins was taken ill in London in August 2001. He fell into a two-day coma after being found in his Kensington hotel, sending the rumour mill into overdrive. It was just two dates into a tour of Britain and Ireland, causing the cancellation of gigs in London and Edinburgh, plus a mammoth outdoor show at Slane Castle in Ireland.

Hawkins survived. A passion for mountain biking, combined with the physical pressures of drumming for a living, had caused him severe back pain, and it had been an excess of prescription painkillers rather than the rumoured heroin that had caused the incident. Even so, his hotel-room 'overdose', reported at the time as 'exhaustion', has refused to go away. The band now resignedly refers to it as 'Taylor's nap'.

Since this episode, communication within the band has improved immeasurably. 'Foo Fighters is Dave's thing,' Hawkins explains, 'but he's not the kind of guy who wants to be anyone's boss. Everyone respects that, and doesn't put him in a position where he has to be a dick about anything.' In fact the bond between the two of them has overtaken the one Grohl enjoys with the longer-serving Nate Mendel to become the crucial relationship within the band. 'He's like my brother,' Dave explains, adding, 'At times we communicate by not even having to speak – other times I reveal more to him than anyone.'

It was because of this unusual closeness that Taylor's addiction to painkilling drugs hit home even harder to Grohl than it might otherwise have done. 'When you see your best friend in trouble it turns you're world upside-down. It was the first time I've actually felt inclined to pray,' he said of the problem period, 'and it worked.' Grohl knew his buddy was going to make it when he came to visit him in rehab. 'The first thing I said was, "Hey, man, you're looking great." He looked at me and said, "Fuck off!" That's when I knew he was okay.' It would be December before Taylor was back behind the kit.

If chart positions told the story, then *One by One* (working title 'Tom Petty'), when it finally came out in 2002, achieved everything expected of it. In Britain, where it was pitched against the Nirvana box set *With the Lights Out*, it still entered the album chart at the very top, two rungs higher than its rival, while in the States it made Number Three.

The recording of *One by One* had, by common consent, not been the perfect way to make an album. Having had one go at it, which was considered substandard, they then went back in and had another. But while the basis of the record was there, Dave was still unhappy with the situation. His motivation was sorely lacking. And this was the point when another obstacle to the Foos' progress reared its head. Because when he agreed to play drums at a one-off Queens of the Stone Age gig at Los Angeles' Troubadour Club, he found himself agreeing to tour with the band. In his own terms, he went 'MIA' (missing in action).

He'd later explain that he needed to escape from a situation which reminded him of the last days of Nirvana. 'After going through all that chaos and misery and pain as it happened, having to go into a miserable situation again would have been a bad idea,' he explained to *Kerrang!*

This was all very well, but it left his own band potentially leaderless and rudderless. It was left to producer Raskulinecz, whose previous form encompassed acts as diverse as System of a Down and alt.country singer Gillian Welch, to take the reins, referring back to the demo tracks and making suggestions for guitar overdubs. 'He said things like, "I think you should play a little something in there,"' recalled Chris Shiflett, '"Play a little melody on that chorus." And we went through every song and sort of figured out what was needed. Dave just left me and Nick to record my guitars and that was that – I didn't even know what was going to make it on to the disc or not. But a lot of it did, even though it was a weird, broken-up way to make a record. Everyone did their parts separately.' If truth be told, Shiflett admits, he 'thought Dave was going to break up the band. I think we all did.'

So what of Grohl himself? 'I think everyone was uncertain whether I would come back. I know that I was. And I was having a blast every night playing drums with those guys. But at the end of the day I had to come back because, much as I loved Queens, they're not family. These guys are family. This is where my heart has always been. And it's 12 other people, not just the guys on stage.' However, he did add that 'I know I'm a better drummer than anything.'

Many people listened for the influence of Queens of the Stone Age to rub off on Dave's Foo efforts – and it is certain there are sonic echoes of the Queens' front man Josh Homme in places. Something else that came from that connection was the distinctive album art of Raymond Pettibon, a legendary punk artist of the early 1980s who also contributed several pieces to the CD booklet. The brother of Black Flag guitarist Greg Ginn, he made his name designing fliers and covers for that band and the Minutemen, among others, on the seminal SST Records label, and his cartoon-style imagery became synonymous with the independent American hardcore scene of Southern California. Dave met Raymond courtesy of Queens of the Stone Age when he came to a show with ex-Minutemen bassist Mike Watt.

'Watt was like, "Hey, Dave, this is Raymond." And I said hi, and noticed he had paint all over him. A little while later, I asked Watt, "Is that Raymond Pettibon?" And it was. It's a really crazy scene. He still lives with his mother, he's like 46, he's really tall and he's socially inept. No social skills at all. We call him Rainman. He invited us to come to the gallery where he keeps most of his shit, and we went down there and it was, like, 10,000 pieces of Pettibon stuff, just stuffed into boxes! We're going through all of it, and you'd come across something like the original [Black Flag] 'Jealous Again' single cover, and I'm like, "Oh my God!" So I figured we had to somehow pay tribute to Pettibon as a hero, because his stuff, those images, just stuck with me my whole life.'

The distinctive, hand-drawn 'heart' cover of *One by One* was the result. Two versions of the sleeve exist, one with a white background and the other black, while more illustrations, all variations on the cover theme, adorn the inner pages of the booklet. The group picture on the reverse of the CD, the band unsmilingly posed against a concrete wall, was as uncompromising as the front had been intriguing. Perhaps recent events had taken their toll.

The Foos had operated a schedule of recording demos for three weeks at a time, then taking a couple of weeks off to recuperate. The result was 18 or 19 almost complete songs, unlike the predecessor, which was practically written in the studio. And while the last album was written on acoustic guitar before being translated into high-volume rock noise, the new songs had all been written and rehearsed 'with amps at ten,' said Grohl. 'There are a few that could go the way of the ballad, but we're trying to avoid that. It's a lot more fun to go out and play a festival with your amps blistering at ten than to sing some sleepy ballad about one more heartbreak. With the touring last time, we realised how capable we are of being the rock-est live ridiculous experience, and we're trying to incorporate that into the record.'

When an album appears a year after its scheduled release date, expectation levels inevitably soar, as does the microscopic critical attention it receives. Yet as with its predecessor, *One by One* came out of its corner with fists flailing. Instead of 'Stacked Actors', this time it was 'All My Life', an obvious candidate for single release, that opened proceedings. 'All My Life' would reach Number Five in Britain, deservedly equalling the performance of debut 45 'This is a Call' seven years earlier.

The BBC website was typical in believing the cream of the crop had come first, reviewer Nick Reynolds reckoning it 'the best thing [Grohl] has ever done. With its atmosphere of claustrophobic sex, ghosts and frustration it sounds like some personal demons are being cast out. It's manic, tight and the guitars sound fabulous. It reaches deeper than the entertaining but lightweight pop grunge that the Foo Fighters have delivered up to now.' Would it, listeners wondered, set the tone for the album?

Dave himself proudly described 'All My Life' as 'one of the most aggressive songs we've ever written – it's kinda dark and dissonant but really in your face. It begins with a vocal and a guitar then it explodes and gets even bigger and just keeps on going and going. It's fucking great.'

'Low' keeps the aggression level high, 'like a machine roaring,' as Dave put it. He acknowledged the dual influences of Soundgarden and Black Flag, resulting in something 'unlike anything we've ever done.' The lyrics are 'kinda sultry – it's about two people getting together because they realise they have more fun fucking each other than anyone else – it's kinda deep.' Released as the album's third single, it would peak just outside the UK Top 20 in the summer of 2003.

The sweeping three-part harmonies of 'Have It All' release the tension three tracks in – in Dave's opinion, the song has 'a cool uptempo groove … and the end is the most fucking rock thing we could possibly figure out … then it just stops on a dime.' The 'fucked-up Beach Boys melody' took the sting from

175

what could otherwise have been a real slammer. 'Maybe that's what we do the best,' he acknowledged, 'those two ingredients complement each other well.' A fourth and final single from an album all Foos fans must surely have had by now, it peaked at Number 37 in Britain in October.

The mid-tempo 'Times Like These', with its 'one-way motorway' chorus, would also prove a popular single choice, hitting Number 12 in Britain where the charts were awash with reality TV winners. It was quickly co-opted to the soundtrack of *American Wedding*, third in the *American Pie* series of films (and directed by Jesse Dylan, son of Bob), keeping company with the likes of the Good Charlottes and New Found Glory. Another candidate for Dave's enthusiastic but oft-repeated accolade of 'best song I've ever written ... it's very emotive and passionate and universal', 'Times Like These' boasts a jangly feel pitched somewhere between Neil Young and Tom Verlaine's influential new wavers Television. Dave was learning to live and love again ... and clearly enjoying both experiences.

With its echoes of his Queens of the Stone Age spell, 'Disenchanted Lullaby' inspires another throat-scouring performance from Dave, and offers, with a combination of verses that are 'trippy as hell' and a chorus he admitted was copped from the Smithereens, 'a little jab at the end ... That's the melancholy, the bittersweet, it's always nice.' Its ever-changing mood also fits with the fact that this was, he claimed, 'the least predictable album we've ever done.' It was one of Dave's favourites on *One by One*.

'Tired of You' would have been, in Dave's words, 'a really sparse one guitar and one vocal song' had it not been for Brian May's trademark four-part guitar harmonies weighing in on the chorus to take the whole thing into another dimension. 'It sounds like a string section,' said an impressed Grohl, 'but he

A tumultuous reception at Glasgow's T In The Park Festival in July 2002 proves too much for our man.

No doubting who drives the Foo Fighters bus as Dave Grohl takes control.

This page: On stage at the Ambassador, Dublin, in July 2002. Footage from the gig appeared as a hidden 'easter egg' in the 2003 DVD release *Everywhere But Home*.

Opposite: Finns ain't what they used ta be: the Foos rock Helsinki, 2003.

Right: At the Rock In Rio Festival, Lisbon, in May 2004. The Foos saved the day when Guns N'Roses pulled out of the show.

Below: The fourth album dream team: Shiflett (left) joins Hawkins, Grohl and Mendel.

Above: Dave Grohl and wife Jordyn pictured at a 2005 pre Grammy party in Beverly Hills.

At the MTV Europe Music Awards in Lisbon, May 2005, where new single 'Best Of You' was nominated.

Left: Once a Kiss fan... on stage at Punchestown Racecourse, Ireland, in 2005.

Above: Oracle Arena, Oakland, California, 2 February 2008.

did it with a guitar and it's fucking amazing.' This was, as previously noted, the sole track to have made it from the original, scrapped recordings, and as such was quite a tease for fans.

Introduced by countryish strumming, 'Halo' is the song that seems to have inspired the album's working title of 'Tom Petty', but as Dave himself acknowledged there are other echoes of classic American rock to be heard: 'The middle section reminds me of Cheap Trick, the chorus kinda reminds me of Guided By Voices with the melodic kinda walking-down-the-street rhythm.' The result, he said, was 'a great driving song' that reminded him of 'My Poor Brain' – 'but it's fucking way beyond that.'

The volume increases again for the multi-segment 'Lonely As You', in Dave's words, a 'really weird Sergeant Peppers heavy metal kinda song – really bizarre, but really hooky. Then it gets huge at the end and I'm screaming my fucking balls off.'

If the Foos had generally steered clear of what Dave called their 'signature fucking retarded sound or whatever', then track nine, 'Overdrive', is the exception that proves the rule. 'This is our one uptempo punk pop song on the record – the one song you'd hear and say "Oh yeah dude – that's the Foo Fighters."' Indeed, another song, curiously called *The Colour and the Shape* – which had been a contender for the last record (they liked the title so much they kept it) – was rejected a second time for that very reason. 'It was almost like another 'Weenie Beenie' sort of song,' Dave explained, 'just another screaming, fast, hardcore song. But we decided not to put it on, because it was a step backwards; we've done that already!'

The tuned-down guitar riff powering 'Burn Away' makes it one of the heaviest songs the Foos have ever recorded, although the lyric is basically a love song. But this is just a curtain-raiser for the closing 'Come Back', a track that, at eight minutes, could be considered the album's magnum opus, but in fact owes its great length to the fact that it's two songs glued together. 'The verses are really heavy with a tribal beat and fuzzy guitars and then there's a middle instrumental section that begins with acoustics that build up to electrics and then the percussion sets in and it turns into an explosion.' Lyrically, Grohl felt it revealed 'all these dark, shitty sides of myself ... saying out all my faults.'

Among the songs they tried at the session that didn't make it to record was 'Danny Says', a track that marked Chris Shiflett's lead vocal debut. 'That was the first time that I ever sang for real in a studio. I was really nervous but once I did it, it gave me a lot more confidence. I was like, "Wow, I can do this if I just double [track] the fuckin' thing. Sounds pretty good."' It was good enough to make a bonus track on the 'All My Life' single.

For an album completed in less than perfect circumstances, *One by One* was an exceptional performer. It won the 2003 Grammy Award for Best Rock Album, while the single 'Times Like These' was nominated for Best Rock Performance by a Duo or Group with Vocal. 'All My Life' won the 2003 Grammy for Best Hard Rock Performance and was also nominated for Best Rock Song.

The most fascinating part of the Grammy experience came just after the band's name was called. While Dave and Taylor were at the podium making their acceptance speech, a large, unidentified man was standing behind them cracking his knuckles and waving to the audience. As Grohl ended his acceptance speech, the man leaned into the microphone to comment, 'And rock would not be anything without BB King. Rock would be nothing without him. Thank you.' A clearly surprised Grohl responded, 'I was gonna say that.' Backstage after the incident, Grohl and Hawkins were still none the wiser about the interruption. 'Does anybody know who that dude was?' said Hawkins. 'I have no idea!' Half the audience assumed it was a Tenacious D-style set-up.

The press, too, were impressed. 'Potent guitar riffs define every song,' said *Rolling Stone*, pinpointing the album as 'rock that draws power from its determination to struggle onward.' *Q* said the band had 'grown in craft and attitude,' while *Mojo* found 'many moments of greatness' on an album that 'trumpets its own qualities to the world beyond the faithful.' *Uncut*, meanwhile, gave it four stars out of five and added a sobering thought: 'The Foos have now made more albums than Nirvana. Fittingly, *One by One* is their best yet.'

But that wasn't a view shared by Taylor, who felt *One by One* might better have been titled 'Half And Half'. The drummer freely admitted that this was 'half a good record and half one that is a little bit shoddy. It's probably not the best outing, but it is a picture of that time when we nearly broke up. We didn't know what we were supposed to do.' He hadn't been surprised when the demo album was binned. 'I was thinking, "Should we even be making records?" It was such a disorganised, unfocused time. I don't think Dave was sure of what he wanted to do, and he is the leader. I think he was still in love with the Queens of the Stone Age stuff, he really wanted to go and play with them. But when he came back I think he also realised that he didn't just want to play drums for someone else. Now he's learned to balance it out...'

Something else Grohl had learned at long, long last was to enjoy the rewards stardom brings without feeling guilty about it. As he finished the recording of *One by One*, he took delivery of a $75,000 BMW M5 car in battleship grey. He'd never, he explained, taken his affluent lifestyle for granted, largely because he didn't have a high school diploma to fall back on should things take a downturn. 'I'm going to be really careful with what I've got,' he said, adding that 'I've got tons of money, but I'm afraid to spend it.' Hence the ubiquitous Chevy truck.

When, in 1995, he got into an accident, he'd rejected the luxury car option even though he knew he could afford it. 'I remember looking around at BMWs and Mercedes and thinking, "These are amazing, but if I get this now, what will I have to look forward to?" That's why I waited. I'm 34 now, so I thought, "OK, I suppose I can get something nice."' Hence the BMW M5, the driving of which ranked alongside skeet [clay pigeon] shooting and eating as his leisure priorities. 'I wouldn't want to sit in fucking Los Angeles traffic in any other car,' he laughed.

To split after four albums would in some ways have been a less tragic mirror image of his Nirvana experience. That, of course, is not what happened. Yet the band's commitment to play two UK Carling weekend dates at Reading and Leeds inspired Dave to take stock as he looked from the stage and saw 55,000 adoring people singing his songs back at him. 'I never imagined it would reach such a point, not for a second,' he confessed years later, before revealing that it had crossed his mind there and then to 'do a David Bowie' (who retired from live touring on a whim in 1973 on the Hammersmith Odeon stage) and go out at the top.

Yet reaching such a level of popularity needed addressing. Would the Foos split? Or look for a new musical direction in which to take those ever-loyal fans? The result would be the latter, even though it would take the best part of three years to come together. The key for the Foos would be to free themselves from the stylistic shackles that had (admittedly profitably) chained the likes of the Ramones, Green Day and AC/DC and create not 'rock music' but 'just music'.

The Foo Fighters' London Astoria date on 26 August 2002 fell on a day that, by coincidence, was exactly seven years on from their debut Reading festival date. Tickets, which sold out in three minutes, were so hard to come by even Tim Wheeler of opening act Ash admitted the main reason they were playing was so they could be on the guest list.

The timing, the day after the Carling weekend and the date before the *Kerrang!* Awards, made certain this would be a gig to end all gigs. From album opener turned concert opener 'All My Life' to the more familiar finale of 'Monkey Wrench', it hit a level of excitement that took even long-time fans aback. Grohl was certainly excited enough to scale the security fence by the stage and peer monkey-like over the top. With so many new songs to showcase, 'Next Year' was an unfortunate casualty, but newcomers like 'Tired of You' made up for the omission.

The Foos' Reading spot was the first time they had headlined a major rock festival, and as such was one of the most moving in Dave's life. 'For us to headline a festival that meant so much to me – Reading was the first festival I'd ever played with Nirvana – made it very emotional. My family was backstage in tears, my sister Lisa was at the side of the stage crying, but it was a great feeling.'

He'd long felt that British audiences were among the more receptive to be encountered during his long bouts of world touring, so UK dates were always keenly anticipated by the band as well as fans. 'It always seems like there's the English audiences and the Japanese and they both kinda go nuts. In America we don't do the hop, y'know the thing where the crowd bounces up and down? They're just too stupid to realise that it's a great way to bounce around and have fun without beating the hell out of each other.'

When you're competing with U2, it's not a bad idea to have a gimmick. But whoever decided that the Foos should strip off and be photographed in a rooftop hot tub for an issue of monthly music mag *Q* in November 2002 was definitely out of order. The fact this bizarre scene took place in Dublin's Temple Bar district at the Clarence Hotel, which Bono and the Edge happen to own, just added to the surrealism. The Irish band dominated the magazine cover without having to change out of their drab 'work clothes', while Dave and friends just looked stupid.

The touring to promote *One by One* would take up much of 2003, a year the Foos had begun at the Grammies in February. The following month, Dave fulfilled a dream he'd nurtured seemingly all his life by contributing drums to an album with childhood heroes Killing Joke. There was to be no repeat of the Queens of the Stone Age flirtation, however, and he did not join their world tour – he had his own dates to play.

The expected slew of singles to be taken from *One by One* began with 'All My Life' in October 2002, and continued in the new year with 'Times Like These', 'Low' and 'Have It All', which threw up some interesting cover versions, including the B-52's track 'Planet Claire' (with the original's Fred Schneider on backing vocal), Prince's 'Darling Nikki' and Joe Walsh's 'Life of Illusion' plus, increasingly, visual content. Being a Foo Fighters completist wasn't getting any cheaper, but there was no shortage of interesting material to savour.

Dave's upcoming wedding to Jordyn Blum in August 2003 was naturally high on his list of priorities, even though they would be following their honeymoon with a tour of European festivals. A stag party took place at the end of the Foos' US tour, when 60 male friends joined Dave for a very long night in Las Vegas. 'It went ... just fine,' he revealed, adding with typical caginess: 'I made everyone promise they wouldn't talk about it.' There would be a honeymoon 'somewhere tropical', and he was looking forward to 'a good seven or eight days of, um, tantric sex.'

On the rare occasions where the Foos found themselves opening for a megaband, their aim was to blow the headliners off stage with a set that, by now, could comfortably be called a 'greatest hits'. Such was the case on 24 August 2003 at Glasgow's Big Day Out at the Green. The nominal headliners were the Red Hot Chili Peppers, great friends of the Foos from tours and times past, but this certainly didn't stop Foo Fighters from turning in what many observers insisted was the performance of the day. They'd find themselves in competition again in the summer, but neither the Chilis nor fast-rising British band Coldplay could shake the Foos' resolve.

Dave took time out the following month to support a friend in need – Steve Lamacq, the BBC Radio 1 DJ and champion of new music whose patronage had been crucial in introducing both Dave's bands to the British public. The midweek, mid-evening *Evening Session* was to disappear and be replaced by a broader-based show, denying new bands the chance of much-needed radio exposure. 'Steve's always been a supporter of rock music in general', Dave stressed, 'but also he's a man of integrity and good taste. And when someone has those qualities and is in the position that he is, then absolutely he has influenced a lot of people. People like him need to take a hand steering music in the right direction. He always seemed like he was doing things for the right reason – the music.'

*   *   *

A large proportion of 2004 would be spent on things other than music. Grohl was to spend time on the road with John Kerry's presidential election bandwagon, increasing his political consciousness, while the other band members took time out for their own side trips. Dave also opened Studio 606, Foo Fighters' newly built recording studio and nerve centre modelled on ABBA's legendary Polar Studios. And the pause between Foo Fighters releases made this the ideal time to release *Probot*, Dave's heavy metal fantasy album with guest stars that had lain on the shelf for the best part of three years.

While many bands would, at this point, have bought themselves time with the old tactic of a compilation or live record, the Foos were made of sterner stuff. Besides, as Dave remarked, 'It's not like I'm going to do this for 20 years and then move to Hawaii – I feel like I'm on vacation all the time!' But then the fact that their new record contained no fewer than 20 previously unheard songs (plus one little-known number revisited) in its double-disc format confirmed that the wellspring of inspiration had yet to run dry. In fact, as Dave said to *New Musical Express*, it had overflowed to produce an album 'so good there isn't a single song on it that we're not looking forward to playing live. We said it about the last album, but we were lying. This time we're telling the truth.'

What he didn't mention was the fact that there had been pressure from the record company (RCA) to put out a 'Greatest Hits' collection – pressure he was ready, willing and able to resist. 'We didn't want to do that. Fuck it. This is our greatest hits – you've just never heard them before...'

His band's fifth album, titled *In Your Honour* (the extra 'u' appeared on the artwork outside the States, where it was just 'Honor'), separated the rockers from the ballads – or, to be more accurate, the plugged from the unplugged. But then you could also have labelled the discs band and solo, because the 'acoustic' disc was very much Grohl's own work in a bigger way than anything since the very first, one man band effort that had kicked the story off. And it was certainly the case that the songs on the 'rock' album seemed purpose-built for live performance. 'For the first time we can take a whole album out on stage every night ... it only took us ten fuckin' years!' Grohl noted.

As Chris Shiflett revealed, the first disc had been recorded in segments, instrument by instrument. 'First drums, then scratch guitars, I'd take home a Pro Tools file and write a bass line. I would run it by Dave and the producer; we'd talk about it, make changes, and then put it down. I would usually come in with this elaborate bass line — but over time, I've come to appreciate simplicity and what it can do for a song.'

The title track, with its Gothic guitar riff and opening vocal challenge ('Can you hear me, hear me screaming?'), was particularly notable: when the band were rehearsing it before recording, a passing guitar technician was informed that this would be the song the band would be opening the show with for the next two years. 'Wow!' came the response. 'After 'All My Life', I didn't know how you guys were going to open a show ever again.'

Taylor had been sold immediately on a track he happily explained had been described by someone as 'The Who meets Fugazi. It's not really a song, it's a manifesto, if you will. And the heaviest thing we've done.' It had always been intended as the opener for the record. The lyric, however – described by one review as 'marriage vows set to caveman riffs' – is not about Grohl's wife. 'It's actually for the people who are suffering under the Bush government,' its writer explained. 'I travelled round the midwest with John Kerry and I was almost in tears meeting people in places like Madison, Wisconsin, seeing that they were desperate for hope, for help.'

The pace rarely lets up thereafter, the first half-dozen songs keeping up a remorseless, relentless pace. 'No Way Back' progresses from a Queen-like introduction (there's also a 'We Are the Champions' feel to the later 'The Deepest Blues are Black') to a thrash-out, while the similarly dark-titled 'DOA' (dead on arrival) rehashes the over-used idea that no one gets out of the world alive. 'I suppose this album is a little darker,' Dave told *Kerrang!*, ascribing his downbeat lyrical slant to the fact that he'd had to come up with double the number of words in the time usually allotted to an album's worth. 'Lyrics are fucking tricky, man.'

Track four, 'Best of You', was selected as the first single and is one of the first disc's undoubted highlights. But at a shade less than two minutes 'Hell' is hardly hot, despite a Roger Daltrey-styled vocal, while the 'Breakout'-reminiscent 'The Last Song' seems to have been buried halfway through the running order just so that nothing too much could be made of its title and the promise that it is 'the last song I will dedicate to you'. The frantic riffing of 'Free Me' approaches the intensity of back-catalogue gems like 'I'll Stick Around', but by the mid-pace jangle of 'Resolve' and 'End Over End' the listener is ready for the contrast. 'Resolve' has shades of 'Everlong' and had been tried in three or four arrangements before it settled: the slowest, Taylor revealed, sounded like 'fuckin' Bon Jovi!'

Dave stated that separating the songs 'gave us more room to move, instead of having eight rock songs and then schizophrenically throwing three softer songs in the mix.' It did, however, leave listeners feeling as if they were being beaten over the head by a sledgehammer. And final track 'The Sign' – a bonus on European recordings – kicks off with 'Paperback Writer' feedback before delivering the heaviest riff of the whole album.

The acoustic disc of *In Your Honour*, Dave revealed, had started life as a potential film soundtrack. 'I started demo-ing all this acoustic music with that in mind. After an hour or two of listening to it, I thought why can't this be a Foo Fighters record? Maybe we should do this kick-ass mellow acoustic record. And then I thought no, I have to have loud rock music in my life somewhere.' The two-disc format was the perfect compromise, and one that helped him overcome being pigeonholed. 'I can write a bossa nova, I can write a thrash tune. It's such an incredible freedom.'

'The success of the acoustic album had set standards the first record had initially failed to reach,' said Taylor. The drummer believed that, at first, hearing 'the acoustic stuff was kicking [the rock stuff's] ass. We knew we needed to stay loose instead of always trying to perfect everything. Only two songs made it from the original rock sessions – 'Best of You' and 'No Way Back'. We redid a bunch of stuff. We always take the long road.'

The division of unplugged and rocking discs is somehow reminiscent of Neil Young, who also likes to have a foot in both camps. The acoustic disc came together in just two weeks – so quickly, in fact, that a list of star names pencilled in to be invited to appear never got acted upon, the songs being completed before the opportunity to call came up. Ry Cooder, Greg Norton of Hüsker Dü and Jim James of My Morning Jacket were among those who missed out.

First song 'Still' has echoes of Dave's childhood love of the Beatles, with its 'Dear Prudence' feel. As the first track recorded for the second disc, it also unlocks many possibilities. 'The idea was we'd do a song a day. By the end of the [first] day I thought, "We're capable of doing things that I've never imagined."' Strangely, the lyrics of 'Still' relate to an incident that happened when Grohl was ten years old and a boy committed suicide on some train tracks. 'After the ambulances split, we found pieces of his skull and played with his bones,' he told *Rolling Stone*. The inspiration might have been creepy, but of the song Grohl also said: 'I couldn't believe that our band is capable of making something so beautiful.'

Led Zeppelin bass player John Paul Jones appeared on the next two tracks, playing piano on the Ryan Adams-ish 'Miracle' and mandolin on the REM-reminiscent 'Another Round'. It was quite a star trip for youthful Zep fan Grohl. 'Here in the studio, I have an original 'Zeppelin II' gold record up on the wall, pictures of John Bonham and Jimmy Page. I didn't know if I should take them down before he showed up. But I figured, you know what? He's probably used to it.'

Nate Mendel's reaction to the Zep legend's presence had been somewhat different. 'It was Dave's idea to have him in, and initially I was like, "Okay, how many songs are not going to have my bass on them?" But it was great, and when he was tuning up his Mellotron he played a couple of Zeppelin riffs, so that was a treat.'

Track five, the seemingly innocuous 'Friend of a Friend', caused a stir when Grohl revealed it had been written 15 years previously in Nirvana days. Tellingly, it was sung and played by Grohl alone. The inclusion of the phrase 'never mind' was a deliberate act of mischief by its writer, who admitted, 'I don't know if I want to field a load of crap about that for a year and a half. But it's a great song!' The title was inspired by how he joined the band: 'They were friends of a friend of mine; I wrote it right as I joined the band.'

He'd been nervous about putting it on the record, he admitted. 'Pretty much any song I write people are usually willing to pick it apart for specific references, obvious references. Whether it's Courtney or Kurt or Nirvana or whatever. And it's not that simple. There are a lot of other people in my life that I love and hate. It's not just The Two.'

When it came to do the acoustic record, time was running low, denying Nate Mendel the chance to write bass lines out of the studio. 'So they ended up being much simpler. A couple of times, I hadn't even heard the song before – Dave and Chris would put down their guitar lines and I'd be in a room with the bass, and Nick Raskulinecz would go, "Okay, let's run it a couple of times and see what happens." I was concentrating on just finding the notes and getting the rhythm right.' The result was spontaneous, simple and effective.

'Over and Out' was a song Dave had demoed in his home studio five years earlier and jumped out as a candidate for re-recording. Its acoustic sound, with 'mics in front of instruments and not a lot between that and the tape', to his mind typified the disc as a whole. 'On the Mend', by contrast, was written several thousand miles away from Virginia in a London hotel room. 'It's another example of how we'd start with an acoustic guitar, do that first, and then start adding to it.' Certainly, a keyboard swell underpinning the picking was a subtle touch.

A bossa-nova styled 'Virginia Moon' had been in the songwriting locker for some eight years – 'We tried to put it on *There is Nothing Left to Lose* but it just didn't make sense' – but many other tracks were of more recent vintage: certainly, it was hard to 'see the join'. It was the piano skills rather than the smoky vocals of Norah J that got her the gig on 'Virginia Moon'. 'I thought it would be cool to have some piano on there; I heard a Norah Jones record and thought "Maybe she's the one I should call."' Certainly there were few stars who would turn down such an invitation.

Grohl revelled in the fact that Foo Fighters fans would be unlikely to have a Norah record in their collection – and while they could have accepted the likes of Charlotte Hatherley from Ash, they were uncertain about liking a track featuring someone more likely to be found in their parents' record collection. 'That's dumb,' insisted a grinning Grohl. 'It kicks open another door for the band, which is what this album is about in many ways. Who's to say what we can't do? We might start doing show tunes, or even reggae!'

Penultimate track 'Cold Day in the Sun' sees the usual roles reversed and Dave playing drums to Taylor's lead vocal. 'It's a song Dave liked,' Hawkins explained, 'and it lightened up the acoustic record. Everyone says it sounds like the Eagles!' He even felt bold enough to offer his friend some drumming tips. 'When Dave was recording the drums I went from the control room into the live room and made a suggestion. He was like, "No. I like what I'm doing."'

Final track 'Razor' features second guitar from Josh Homme, and was considered by many the best track on the disc if not on the album as a whole. Unusually, it had been played in public, at a tsunami benefit in Los Angeles, before being committed to tape. 'I sat up all night trying to write this song, and it didn't work. I woke up early and started writing lyrics and got it right as the car was coming to pick me up.' Grohl was practising it in the dressing room he was sharing with Homme, and suggested he play a guitar harmony line. This worked so well that Dave invited him to reprise it in the studio. The overall effect isn't unlike the late Nick Drake.

For Grohl, the second disc pointed the way to the future. 'Every record we've made I've always imagined being our last,' he concluded. 'But for once in my life I've made a record I don't want to be the last ... it's opening doors I can see through for ten more years.' He reflected that 2005 had not only seen him completing the double album but building an enormous recording studio and 'going in with this hare-brained scheme of doing a half acoustic/half rock album, writing 40 songs and choosing the best 20 for the record. I am so proud that we pulled it off and that it has led to the biggest tours, the biggest shows and the biggest singalongs we have ever had.'

The whole thing proved so successful that the possibility of an unplugged tour in 2006 was quickly put into action.

Drummer Taylor Hawkins, for one, couldn't wait: 'We told everybody we're gonna do some acoustic touring, so I guess we'd better. Instead of going out there and sweating my butt off every night, I'll be playing with my brushes quietly and stuff. I think it'll be good for us, though, as musicians, to go out and explore that dynamic.'

There were those who considered the two-disc format a marketing ploy, but Chris Shiflett was at pains to deny the accusation. 'We really went to bat to keep the cost of the record down, and it's only going to be about a buck more than the price of a single album. So it's not like we're making twice the money. We never discuss marketing or even how things will be perceived in the public eye. We just do it for the joy of doing it.' For Shiflett, the acoustic album was invigorating and 'the most enjoyable part of the process. It seems to have really struck a chord with people who have heard it. That stuff was great to record; it only took a couple of days. Doing *One by One* was the polar opposite to the way we made the new record, with everybody here, which is a much better way of doing things.'

In Dave's view, *In Your Honour* is Foo Fighters' counterpart to Zeppelin's *Physical Graffiti*, the 1975 double that is regarded as their definitive statement. 'If somebody asked me which Zep album to buy I would tell them that one because it has such a wide dynamic and shows the range the band had. And that's what we wanted to do with this album.' Taylor Hawkins chimed in with his verdict: 'We don't make cool-guy rock; we make heart-on-your-sleeve arena rock, or classic rock with punk-rock energy.'

An interesting controversy arose from the fact that the CD was issued in copy-protected form, and would only allow you to play it on a PC computer via technology automatically installed. Though it would not allow the songs to be moved to an Apple iPod, the album was available at the iTunes Music Store – meaning a fan who wanted to play the disc on a PC and access the music via their iPod would need to buy it twice.

Foo Fighters toured the States in September and October 2005 with Weezer in support, and were joined on stage by Queen's drummer during an October show at New Jersey's Continental Airlines Arena. Roger Taylor took time out from touring the US with Paul Rodgers on the 'Return of the Champions' trek to link up with the band for a rendition of the classic 'Tie Your Mother Down'. Taylor performed lead vocals on the track.

Foo Fighters celebrated their first decade in 2005 with a move into rock's big league. For Chris Shiflett, this translated as 'Lasers and wacky shit, things projected on screens,' while Nate Mendel was happy to accept that, while they'd been on the slippery slope to arena rock for the best part of ten years, they had accepted it now. 'And to declare that we've arrived, we're trying to outdo Pink Floyd!'

A major factor was that, with a fifth (and sixth) album to choose from they had extended their show to two hours in length. This, Dave explained, would enable them to feature at least three songs from each of their releases, including 'the deep album cuts' which had never been extracted as singles but were the band's personal favourites.

Australia and New Zealand enjoyed the Foos' company during their winter – and Dave, for one, relished the experience. 'I know that when I get to Australia, there's going to be 20,000 screaming kids singing their hearts out to 'Best of You' or 'Everlong'. That's something to look forward to every night, no matter how bruised you get or how thrashed your voice is.'

The Foos ended the year of 2005 with a December tour of Britain, a country with which they had enjoyed a close affinity. While Birmingham's NEC, Glasgow's SECC, Manchester's

Evening News Arena and London's Earls Court (twice) all welcomed capacity crowds, Cardiff's Millennium Stadium was as full to the rafters as for any rugby international – albeit this time with the roof firmly closed – as the Foos repaid a favour and opened the show for Oasis, who'd supported them Down Under in Perth. 'You have to respect them, they write great pop songs,' said Taylor.

Dave admitted to loving Oasis, a band who were already chart-toppers when the Foos kicked off but who they had now caught up with, and arguably overtaken, in commercial terms. 'There are really very few bands that make it that difficult to hate them just by being so fucking good,' he said. 'I know in interviews they come over like touchy bastards or whatever but you can sit down with them in a bar and have a couple of drinks and you will have the night of your life. I get on with anybody,' he continued, 'but those guys are great. The last time I saw Noel [Gallagher] he was in Covent Garden and he just tapped me on the shoulder and was like "Alright mate?" He was happy because he'd just got out of an interview. Their music is fucking good and their songs are contagious.'

There'd rarely been a summer that Foo Fighters hadn't played at least one major festival show in Britain – and 2006 was to be no exception. In a summer when the Who and Pink Floyd founder member Roger Waters were due to take over London's Hyde Park and play to 60,000 people, the Foos announced they'd finally joined the big league by staging their biggest-ever UK show in June. This would rival or maybe even eclipse Green Day's massive concerts at the Milton Keynes Bowl the previous year. Queens of the Stone Age were the main support act, with the Subways opening the show.

It was just another gig in the life of Foo Fighters, but as ever they were going to give it all they had. For Dave Grohl, there was simply no other way.

SIDE TRIPS

'When I go into the studio – whether it's with Queens of the Stone Age, Killing Joke or Probot – I'm there to make the song sound good. A song like 'Song for the Dead' by Queens deserves as much power as you can give it, and something like 'The Death and Resurrection Show' by Killing Joke deserves something cacophonous like a marching band. The challenge is finding exactly what the song needs or deserves; that's the biggest deal.'

It has already been mentioned that, by touring with Queens of the Stone Age in 2002, Dave had unwittingly placed the Foos' very existence under threat. The whole thing came about after he jokingly remarked, when asked to name his greatest disappointment of 2001, that it was the fact he hadn't been asked to play on their record. 'I've known those guys for a long time. I was a huge fans of the first Queens album ... so they were nice enough to ask when it came time to make another record.'

This mutual adoration meant that he played on all tracks but one of the album *Song for the Deaf*, and touring naturally followed. 'The time with Queens of the Stone Age really kind of opened me up, because I hadn't really played the drums with anyone seriously for eight years. When Queens asked, they were the only band I would've done it for. They're the only band that I would join and play drums with. But y'know, it was great to play with those guys and when you're in a band with people and it just fuckin' clicks, and you don't have to talk or say anything, it's easy to make music. After doing that I realised, like, "That was great fun, we toured, we made a record ... I'd like to do that more often." I love playing the drums. I don't even have to think about it.'

QOTSA bassist Nick Oliveri was enthusiastic about Grohl's temporary recruitment, as he told *Record Collector* in July 2002: "He's just enjoying himself playing with us because it's a stress-free environment. He can just relax and play drums and smile and have a good time. He's one of the best drummers in rock and I'm happy to see him behind the drums again. You know, I haven't taken my bass home in years. But with Dave behind the drums ... I need to practice!"

Grohl's first musical 'side trip' took place when he recorded the Pocketwatch sessions as a way of satisfying the songwriting cravings that could never find an outlet with Nirvana. It should perhaps not be surprising, then, that he had a similar desire to 'stray' when he felt the Foo Fighters sound had been so tightly established that it was unable to accommodate every song that came into his head. 'When I was 16 I wasn't the singer of the Foo Fighters or the drummer of Nirvana,' he explained. 'I was a fan of heavy music. I still am.' Dave felt that, after making *There is Nothing Left to Lose*, he became 'sick of hearing 'Learn to Fly' and feeling that was my life direction. It just seemed funny to me that a person who grew up listening to hardcore punk rock and death metal was writing Top 40 pop songs.'

Hence *Probot*, the album of metal originals he recorded with a variety of guest vocalists in 2001, in the long gap between the Foos' third and fourth albums. The first stage was laying to tape seven instrumentals cut with nothing particular in mind. Then, after guesting on Tony Iommi's solo album, the idea hit him like a ton of bricks: why not select other

singers to match the songs? The next session consisted of
five more songs written after having come up with this idea.
'I wanted to match vocalists with songs that were within their
realm, without making it seem like I was parodying them.'
Hence ex-Napalm Death/Cathedral singer Lee Dorrian's song
'Ice Cold Man' was written with him very much in mind, while
'The Emerald Law', featuring ex-St Vitus/Obsessed
vocalist/guitarist Wino, began life as an instrumental.

Grohl's intention was not to select the likes of Ozzy
Osbourne, Tony Iommi's 'mouthpiece' in Black Sabbath and
now on his way to becoming a self-parodying Reality TV star,
but singers whose obscure yet influential metal of the 1980s
had reached him as that 16-year-old fan. There was, he
explained, an element of payback involved. 'The spotlight is
supposed to be on the singers. I'm just the background band.
Probot's not my status symbol, although it's a dream come
true for me. But it's important to make sure that this is not a
record by "the Foo Fighters guy."'

Typical of the participants was Cronos, mainman of British
death metallers Venom, who took the lead on opening track
'Centuries of Sin'. 'Dave sent me an email, in which the first
hundred lines he was talking about how much he loves us and
how often he's seen us play live. A real fan letter! Back then he
was only playing with the idea of recording a metal album
with all his metal-heroes and Venom having a part in it. He
wrote that he'd have to get something off his chest. I answered
instantly: "Of course, man. Send this shit over! Let's fucking
do it!" I'm not preoccupied. I'm open for everything. And
Dave's cool.'

The roll of vocal honour included exotic-sounding names
known only to those who had drunk deep of the metal chalice:
Max Cavalera (Soulfly, Sepultura), Tom G Warrior (Celtic Frost)
and Snake (Voïvod) were three. In addition, guitarists Kim

Thayil of Soundgarden played a memorable solo on the King Diamond track ('Sweet Dreams') and Bubba Dupree of Void on Mike Dean's 'Access Babylon'.

Perhaps the most famous singer in mainstream terms was Lemmy of Motörhead. He entered the studio clad in a long tailcoat and white boots, knocked back a couple of Jack Daniels and Cokes with Dave and then slayed him by nailing the vocals straight away. 'After meeting him, I don't think I've ever met a rock 'n' roller in my life,' gushed Grohl. This was the track selected as a single, with a video that no one involved will ever forget. Sunset Boulevard was the place to be on 16 November 2003 as 66 'Suicide Girls' added their photogenic talents to the mix, writing on specially designed 'bondage furniture' as Lemmy, Dave and guitarist Wino hammered out the track.

Probot was destined to wait many months for release as Grohl pondered the best way to unleash it on an unsuspecting public. In addition, with the Foo Fighters now back on track, it would be politic to release it in a way that stole none of their thunder. Grohl decided the album would come out via indie hardcore label Southern Lord, whose owner Greg Anderson was an acquaintance dating from his days with Scream and now played in a band called Goatsnake with Peter Stahl, brother of Franz, Foos road manager and the former singer for Scream. It was the next best thing to keeping it in the family. 'It was important for me to keep *Probot* as personal as possible, not with a huge company. The underground spirit of the record is straight. Metal was an underground-movement in the '80s. The loyalty was an example. Sixteen years ago I slept on Lee [Dorrian]'s floor. At that time he still was in Napalm Death. The metal family is all over the world, every member is making music out of the right reasons.'

As you might expect, the vast majority of singers approached were only too willing to add their voices to the

Probot project. The only names on his wish list whose services remained unavailable were Tom Araya (Slayer) and Phil Anselmo (Pantera). 'I sent packages with tapes and hoped that that the addressee would like them. That's why it took three years from the first take until the last take. I also sent a tape to Tom Araya, but it didn't work in the end.' The Slayer singer would prove hard to replace, as the song 'Silent Spring' had been intended specifically for him. 'It had to be someone who fits into the family. It took a while, but then I thought of Kurt Brecht from DRI. DRI, Corrosion Of Conformity and the Cro-Mags – these were the three best bands from the punk or hardcore side that in reality were making metal.'

Probot finally emerged in early 2004 on the previously mentioned Southern Lord label. Reviews were mixed, metal mags uncertain what to make of this detour into their territory and mainstream reviewers flummoxed because Grohl had 'thought outside his box'. 'The most disappointing aspect of *Probot* is that many of the songs sound more like Foo Fighters turned to eleven than actual metal,' was a typical example of the former, suggesting that 'The Emerald Law' 'could have been Foo product, or a hard-edged Nirvana B-side.'

For Dave the release of the album was its own reward, and live performance never a realistic possibility. 'The logistics of making the album were so insane,' he explained, 'I can't even imagine getting all these people into one room at the same time. It would have been amazing to do one show for a record release party, but it's kind of great and special that it's a once in a lifetime thing. And it should remain that way.'

One meeting that took place in Auckland, New Zealand during the Big Day Out in early 2003 would lead to Dave recording with long-time heroes Killing Joke. The two bands were on the same bill, and a meeting was convened with their mainman Jaz Coleman at a pub. 'I was waiting for him,' he recalled later, 'thinking I hope I recognise him, and in walks this fucking priest.'

'The first night we really did get everything out of our system; what very disgraceful behaviour,' said Coleman, referring to how he and Grohl got so drunk they ambushed a pair of Americans deemed guilty of being George Bush sympathisers. 'Jaz caught hold of them and started screaming at them,' Grohl relays, smiling at the memory. 'I had to fucking drag him away from mauling them. He was trying to bite their ankles at one point. So we wound up rolling down the hill together.' 'It was very funny,' laughed Coleman. 'Poor fuckers didn't know what happened to them. It was a good blowout. It was, "Let's see absolutely the worst sides of each other straight away – see what we're dealing with."'

It hadn't been all smiles, though, since bad blood had existed between Killing Joke and Nirvana over 'Come As You Are'. The track from *Nevermind* had a riff lifted straight from the Joke's 'Eighties', and Kurt had been reluctant to release it as a single for that reason. Dave and Killing Joke's Paul 'Raven' Ferguson had encountered each other at a Pantera show when the subject came up. And while legal action had been as close as this, Jaz duly joined the Foos live to sing 'Requiem'. He also suggested Dave might want to help out on a new album they were planning. Did he ever?

The drum tracks for the eponymous CD were recorded at Grandmaster Studios in Hollywood at the end of March 2003 – and though it had been suggested that Danny Carey from Tool and John Dolmayan from System of a Down would share the percussion duties, Grohl proved an immovable presence on the drum stool. Jaz: 'When Dave came in and heard everything he said "I want to do this. This is mine."'

In the end, he played it, in one reviewer's words, 'like a Killing Joke drummer rather than fitting the band round his muscular style' – evidence of his pride in having been selected. And it seems he truly enjoyed the experience. 'The funny thing about meeting Jaz and then hearing the music and the lyrics we recorded together on *Killing Joke* is that everything's so relevant. It almost seems prophetic. You'd always heard that Killing Joke was more than just a band, it was almost like an extended family or a network of individuals with a common goal or cause. I feel like I'm a part of it now.'

If that was the fulfilment of a childhood dream, perhaps Grohl's least expected collaboration came in 2004 when he took a phone call from Trent Reznor of industrial-rock giants Nine Inch Nails. Reznor had tended to be something of a one-man band on his studio albums, which typically emerge about every five years. But for *With Teeth*, the follow-up to 1999's *The Fragile*, he opted to replace the usual programming and synthesisers with 'real' instruments – guitar, bass, piano and, of course, Grohl's so-distinctive drums.

Reznor still played most of the music himself, but planned to bring in members of the latest live Nails line-up to give the human touch he desired. He found he kept asking drummer Jerome Dillon to play like Grohl, whom he had met at a festival in Australia some years earlier. 'Finally I thought, "Why don't I just call Dave and see if he'd do it?" A few days later we were in the studio.' The experience proved a pleasant one. Importantly for Reznor, Grohl proved 'a really nice guy', but, more importantly, 'as a musician he brought an understanding to the material.'

The main reason why real drums were used on this record, as opposed to programming, was the unpredictability factor. 'I want the excitement of when you have an exciting guy playing an instrument. It takes it up a notch.' A by-product of the recording process was that each song on the album was laid down with live performance in mind: all could be played by the current tour line-up without reliance on pre-recorded backing tracks. 'There is a much less refined approach to most of this record,' Reznor confirmed, 'and I wrote a lot of the tracks envisioning powerful live drumming – enter Dave Grohl! Working with him has been one of the most inspiring and exciting experiences I've had in the studio. The tracks he's played on have come alive in a "better-than-I'd-even-hoped-for" type of way.'

When he entered Sound City Studios in Van Nuys, California, in July 2004 to pound out the backing tracks, Grohl was amazed that this was Reznor's first new studio record in five years. Reznor forced himself to write two songs every ten days, and they were recorded even more quickly. 'I wanted it to sound "played". Not like a garage band, necessarily, but with computers it's easy to fix things and make everything perfect, and sometimes you can lose an element of humanity and imperfection ... We treated things as performances.'

After the album opens with 'All the Love in the World', its electronic drums more typical of past NIN music, Grohl's role in pushing the band's new hard-rocking approach becomes evident on tracks two and three, 'You Know What You Are' and 'The Collector', Grohl's constant pounding adding a no-frills rock edge. The title track, the longest song on the disc, finds Grohl hammering home a simple yet effective chorus, while 'Love Is Not Enough' is another song built on a complex percussive foundation.

One unexpected by-product of Dave's involvement is the presence of piano on nearly every track. 'When it came time to pick the best of the best and arrange them in the studio,' Reznor explained, 'I found a lot of the space the piano took up sat nicely. It was an odd sound with violent live drums and this cold, brittle environment of a piano to anchor everything together.' But it worked. Reznor produced the album himself, which was then completed in New Orleans by master mixer Alan Moulder, who ensured the drums were prominent, giving full rein to Grohl's very distinctive style.

Reznor and Grohl seemed unlikely collaborators, both having 'enjoyed' the company of Courtney Love in slightly contrasting circumstances. More importantly, the pair are both hands-on bandleaders, used to having their own way and making the musical decisions that matter. Yet, like most drummers, Dave was able to knuckle down, take direction and revel in doing a professional job enhancing the vision of others. He did it to legendary effect in Nirvana, and was happy to do it again here.

*   *   *

As if to show that his boss was not the only drummer in demand, Taylor Hawkins decided to develop his own extracurricular activities. His activities began with Chevy Metal, an informal covers outfit which convenes weekly to play versions of 1970 British classic rock, Yes and Electric Light Orchestra among their targets.

The March 2006 release of a debut album from the Coat Tail Riders, a band named after a song by the Supersuckers, took things to another level. 'I really wanted to make a record and have a project outside of the Foo Fighters,' Taylor told *Rolling Stone*. 'I had to kind of create another little environment for myself to keep busy and excited.' Hawkins planned a solo tour of the US and the UK, playing drums and singing lead vocals at the same time, after Foo Fighters had finally ended promotion of *In Your Honour*. The album was the result of more than a year's work, he told the magazine. 'I think it [was] Oscar Wilde who said, "Why go on vacation when working's so much more fun?"' Hawkins said with a laugh. 'I'm no good when I have nothing to do.'

The summer of 2004 had seen him ensconced in the home studio of friend Drew Hester. In Grohl-esque fashion, Hawkins took care of drums, vocal and guitar duties alongside guitarist Gannin and Jane's Addiction/Alanis Morissette bassist Chris Chaney. The new record was influenced by Hawkins' childhood listening – the Police, prog-rock from the 1970s, Queen and Devo. 'Everything I grew up listening to is on there. I don't think I'm John Lennon, but I like writing songs and making music, I really do.'

Touring with the Coat Tail Riders was planned to be on a much more manageable scale and with a more informal approach than the Foos' slick rock show. 'We're really stretching the songs out,' Hawkins said. 'Our template in a way is Cream, where the song is the germ of what we're going to do and we'll just take it from there.' The eponymous debut from the trio received a lowly two out of five review from *Rolling Stone*, who said it mixed 'palatable post-grunge darkness with controlled punk splatter and an array of subtle electronic embellishments. Hawkins' throaty singing is steady if nondescript, but barnburners like 'It's OK Now' are lacking in both personality and hooks.'

*   *   *

Meanwhile, Nate Mendel had reunited in 2003 with William Goldsmith and Jeremy Enigk as the Fire Theft; only Dan Hoerner was absent from the original Sunny Day Real Estate line-up. It wasn't Mendel's first reconnection with old friends: indeed, rumour had it that a full-time reunion had been on the cards after the band had re-formed in 1997 to record tracks for a Sub Pop rarities compilation. Re-establishing his rhythm relationship with William Goldsmith, by now an ex-Foo, was clearly an attractive proposition, but he had proved unable or unwilling to commit himself on a permanent basis. 'Waiting for Nate became the theme to our lives,' guitarist Hoerner had commented.

The vacancy had eventually been filled by Mommyheads four-stringer Jeff Palmer, but by 2000 singer Enigk was also handling bass duties. That year's 'Rising Tide' wrote the band's name on *Billboard*'s Top 100 album chart for the first time but they disbanded the following year, unhappy with their label's distribution. The Fire Theft was their next step.

Nate was absent on official business when they tested the water with a sellout booking in January at the compact, 300-capacity surroundings of the Graceland nightclub in Seattle, Nick Macri deputising. Brad Wood, who produced/engineered the first two Sunny Day albums, helped out on keyboards, and they performed a set of all-new material with aplomb. A reviewer from *Decoy Online* defined the fare on offer as 'equal parts indie rock, 1970s prog, and 1980s new wave. You can definitely feel the pull of Pink Floyd and Zeppelin's influence,' concluding: with 'You can't keep a good band down.' But the lack of an encore underlined the fact that there was to be no looking back to their previous incarnation for crowd-pleasing material: the new stuff and the new band had to stand and fall on its own merits.

March found them at New York's 500-capacity Bowery Ballroom, by which time Nick Macri had switched to keyboards, displacing Brad Wood, and second guitarist Billy Dolan (5ive Style, Heroic Doses) had joined. Recording sessions followed, an eponymous long player finding its way to the shops in late 2003 via Rykodisc. It was well reviewed, *Esquire* calling it 'a mesmerising debut' and *Entertainment Weekly* praising its spectrum of sound from 'delicate pop miniatures to grandiose rock epics'. It suggested that SGRE fans might not go for the Fire Theft's 'classic rock ambition and orchestral gloss', but concluded that this might be the rare spin-off band that equals its progenitor.

A North American tour kicked off in Seattle on 27 September 2003, but scheduled European festivals in summer 2004 for some reason didn't happen. Dates were scheduled for the Lollapalooza festival, which was cancelled, leaving the story open-ended. Nate stayed busy, however, scoring and appearing in the independent film *Our Burden is Light*.

Unfortunately, William Goldsmith was then diagnosed with repetitive stress disorder and told that, without treatment, his career as a drummer would be over within two years. 'I was asking for it,' he explained, 'because I'm self-taught and never really learned any technique. I play more with my arms, and that's not good.'

Goldsmith decided to become more restrained. 'I find you can play heavier the more relaxed you stay. I'm trying to let my wrists do the work and give my arms a break. When I was a kid, I wanted to be exactly like Keith Moon, and that's how I played for a long time, just completely insane. Now I'm really starting to enjoy simplicity. I don't like playing things that are unnecessary. I want to leave room for all the colours to really swirl around me.'

*   *   *

No chapter on Foo Fighters spin-off activities could possibly close without mention of Tenacious D. A spoof metal duo formed way back in 1994 by actors Jack Black and Kyle Gass, they had first interacted with the Foos on the video for 'Learn to Fly' when they played the drug-smuggling ne'er-do-wells whose activities threaten to down the airliner on which Dave and pals are flying.

It was inevitable that Black, a rock-star wannabe whose films have included *School of Rock* and *King Kong*, would get into the recording studio, and Grohl was a participant – along with Page McConnell (Phish), and Warren Fitzgerald (Vandals) amongst others – on the pair's eponymous 2001 debut album, which saw them revisit the classic rock era with much humour and schoolboy sniggering. Tasteless it was, but great fun too. As one amateur Amazon reviewer put it, 'if swearing and songs about anal sex aren't to your taste, the music alone more than makes up for it!'

Dave also starred as a 'shiny demon' in the video for their hit single 'Tribute', appearing in a red suit and playing a preposterous guitar solo before melting down in the face of a challenge from our two heroes. Further elucidation is impossible; if you haven't seen the video, make every effort to.

Jack Black was unstinting in his praise for Grohl. 'Ronnie James Dio in 1983 was definitely rocking harder than Dave at that time, but the thing is Dio never achieved immortal, Mount Olympus status ... Dave is on the mountain, he's there with Jim Morrison, the Beatles, Jimi Hendrix...'

pubLic and private

'G rowing up [as a] punk, 'rock star' was a derogatory term. As far as I'm concerned, it still is. Being a 'rock star' is about celebrity, not about music, which is why you're supposed to be doing this in the first place. Being a rock star shouldn't be considered a career option ... If you don't love to play music – and you're not doing it purely for that reason – then quit.'

Dave Grohl's philosophy is commendably simple, and one that has not varied one iota despite the success he has achieved. U2 biographer Bill Flanagan recounted an incident in his book *U2 At The End Of The World* when Grohl, then of course Nirvana's drummer, came to a show during the first leg of the Zoo Tour in 1992 to pay his respects to opening act the Pixies: 'Bono invited him in for a talk. Bono mimicks Grohl chewing gum and saying, "Hey, man, nothing against you, but I don't know why the Pixies would do this." Bono asked if Grohl didn't think it was brave of the Pixies to try opening for U2 in arenas. Grohl didn't buy it. "We'll never play big places," he said of Nirvana. "We're just a punk band. All this success is a fluke. Tomorrow I could be somewhere else."'

After that meeting, Dave had reportedly declared that 'It was a bummer meeting Bono. He reeks of rock star-ness ... It made me want to give up being in a rock 'n' roll band.' And even though the 'fluke' of success had continued via Foo Fighters, his attitude remained the healthy one that it could all be over tomorrow. Ironically, the Foos linked with U2 in November 2005 to pay tribute to late, great country star Johnny Cash in a US TV special coinciding with the release of the long-awaited biopic, *Walk the Line*.

Life as a Foo Fighter had never exactly approached Dave's experiences with Scream, sleeping on people's floors and driving from gig to gig in clapped-out cars. But then again, as he remarked in 2005, he'd earned the right to enjoy life's little luxuries. 'I've been on the road since I was 18 years old; I'm about to turn 37. The most important thing for me now isn't getting obliterated ... but that the shows are good. I've had a lot of parties out there. Now it's time to get out there and sing along with the crowd.'

And there remained the realisation that, as he prepared to welcome a little Grohl into the world, rock 'n' roll wasn't the be-all and end-all of his life.

Dave's freelance drumming efforts had at least kept his seat warm on the high table of rock percussionists. 2005 saw him take his place alongside Keith Moon. Buddy Rich, Elvin Jones and (his biggest hero) John Bonham in *Rhythm* magazine's Hall of Fame. 'It's the greatest honour for me as a drummer,' he gushed excitedly. 'It's funny to still think of myself as a drummer because I've been doing the Foo Fighters thing for the last 11 years, but I am constantly reminded every time I sit down at the drum set, or every time I jam with new people, that I am a drummer at heart. It's my first love and it's the instrument that I feel most comfortable playing, so being inducted into the *Rhythm* Hall of Fame is a badge that I am going to wear very proudly.'

Someone else who remained very proud was Virginia Grohl, who continued to be seen supporting her son on the live circuit, not to mention supping with the famous. 'We can go out and play a festival,' laughed Dave, 'and after we are done playing I will come back to the dressing room and my mom is having a Guinness with Billie Joe from Green Day. I basically just hand her a pass and let her do her thing now. Early on I would have to, you know, make sure that she had her room and she was comfortable and she wasn't getting accosted by other people. Now, you bring mom to the show and it's like she is in the band. She is like part of the crew. I'm the guy with the cool mom.'

*   *   *

Dave Grohl rarely backs a loser, but when he took the decision to back Presidential candidate John Kerry in 2004 he was sticking his neck out in a hitherto unprecedented way.

Foo Fighters had weathered controversy when, in 2000, they played a Los Angeles benefit gig for Alive and Well, an 'alternative AIDS information group' whose unorthodox beliefs flew in the face of accepted medical science. It was a cause backed by Nate Mendel, and the Foos had attracted a significant amount of adverse publicity because of it. They'd also played Free Tibet events at the invitation of the Beastie Boys, with no repercussions.

The commercial complications of rocking against President Bush had been felt by country trio the Dixie Chicks, who had received much flak from the country music establishment after condemning the Iraq war from the stage in 2003. But Grohl was the man who felt indignant when the Bush re-election campaign used Foo Fighters' 'Times Like These' (from the *One by One* album) without first seeking permission. It was an echo of Ronald Reagan appropriating Bruce Springsteen's anthemic 'Born in the USA' back in 1984. Never mind that the lyrics questioned American foreign policy and lamented the lot of the Vietnam veteran, Reagan never got further than the supposedly patriotic chorus.

And just like the Boss two decades earlier, Dave was less than amused. 'I don't give a shit if he [Bush] likes our band,' he blustered, 'but I take it personally when a politician that doesn't represent my personal beliefs uses music that I poured my heart and soul into for his personal gain.'

This entry into the world of politics represented a significant shift in Grohl's world view. 'I don't think people have to use their fame or their band as a platform to be political,' he'd told the *Sun-Herald* newspaper in 2003. 'I have a lot of respect for bands that do. Whether it be Rage Against the Machine or Fugazi or Atari Teenage Riot.' One year later, his perspective had changed. 'Traditionally I've stayed away from political activism, but the policies and actions of the current administration have made me realise that I no longer have a choice.'

Up until this point, Grohl had made a point of not linking his political views to his music, save for the occasional benefit, as listed above. But when Bush played his dirty trick, the gloves came off with a vengeance. 'It just goes to show how out of touch that man is if he's using our songs at his rallies.'

Rather than issuing a cease-and-desist letter, Grohl nailed his colours to the mast when he went on the campaign trail with Democratic Presidential candidate John Kerry. 'There's no way of stopping the President playing your songs so I went out and played for John Kerry's people instead, where I felt the message would make more sense.' A rally in Iowa saw him play 'My Hero', 'Times Like These' and 'Learn to Fly'. He explained: 'I sang those songs, which are supposed to represent love, hope and compassion, for a person that I believe represents all of those things.' The response was enough to get him on board the Kerry bandwagon – a curious echo of his father, who had at various times acted as a Republican campaign manager and speechwriter in the Washington DC political scene.

Dave's earlier reluctance to be politically 'engaged' was perhaps understandable given his father's political leanings. 'I've never been an outwardly political person,' he acknowledged. And, while stressing he had always voted and been active in his community, he agreed that politics had never yet found its way into his music.

But travelling from town to town through middle America in John Kerry's entourage left an indelible mark. 'What inspired me most wasn't necessarily political. It was the strength of community and human will. Seeing so many people come out because they either desperately needed to be rescued or they genuinely wanted change. It really hit me. I'd never been so deeply involved in something so important. It was unbelievably inspirational.' Grohl would play acoustic shows at these rallies, claiming somewhat unrealistically that 'nobody knew who I was.'

The title of his next album, *In Your Honour*, would pay explicit homage to Kerry, as the singer-guitarist explained to *Rolling Stone*. 'We'd pull into small towns, and thousands of people would come to be rescued by this man.' The Kerry camp returned the compliment by describing Grohl as a 'hero' on the campaign trail who 'inspired a record number of young voters' to support the Democratic senator. What was more, spokeswoman Katharine Lister said that one-time high school bass player Kerry 'is ready to return the favour and go on tour with Dave Grohl and open for the Foo Fighters anytime.'

Dave's first stop was Milwaukee, and he immediately used an internet weblog to contrast the political caravan with the Foo Fighters touring machine. 'I've never seen such a massive group of people move with such organisation and ease, and still make it seem like a family trip,' he stated admiringly. His audience at this 'mini gig' was 'definitely different than the crowd I'm used to rocking. Can't say that we get many WWII vets at Foo Fighters shows, but there's always time! The crowd was great, though, and I think they got what I was trying to say with my song 'My Hero'.'

The trip across America with Kerry even led him back to his former Nirvana rhythm partner when Krist Novoselic showed up at Las Vegas to introduce him. Addressing the crowd, he asked, 'When was the last time I was on the stage with Dave Grohl? I love the man.' The pair embraced, all smiles. Then, standing in front of a banner reading 'Kerry & Edwards: A Stronger America' and under Novoselic's intense gaze, Dave strummed his acoustic songs.

One reason he was voting for Kerry, Grohl explained from the stage, was so people in other nations might like Americans, the way they used to pre-Bush. 'Everyone would want to meet an American. Meeting Americans was like meeting Elvis,' he said, raising laughs. But now people overseas 'don't see me, they see Bush.'

At the end of the day he was thankful that the Kerry campaign 'gave me this wonderful opportunity. I've done a few things in my life that I'm very proud of, but this one might take the cake: Using my music to stand up for something I believe in. Not as a 'celebrity', not as a 'rock star', but as an American kid from Springfield, Virginia. Don't worry, I won't be running for office any time soon ... but this sure is fun!'

Grohl spent some time on the campaign trail, and was impressed by what he saw from the stage when he played benefits. 'The first 20 rows of the audience would be people in wheelchairs. Then there were farmers, schoolteachers, and blue-collar factory workers and I got to see how all these really strong people came together devoted to this one honourable cause. The strength of community and human will was inspiring.'

There was an inevitable reflection of this in the album he was about to make, and though he insists that *In Your Honour* 'isn't actually a political record', he admits he was 'really, really inspired by how passionate people were to make a change.' Sadly for Dave and fellow Democrats, and as we now know, President Bush amassed enough votes to secure a second White House term.

The groundswell of youth opinion against Bush's re-election was headed by an organisation called PunkVoter, backed by out-fits as well known as Good Charlotte, Blink 182, the Offspring and NOFX (whose Fat Mike Burnett was a spokesman), as well as individuals like Jello Biafra (the Dead Kennedys), Wayne Kramer (MC5) and Billy Gould (ex-Faith No More). In total, over 200 bands signed up to aid the cause of mobilising American youth to register to vote. Chris Shiflett was quick to add his backing. 'I think it's important to get the message out as much as you can to young people, to get them involved in the political process and make sure they're not complacent ... The kids can really swing this thing if they all go out and vote.'

Though the thing wasn't swung, it's reckoned that between 100,000 and 200,000 young people registered to vote as a result of the PunkVoter campaign. And that can only be helpful for democracy, whichever political colour you are.

Foo Fighters donated the track 'Gas Chamber' to a various artists fundraising CD called *Rock Against Bush Vol 2*, released in April 2004. The track, originally by obscure Californian hardcore band the Angry Samoans, had long been a favourite of Dave's and had first been recorded by him during down time on the last Nirvana sessions in January 1994. The version on the album, from a November 1995 session at BBC's Maida Vale Studios, had been a bonus track on the 'Big Me' single and was otherwise unavailable. The other big name to contribute to the album was Green Day (the unreleased 'Favorite Son'), the likes of Dropkick Murphys, Sleater-Kinney and Sick of It All seeming second division by comparison.

Unlike Grohl, Krist Novoselic was no stranger to matters political. He had been instrumental in creating a political action committee, JAMPAC (Joint Artists and Musicians Political Action Committee), to fight a number of different issues, including the Teen Dance Ordinance, a 1985 law that severely limited the ability of minors to attend shows.

As successive musical endeavours – Sweet 75, who released a single self-titled album, followed by the No WTO Combo with Jello Biafra and former Soundgarden guitarist Kim Thayil, and Eyes Adrift with Meat Puppets frontman Curt Kirkwood – failed to take off, politics took precedence.

Novoselic would remain active in politics as an elected Democratic State Committee man, making appearances to advocate electoral reform (especially instant-runoff voting and proportional representation) and running the website fixour.us. He considered a 2004 campaign for Lieutenant Governor of Washington (as a Democrat, challenging an incumbent of the same party), but decided against it. He'd always felt Nirvana was a political band: 'We were the prophets of the disenfranchised. We spoke to the disenfranchised because we ourselves felt that way.'

Having publicly politicised himself, Grohl decided to let Campus Progress volunteers accompany his band on the North American leg of their 2005 world tour. The object of Campus Progress was 'to strengthen progressive voices on college and university campuses nationwide; counter the growing influence of right-wing groups on campus; and empower new generations of progressive leaders.' The organisation claimed that, while the media perceived US campuses as hotbeds of liberalism, conservative groups were spending over $35 million annually to push their agenda at students.

The sixteenth show of the tour brought Grohl back to home turf – George Mason Patriot Center in Fairfax, Virginia, to be precise – and some 30 friends and family members were in attendance as his guests, including his wife, to whom an acoustic 'Everlong' was dedicated. At another point Grohl apologised to his mom and dad for his childhood misdemeanours, then sang to them with spotlights on the singer at the front of the stage and his parents at the back of the arena.

Foo Fighters and support act Weezer were happy to endorse Campus Progress, though the crowd was far from exclusively college students: reports suggested the presence of a handful of parents and children 'and a whole lot of Nirvana hanger-oners'.

If Dave Grohl saw his future in politics, he wasn't declaring his hand just yet. But there seems little doubt that the interest ignited by his John Kerry involvement will continue to smoulder for some time to come – whether detectable in his music or not.

* * *

The private Dave Grohl lives behind high walls. It's part of his post-Nirvana strategy to allow the press unlimited access to Grohl the rock star in exchange for privacy for Grohl the individual.

In 2003 he gave *USA Weekend* a rare insight into his off-duty life. 'I'm an early-to-rise kind of guy. I usually wake up around 6.30 or 7. Maybe I'll put on the new Beck or Coldplay album. (I'm a delicate flower at that hour.) I make coffee, and I'll throw a few eggs and half a pack of bacon on the frying pan. (Man, I have the metabolism of a gerbil!) Once I've got plenty of animal fat in the old system, I hike in the hills around Hollywood.'

The weekend, for carnivore Grohl, would not be complete without a barbecue. He claimed to have 'packed 130 people in my back yard around my sweet grill. I'll grill up asparagus, peppers, onions and, being a carnivore, lots of meat. Steaks

and chicken, or I'll do a brisket or shrimp tacos.' His house –
1800 square feet, with a small 1950s-style kitchen and a patio
in the back with a small pool – is clearly his domain, as he
proved by getting married for the second time there.

His first marriage to Jennifer Youngblood between 1993 and
their divorce four years later was kept under wraps.
Subsequent girlfriends – Smashing Pumpkins and Hole
bassist Melissa Auf der Maur and Louise Post, frontwoman
of Veruca Salt – were relatively high-profile individuals, yet
curiously next to nothing hit the public pages. A relationship
with allegedly kleptomaniac actress Winona Ryder was all
but denied; 'I'm a musician,' he deadpanned. But then her
ex-musician boyfriends included Ryan Adams, Evan Dando
and Adam Duritz, so it's likely he was being ironic.

With remarriage in his sights, he fully admitted that his
past choices had been off the wall. 'Pretty much every
girlfriend that I've ever had has been relatively insane, OK? If
I were in a roomful of women, I'd find the biggest fucking
nutcase.' The reason was his nurturing nature. 'I love being
the provider, emotionally and otherwise – that's what I do.'

The biggest story to circulate concerning Grohl's love life,
that he was dating Christina Aguilera, was in fact completely
untrue. 'We were both in the same studio and we bumped into
each other in the kitchen and talked. But she's a kid, man –
what age is she, 21 or something? She's a child and I'm an old
rock guy. It was huge news, to my amusement.' It wasn't that
amusing, however, as he was already dating the girl who would
become his second wife. Tellingly, when a local radio station
carried the story, Dave 'phoned and told them to get real.'

The roles were reversed in his new relationship, as he
explained. 'I never met anyone who could take care of me, but
I finally found one. And this person makes me feel like I'm
the crazy one that needs to be taken care of. I like that, it feels

good.' Wife number two, TV producer Jordyn Blum, some eight years his junior, became Mrs Grohl on 2 August 2003, and every indication was that this was a keeper.

At 34, Dave now knew his mind. 'I just don't take any of this for granted. I mean, there are times when it all seems like a dream. Having been in a band like Nirvana, coming through that terrible demise and then deciding, "Fuck the world, I'm gonna pick up a guitar and write some songs" never expecting, eight years later, to be doing an interview about the last eight years. It amazes me. So what could be better than that? What could possibly make it bigger? Well, for one thing, have a family ... I dream about having kids, man.'

There were no Hollywood stars present at the nuptials, just friends and family, though the day had a rock 'n' roll theme. 'I just decided to have a Wedding Festival rather than a Reading Festival,' he explained with a smile. 'My backyard kind of looked like a festival site because I had a tent, 250 people, a Beatles tribute band playing and a wonderful DJ.' At one point he had considered calling the Reverend Al Green and asking him to marry them. 'But I figured it would turn into an Al Green show.'

He recommends the Fab Four to anyone – 'They start in Hamburg, wind up in the Sgt Pepper suits and before you know it, they're doing 'Let It Be'" – and admits in the middle of the gig to shouting 'Where's Yoko?' Something Grohl turned down, however, was the choice of opening number, 'In My Life'. That, he explained, 'is a big song for me because that is what we played at Kurt's memorial. I find it difficult to listen to now because it was so perfect for that day. At my wedding the band suggested this for the first dance. We didn't pick it. It breaks my heart to hear it even now.'

Grohl had taken steps to avoid it becoming 'a Jennifer and Brad wedding. Apparently, J-Lo and Ben Affleck have invited everyone to take pictures of their wedding. That's really funny! In an attempt to seem like normal people they've invited every paparazzo helicopter in northern America to take pictures. I can honestly say that no one gives a shit enough to spend fuel on a helicopter to go over my backyard.'

Taylor Hawkins was an usher, and Krist Novoselic was present, but otherwise it was buddies 'Jimmy, Richie and Mike from Virginia, people I've known since I was five years old.' Add 'friends from Virginia, relatives from Ohio and Louisiana, my fiancée's family from California and Baltimore ... plus I think Jack [Black] is probably going to come, and maybe Kyle [Gass] might show up.'

In 2003 Grohl told Australian *Kerrang!* that he'd finally grown to love his adopted city. 'I used to not like Los Angeles. I lived there on my own, this is maybe about five years ago, and it just didn't feel like home. But now I've got a nice place with my girl and I live down the street from my sister, there's family in the neighbourhood, so I'm digging it, it's nice.' He could even put up with being recognised every day. 'But people don't come up screaming. They walk up and say, "Hey, Dave." There seems to be this familiarity, and that's where music crosses boundaries. Music that begins on a notepad or in a basement makes its way into a stranger's heart. People come up to me and say, "Your last record really helped me through a divorce" or "Your last record helped me through an abusive situation." It's amazing you can share something like that with a stranger.'

He might have 'fathered' five Foos albums, but one thing Grohl hadn't done by the end of 2005 was produce an offspring of his own. But that was set to change. Even before his marriage he was trumpeting his desire to be a dad. 'I'm all about family, and everybody who knows me knows that. It's important to stay close to your family, whatever you do, but especially doing what I do. Jordyn and I can't wait to have children.'

He was aware, though, that his lifestyle would have to change unless he was prepared to be an absentee pop – not an option, given his single-parent childhood. 'One reason I never have [had children] is I travel so much. But I've learned you can make music for the rest of your life without playing the game of touring, MTV and everything that goes along with your conventional idea of being a commercial rock band. I would just love to have a family. That's the one thing I don't have. I love children and I love my family and shit, I love being at home. There's nothing better to anchor you at home than a couple of rugrats.'

His role model as a rock 'n' roll father is Neil Young. 'He's living the life I hope I can have one day. He's living on a beautiful farm with his beautiful children and his beautiful wife. He plays concerts now and then. He still makes records. His love of music hasn't diminished. And he's remained a real person.'

The past few years, Dave said, had brought an epiphany. 'I've settled down quite a bit, that's for sure, and realised life is very delicate. It's too short to wait for anything to happen to you. It's too short to waste it on anything superficial or unimportant – you have to fill your days with things that are meaningful and real.'

The Grohls announced in 2005 that they would become proud parents in the spring of 2006. This would punctuate promotion of *In Your Honour* and ensure that the much-mooted acoustic tour would not happen until later in the year. Taylor Hawkins was the man who inadvertently broke the news, letting it slip to MTV. 'Thanks, Taylor,' Grohl said. 'We were trying to keep that private!' Coincidentally, guitarist Chris Shiflett and his wife were expecting their second child.

But workaholic Dave wouldn't be waiting idly for the happy event. 'I've already sat around the house writing lots of new music to just stay productive,' he told *Kerrang!* magazine in late

2005. He added that '2006 is going to be a huge year of discovery' – and it seems he included both the Foos and fatherhood in that statement. 'There's a lot more in life that's way more important to me than going out on the road and making rock records. The most important things are health and happiness and family. That said, I can't wait to go back ... and keep on [making music]. It's just figuring out how you make it last a lifetime.'

Dave and Jordyn Blum welcomed their first child, Violet Maye, into the world on 15 April 2006, though such was the blanket of secrecy that the news took a full week to make it to the wires. Quaintly named after the proud dad's grandmother, Violet weighed 6 lbs 15 oz and measured 21 inches – as her father described her, 'just perfect.'

* * *

One of the hubs of Grohl's life, a true home from home where his future sonic offspring will be conceived, is Studio 606, the recording facility he commissioned at an estimated cost of $700,000. A handy ten minutes from his home in Encino, it is Foo Fighters' nerve centre. 'Eight thousand feet of rock-oriented real estate,' according to one impressed journalist, its wood-panelled interior was modelled on ABBA's legendary Polar Studios.

As well as the studio itself there are storage facilities for the band's gear, while a live room the size of a small club gave them ample space in which to rehearse. Upstairs in the office, state-of-the-art Apple Macintosh computers jostle for space with table-tennis and pinball machines, while chair cushions made by Grohl's mom from his old T-shirts displaying the names of Slayer and Sonic Youth add a homely touch. Outside, flashy autos stand within rebound range of the basketball court beside the car park.

The studio walls groan under the weight of nearly 100 gold, silver and platinum discs the studio's owner has amassed in his career. Names like Nirvana, Queens of the Stone Age and Foo Fighters have proved their popularity from Iceland to India via all points on the rock 'n' roll map.

With his own studio with which to play, Dave has begun dipping his toe into the waters of freelance production, and in 2004 it was little-known quintet Rye Coalition that felt the benefit. Their fourth full-length album, *Curses*, was overseen by Grohl before they parted from Interscope Records and demanded they be given full rights to their record. Their history of touring with Foo Fighters and Queens of the Stone Age did them no harm, while 2002's critically acclaimed *On Top* album had been recorded by Steve Albini.

In Grohl, Rye Coalition claimed to have found 'someone whom they can connect with musically, someone who understands what kind of band Rye Coalition is, and most importantly someone who shares a similar sense of humour in pursuing the creative process solely for the love of making music. Nick Raskulinecz was recruited to engineer, co-produce, and mix the album, recorded at the very same Sound City Studios in Van Nuys, California, where another little-known band had created *Nevermind* some 13 years previously.

It was a coincidence that tended to back up Grohl's smiling assertion that everything that had happened to him was just a happy accident: 'One day the happy accident will be that it ends, I guess.' Millions of fans the world over will be hoping against hope that, just for once, he had made the wrong call...

'THIS DOESN'T GET OLD...'

The Hyde Park, London show Dave had been looking forward to was nothing short of spectacular. And while most mortal men would have been spending the last solitary pre-performance hour contemplating life from a backstage Portaloo, Dave was blithely cooking steaks for his family on a barbecue!

Juliette and the Licks, fronted by actress friend Juliette Lewis, replaced the Subways as the opening act, while Angels and Airwaves and Motorhead were added to the bill, the latter as 'special guests'. Motorhead singer Lemmy took those words literally by coming on during the Foos' set and reprising 'Shake Your Blood', his showcase from Dave's *Probot* project. A further surprise was in store for the 85,000 fans – 25,000 over the original estimate – when Roger Taylor and Brian May of Queen invaded the stage for a semi-jammed medley of 'We Will Rock You' and 'Tie Your Mother Down'.

The week before Hyde Park had, said the Foos chief, 'honestly been the most fun I've had in the band for years.' Few acts would have used the Isle of Wight festival as a warm-up for anything, but they acquitted themselves well, headlining the Saturday night in between the Prodigy (Friday) and Coldplay (Sunday). Then came the first acoustic show in Ipswich, which Grohl admits he found 'jarring. I mean, we were so out of our element – after the gig I didn't know whether it was good or bad because we'd never done that before.' Further unannounced warm-ups in took place in London, the most memorable at the Camden Underworld. 'That was special,' said Dave, 'because we hadn't done a show that small in a long time. It renews your passion for just getting sweaty with 90 people.'

While Hyde Park was the Foo Fighters' largest non-festival headlining concert to date, it wasn't to be the most memorable gig played in support of *In Your Honour.* As a tenth anniversary celebration, Grohl and his boys had been granted special permission to perform at the Roswell Industrial Air Centre in New Mexico, the very location after which Dave had named his record label. Sadly, he didn't get to see the hangar where the fragments of the supposed alien crash-landing in 1947 were stored...

At the end of the tour, instead of returning home, Grohl found he wanted more. 'We were all pretty tired,' he admitted, 'but after the rock portion of the touring we went out and played a bunch of acoustic shows in smaller theatres and that really inspired us to keep playing and writing.'

The acoustic tour that took place in the summer of 2006 featured an augmented line-up, in echoes of Nirvana's MTV *Unplugged* phase. The newcomers included an old friend in former member Pat Smear (who rejoined as an extra guitarist), Petra Haden on violin and backing vocals, Drew Hester on percussion and Rami Jaffee on keyboards. (Jessy Greene would replace Haden in 2007, adding occasional cello as well as violin to the mix.)

While the set list understandably focused on *In Your Honour*'s acoustic half, the band also used the opportunity to play some lesser-known songs such as 'Ain't It The Life', 'Floaty' and 'See You'. The band also performed 'Marigold', the *Pocketwatch*-era song best-known as a Nirvana B-side. They also added a major name to their honours board when, in late 2006, they toured as opening act for Bob Dylan, on the crest of a wave promoting his *Modern Times* album. (This connection could well have been made by Rami Jaffee, a founding member of the Wallflowers, along with Dylan's son Jacob.) The fruits of this extended touring would become apparent when, at year's end, Dave found he had 40 new songs in the bag. He'd demoed these with Taylor Hawkins, and many had emerged from the process as complete entities – unusual for him, as Hawkins explained.

'Dave added vocals to demos really early on – a completely different way for him to work. He'd usually leave vocals off until the last moment. But this time he wanted to have an idea of where the song was going from a lyrical point of view.' The result, the drummer concluded, would be 'the slickest album that we've made so far. I don't mean in terms of the way it sounds or the production techniques or anything, just in the way that it felt "right" in the way we approached it and the way it came together.'

The new album, *Echoes, Silence, Patience And Grace*, would kick off the second decade of the Foo Fighters story in 2007. But it wasn't in fact the next release the band's fans would lap up. That honour would fall to *Skin And Bones*, the first live release of the band's audio career. Grohl had previously fought shy of a concert album because the live versions of the songs were essentially similar to their studio counterparts, but the format of the half-acoustic shows had meant changes to the arrangements that invited some kind of recording.

'The shows were different to anything we've ever done,' he confirmed. 'To me, the special thing about *Skin And Bones* is that you've got songs that go back throughout the whole damn catalogue and they sound completely different to the versions already on the record. So it's almost like an acoustic remix record, except it's in front of an audience.'

The title track 'Skin And Bones' had originally been released as a B-side to 'DOA' but took on a life all its own and became a major part of the Foo Fighters' acoustic shows. It was played on most of their tour and on *The Tonight Show With Jay Leno*. It also appeared on *Five Songs And A Cover*, a US-only EP collecting together the non-album B-sides of singles taken from *In Your Honour*. The cover referred to in the title is Cream's 'I Feel Free' which featured Taylor and Dave swopping roles.

Released in late November 2006, the *Skin And Bones* CD was made up of an acoustic set compiled from three shows at LA's Pantages Theater. A DVD, also called *Skin And Bones,* was released separately from the CD. This included extra songs from the LA acoustic gigs that hadn't been included on the audio release due to time constraints. A second disc of the Foos' headlining set at Hyde Park from the previous June was added to the UK release.

For better or worse, Hyde Park, the biggest gig in Britain that year, had changed the band's perspective on the future. The next gig, at Manchester's Old Trafford cricket ground to 'only' 50,000, was inevitably a little bit of an anticlimax. 'It seemed small,' a stunned Grohl admitted, and he appreciated the underdog status he had cherished for so long had now gone out of the window for good. 'Hyde Park was strange for us. Where do you go after that? Do two next time? It was like a dream. But it really makes you wonder, what next? In order for us to keep this ball rolling we have to do bigger and better things every time we come out with an album.'

Summer 2007 had its highpoint in the shape of Live Earth – a series of consciousness-raising shows in eleven locations around the world, broadcast to a mass global audience. Foo Fighters appeared at Wembley Stadium, second on the bill to Madonna. Taylor had also played earlier in the day as part of drumming supergroup SOS Allstars with Roger

Taylor of Queen and Chad Smith of Red Hot Chili Peppers.

Grohl rated Live Earth 'the best thing that's happened to me this year... We were there for specific reasons, but those 25 minutes we played confirmed to me a lot of things about the band. I realised that we could jump into a stadium like that, somewhere that size, and feel like we owned the place for the time that we were on stage.' Whether the issues of climate change were effectively promoted is another matter... but 'Best Of You' returned to the UK Top 40 in July 2007, reaching Number 38 after their performance.

Live Earth had been preceded by a rare support date in late June at Los Angeles' Dodger Stadium with the Police. Ticket prices had ranged from $300 down to $50 in the upper deck from where, according to one resident, 'You have a better view of the mountains than you do the field!'

The Foos sensibly wheeled out a greatest hits set for the assembled 55,000 crowd – even the Dodgers baseball team didn't usually sell out the stadium, so the pre-gig gridlock in the area was intense. As was the atmosphere inside. Dave braved the crowd to wade across to the back of the stadium, climbing up on the scaffolding around the soundboard tent and rocking out while facing his now distant colleagues. It was an impressive way to turn an impersonal stadium event into a rock'n'roll show by bringing the crowd right into it.

Even Police fans saw the Foos as the stars of the show, since Sting and company delivered what was generally regarded as a lacklustre performance. It was, however, one of their earlier tour dates, so there was plenty of time to improve...

The Foos returned to Britain in August to headline both venues of the V Festival (Chelmsford and Stafford), plus play shows at Edinburgh's Meadowbank Stadium and Marlay Park in Dublin. These were interesting inasmuch as, in an echo of the *One By One* tour, they were playing material from a new album the audience had yet to hear.

Sharp-eared V Festival-goers also enjoyed a surprise hour-long acoustic set the Foos played on the Channel 4 stage under the name 606 (Dave's studio). This lived up to his promise that 'I know we're playing the big stages, but you might want to keep an eye on the side stages too.' The acoustic set-list was: 'Skin And Bones', 'Marigold', 'My Hero', 'See You', 'Cold Day In The Sun', 'Big Me' and 'But Honestly'.

But, for Dave Grohl, the central focus of life was his daughter Violet, now a year old and toddling on tour. 'Ten years ago I'd have had a room full of beer bongs, and now look at me,' he laughed. My favourite way to warm up for a show now is to play with my kid for a half an hour. Whereas before I'd be listening to Voivod, now I'm getting half an hour with my baby before I hit the stage. That gets me on an even keel.'

It was not difficult to understand why they'd chosen to appear in Britain for Live Earth rather than New Jersey's Giants Stadium, where even hometown heroes Bon Jovi were relegated to fourth slot behind the Smashing Pumpkins, Roger Waters and the Police. In Britain, he reflected, 'we're treated like this world-class rock band. Then we go home and we're playing in theatres, much smaller places. I remember at one point thinking, God, I wish our band was as big in America as it is in Britain.'

On the other hand, relentless fame was not something he craved. He admitted that, when he'd been hassled while visiting a department store in Manchester a few years earlier, he'd walked out thinking 'Thank God our band is not as big as that in America!' Back home in the US of A, California was ablaze – fortunately far enough away from the Grohl homestead to allay any fears.

The long-awaited sixth studio release *Echoes, Silence, Patience And Grace* finally made its appearance in September. Dave had targeted Britain for special efforts, and he and his bandmates teamed up with BBC Radio 1 to promote not only the record but the radio station's 40th birthday which fell in the month of release – making it just a year or so older than Grohl himself.

He became a guest presenter on 18 September, following Paul McCartney (who had kicked off the series) and preceding Gwen Stefani, following the brief of playing music that had inspired him in his youth. The previous day had seen him and the band in Brighton for the final climactic day of the radio station's Six Weeks of Summer – firstly being interviewed by DJ Chris Moyles, then playing an acoustic version of 'The Pretender' in Jo Whiley's Live Lounge feature and later playing a broadcast concert from the intimate 550-capacity Concorde 2 club. Other unrelated promotional activities around this time included hosting a backstage bar at the MTV Europe Music Awards and playing second single 'Long Road To Ruin' on Jonathan Ross's TV show.

For Taylor Hawkins, the new release was a record that amalgamated the two approaches that had been kept separate on its studio forerunner. 'I know that Dave wouldn't have been comfortable putting violins on a song before. But for whatever reasons, it just felt like the right time to explore those. This time we embraced the idea of really using arrangements in a more considered way. The last record, obviously, was half heavy stuff, half acoustic songs. It sounds obvious, but this time around we weren't afraid of incorporating everything into one song if it felt right.'

The band hooked up again with Gil Norton, producer of 1997's double platinum *The Colour And The Shape*. This, coincidentally, was to be reissued as a remastered 10th anniversary deluxe edition featuring six bonus tracks. But Norton's role was to be as an anchor, ensuring the Foos didn't lose sight of their roots. In an interview with XFM, Grohl noted that the band was eager to expand on their signature sound: 'The album that we're making sounds like a Foo

Fighters album, but it's definitely moving in a few different directions. It's cool.'

Taylor Hawkins highlighted the music's 1970s rock influences: 'stuff that we've always been into, but it came out more strongly on this record than it ever has done.' *A Night At The Opera* and *Physical Graffiti*, progressive masterworks by Queen and Led Zeppelin respectively, were among the albums mentioned. But Hawkins was initially a little worried about the new producer – after all, the first record he did with the band saw his predecessor on the drum stool, William Goldsmith, quit! 'I heard (Norton) was a complete workhorse and a tyrant and nothing's good enough (but) he was a hard-working guy and he did work us hard.' Hawkins also remarked that 'You have to have your shit together when you're working with Gil,' so the three weeks of pre-production before entering the studio proved a good investment.

For his part, Norton said Grohl was looking to continue the acoustic direction the band had ventured into in recent years. 'One of the things Dave really wanted to do was to combine the acoustic album that he'd done coming off the acoustic tour — the bigger band, string players — and build things from acoustic songs into rock songs. That's the sort of dynamic he wanted,' he said. But one thing hadn't changed since 1997 – Grohl was still possibly the hardest-working man in rock. I swear to God, he never stops. He is so *driven*.'

It was no surprise that bombastic opening cut 'The Pretender' was also selected as lead single for the album. 'Let It Die' began acoustically before taking a leaf or two out of Queen's book for the 'Flash'-like mid-section. 'Summer's End', another highlight, had a Southern-rock feel while 'Stranger Things Have Happened' was almost drumless folk. The closing 'Home' was Grohl alone on what one critic called 'vocals, piano and too much melodrama'. But there was no doubting the man was a homebody now.

The piano Grohl's wife had given him as a birthday present a few years earlier also inspired him to write the mid-tempo, Beatle-esque 'Statues'. The staccato beats of 'Erase/Replace' made it a drummer's dream, while the pop sheen of 'Long Road To Ruin' made it the ideal second single and a future stage favourite. But very much on its own was 'Ballad Of The Beaconsfield Miners,' a fingerpicking bluegrass-tinged instrumental duet with guest guitarist Kaki King.

The song was written after Dave met a survivor of a 2006 mine collapse in Tasmania who, while trapped underground, asked for an iPod loaded with Foo songs to keep him company. The track was Grohl's salute to one man's bravery. 'For years, I've had people come up to me and say, "That album helped me through a really difficult time" or "This song was the first dance at our wedding," but something like the Beaconsfield incident was so much heavier. It was about survival,' he said.

Reviews of the album were generally favourable: *New Musical Express* considered it 'As bloody and primal as major-label stadium rock is allowed to get, and it's brilliant', giving a 7/10 rating, while metal bible *Kerrang!*'s four-star (out of five) review concluded 'The Foos finally remember how to get it right.'

Rolling Stone homed in on the variety on offer, calling it 'an anthology of strong new songs by a great bunch of bands, all calling themselves Foo Fighters... Grohl used to spread this variety across whole albums – the one-man power pop of 1995's *Foo Fighters*; the real-band slam of '97's *The Colour and the Shape*; the unplugged CD in the 2005 set *In Your Honour*. He has finally figured out how to make one record out of all that leeway.'

All in all, things had gone well, and the chart statistics were the icing on the cake. *Echoes* sold more than 530,000 copies in the US in its first four months of release, pushing it to a peak of Number 3, while single 'The Pretender' took up residence atop *Billboard*'s modern rock chart, spending a record 17 weeks there. In Britain the album made Number 1 as expected, the single Number 8, while follow-up 'Long Road To Ruin' peaked at Number 35.

Away from the Foos, Taylor (like his boss a new dad these days) had been taking a leaf out of workaholic Grohl's book by moonlighting on drums for Coheed And Cambria. Their new album *No World For Tomorrow* featured Hawkins, much to frontman Claudio Sanchez's delight. 'Taylor's a songwriter, so when he's playing the drums he's not thinking of it as "Oh, I'm a drummer, how flashy can I be?" he's really "What is going to add to this song and make it the strongest it can possibly be?"'

The early part of 2008 saw the Foo Fighters make their regular round of awards shows. In their adopted homeland of Britain, Brits for International Group and Album were scarcely a surprise, and on their return to home shores two out of five Grammy nominations bore fruit. *Echoes, Silence, Patience And Grace* won Best Rock Album while 'The Pretender' took Best Hard Rock performance. 'This doesn't get old,' crowed Grohl as he accepted one of the gongs.

Best album was Herbie Hancock's Joni Mitchell tribute, *River: The Joni Letters*, a choice that pleased Nate Mendel. 'It seems like the Grammys go with the big sellers. The most popular stuff seems to win. But we were happy we didn't win. Right before the announcement, Taylor goes, "We better not win this. We don't want anything to do with being in that position – all those people being (angry) at us."'

But the ever-lovable Foos made many more friends with a performance of an expanded version of 'The Pretender' in the Staples Centre parking lot with John Paul Jones conducting a 30-piece orchestra that took the 'Foos with strings' theme to a hitherto unimagined extreme.

One of the major future shows in the band's diary was at Wembley Stadium on 7 June 2008, an event that Radio 1 would be hosting and broadcasting. Dave saw this showpiece event of the summer as 'a huge challenge and not one we take lightly... Headlining Wembley Stadium is an incredible honour... Every time I think we can't take things any further, our UK fans prove me wrong!

That same month of June 2008 had seen Dave guest with Paul McCartney when the ex-Beatle played a hometown gig at Anfield football ground. It was the highpoint of Liverpool's spell as European City of Culture, and was televised world-wide. Dave joined Macca for 'Band On The Run', on which he played guitar and sang, switching to drums for 'Back In The USSR' and 'I Saw Her Standing There'.

He reprised his role on the latter song in LA the following February when Paul appeared at the Grammy Awards, while in yet another guest appearance he drummed on the tracks 'Run With The Wolves' and 'Stand Up' on The Prodigy's 2009 comeback album *Invaders Must Die*. Meanwhile the Foos journeyed to Berlin in May to perform 'Wheels' and 'All My Life' at the 2009 MTV Europe Music Awards.

It was time for the Foo Fighters to take a break, a fact Dave had strongly hinted at the previous September. Speaking on Chris Moyles' BBC Radio 1 show, he told fans not to expect any new music for a while. 'We've never really taken a long break, I think it's time,' Grohl commented. 'After doing Wembley, we shouldn't come back there for 10 years because we've played to everybody. We're over in the UK every year, every summer, so I think it's time to take a break and come back over when people really miss us.'

And it soon became apparent what Grohl was up to in his spare time – family matters! On 17 April 2009, Dave and wife Jordyn welcomed their second child, a daughter named

Harper Willow, into the world. But typically he wouldn't be idle, music-wise, for long.

For a confirmed Led Zeppelin fan like Grohl, the chance to collaborate with a band member was not to be sniffed at. Indeed, he'd offered his services to Zeppelin for their 2007 reunion show at the O2 Arena (the drum stool was taken by Bonham's son Jason). But now another opportunity presented itself. Them Crooked Vultures was an old-fashioned supergroup, combining Dave's talents with those of Zep bassist John Paul Jones and Josh Homme, with whom he'd played before when depping as drummer in Queens of the Stone Age. The band performed their first live shows in August 2009 in Britain, including a secret spot at the Reading Festival. An eponymous album followed in November and was critically acclaimed, *Rolling Stone* magazine hailing them as 'the second-best band John Paul Jones has ever been in.

'Sometimes,' the review continued, 'the music sounds exactly like Zeppelin, as on "Reptiles", a sly update of "South Bound Suarez". Other times it sounds like Queens of the Stone Age, with a hot new bassist. But it's not desperately ambitious — the album sounds like the good-natured quickie it probably was.'

Ironically, the Vultures album clashed with a Foo Fighters release – and given the band had been dormant for some months, it wasn't surprising that this was their first *Greatest Hits* collection. As usual with such offerings, the 13 previously released tracks were augmented by three bonus cuts, an acoustic version of 'Everlong' and two new tracks: 'Wheels' and 'Word Forward'. These were overseen by Butch Vig, whose production career had taken off with *Nevermind*.

A deluxe edition of the compilation included a 28-page book and a DVD featuring some of the band's music and live performance videos. The Foo Fighters had played an internet-only live concert beamed to the world via Facebook and Livestream from their Studio 606 complex in Los Angeles on 30 October. The album, which reached Number 4 in Britain and 11 in the US, resulted from the record label exercising a clause in the band's contract that allowed them to release it – despite Grohl stating he would have preferred to wait until after the band had retired.

'This greatest hits record, that's the end of something,' he concluded, adding: 'It's time to move on into this next chapter or another phase. Maybe it will be different in whatever way. I don't know. It's nice to not know what's going to happen…'

Whatever it was, there'd be millions of fans waiting for that next move.

Discography

Based on UK/European releases from Nirvana onwards: previous releases in US only.

MISSION IMPOSSIBLE
Single
1985 7-inch vinyl
1. Helpless 2. Into Your Shell 3. Am I Alone? (Split with Lunchmeat)

DAIN BRAMAGE
Album
1987 *I Scream Not Coming Down*
1. The Log 2. I Scream Not Coming Down 3. Eyes Open 4. Swear 5. Flannery
6. Drag Queen 7. Stubble 8. Flicker 9. Give It Up 10. Home Sweet Nowhere

SCREAM
Single
1990 7-inch vinyl
1. Mardi Gras 2. Land Torn Down

Albums
1988 No More Censorship
1. Hit Me 2. No More Censorship 3. Fucked Without A Kiss 4. No Escape
5. Building Dreams 6. Take It From The Top 7. Something In My Head
8. It's The Time 9. Binge 10. Run To The Sun 11. In The Beginning

1989 Live at Van Hall
1. Who Knows Who Cares 2. U Suck A 3. We're Fed Up 4. Laissez faire
5. This Side Up 6. Human Behaviour 7. Iron Curtain 8. Total Mash
9. Still Screaming 10. Chokeword 11. Feel Like That 12. Came Without
Warning 13. Walk By Myself

1990 Your Choice Live
1. CWW Pt II 2. ICYOUD 3. The Zoo Closes 4. Hot Smoke And Sassafras

5. Fight 6. American Justice 7. Show And Tell 8. Sunmaker 9. No Mistake
10. Take It From the Top 11. Dancing Madly Backwards 12. Hit Me

1993 *Fumble*
1. Caffeine Dream 2. Sunmaker 3. Mardi Gras 4. Land Torn Down
5. Gods Look Down 6. Gas 7. Dying Days 8. Poppa Says 9. Rain

DAVE GROHL as **LATE!**
Cassette
1992 Pocketwatch
1. Pokey The Little Puppy 2. Petrol CB 3. Friend Of A Friend 4. Throwing
Needles 5. Just Another Story About Skeeter Thompson 6. Color Pictures
Of A Marigold 7. Hell's Garden 8. Winnebago 9. Bruce 10. Milk

NIRVANA
Singles
November 1991 Smells Like Teen Spirit
CD: 1. Smells Like Teen Spirit 2. Even In His Youth
7-inch vinyl 1. Smells Like Teen Spirit 2. Drain You
12-inch vinyl 1. Smells Like Teen Spirit 2. Even In His Youth 3. Aneurysm

March 1992 Come As You Are
7-inch vinyl 1. Come As You Are 2. Endless, Nameless
12-inch vinyl 1. Come As You Are 2. Endless, Nameless 3. School (Live)
CD: 1. Come As You Are 2. Endless, Nameless 3. School 4. Drain You (Live)

July 1992 Lithium
7-inch vinyl 1. Lithium 2. Curmudgeon
12-inch vinyl 1. Lithium 2. Curmudgeon 3. Been A Son (Live)
CD: 1. Lithium 2. Curmudgeon 3. Been A Son (Live) 4. D7

November 1992 In Bloom
7-inch vinyl 1. In Bloom 2. Polly (Live)
12-inch vinyl 1. In Bloom 2. Polly (Live) 3. Sliver
CD: 1. In Bloom 2. Polly (Live) 3. Sliver

February 1993 Puss/Oh, The Guilt
(Split Single with the Jesus Lizard)
7-inch vinyl 1. Puss 2. Oh, The Guilt

CD: 1. Puss 2. Oh, The Guilt
August 1993 **Heart Shaped Box**
7-inch vinyl *1. Heart Shaped Box 2. Marigold*
12-inch vinyl 1. Heart Shaped Box 2. Marigold 3. Milk It
CD: *1. Heart Shaped Box 2. Marigold 3. Milk It*

December 1993 **All Apologies/Rape Me**
7-inch vinyl 1. All Apologies 2. Rape Me
12-inch vinyl 1. All Apologies 2. Rape Me 3. MV
CD: 1. All Apologies 2. Rape Me 3. MV

October 1994 **Pennyroyal Tea**
CD: 1. Pennyroyal Tea 2. I Hate Myself And Want To Die
3. Where Did You Sleep Last Night

December 1995 **Nirvana Singles**
1. Smells Like Teen Spirit 2. Even In His Youth 3. Aneurysm
1. Come As You Are 2. Endless, Nameless 3. School (Live) 4. Drain You (Live)
1. Lithium 2. Been A Son (Live) 3. Curmudgeon
1. In Bloom 2. Sliver (Live) 3. Polly (Live)
1. Heart Shaped Box 2. Milk It 3. Marigold
1. All Apologies 2. Rape Me 3. MV
Released in US, Australia and Germany to counter bootleg releases.

Albums
September 1991 **Nevermind**
1. Smells Like Teen Spirit 2. In Bloom 3. Come As You Are 4. Breed
5. Lithium 6. Polly 7. Territorial Pissings 8. Drain You 9. Lounge Act
10. Stay Away 11. On A Plain 12. Something In The Way 13. Endless,
Nameless

December 1992 **Incesticide**
1. Dive 2. Sliver 3. Stain 4. Been A Son 5. Turnaround 6. Molly's Lips
7. Son Of A Gun 8. (New Wave) Polly 9. Beeswax 10. Downer
11. Mexican Seafood 12. Hairspray Queen 13. Aero Zeppelin
14. Big Long Now 15. Aneurysm

September 1993 **In Utero**
1. Serve The Servants 2. Scentless Apprentice 3. Heart Shaped Box
4. Rape Me 5. Frances Farmer Will Have Her Revenge On Seattle 6. Dumb

7. Very Ape 8. Milk It 9. Pennyroyal Tea 10. Radio Friendly Unit Shifter
11. Tourette's 12. All Apologies 13. Gallons Of Rubbing Alcohol Flow
Through The Strip

October 1994 **MTV Unplugged in New York**
1. About A Girl 2. Come As You Are 3. Jesus Doesn't Want Me For A
Sunbeam 4. The Man Who Sold The World 5. Pennyroyal Tea 6. Dumb
7. Polly 8. On A Plain 9. Something In The Way 10. Plateau 11. Oh Me
12. Lake Of Fire 13. All Apologies 14. Where Did You Sleep Last Night

October 1996 **From The Muddy Banks of the Wishkah** *(Live)*
1. Intro 2. School 3. Drain You 4. Aneurysm 5. Smells Like Teen Spirit
6. Been A Son 7. Lithium 8. Sliver 9. Spank Thru 10. Scentless Apprentice
11. Heart Shaped Box 12. Milk It 13. Negative Creep 14. Polly 15. Breed
16. Tourette's 17. Blew

November 2002 **Nirvana** *(Compilation)*
1. You Know You're Right (previously unreleased) 2. About A Girl
3. Been A Son 4. Sliver 5. Smells Like Teen Spirit 6. Come As You Are
7. Lithium 8. In Bloom 9. Heart Shaped Box 10. Pennyroyal Tea
11. Rape Me 12. Dumb 13. All Apologies 14. The Man Who Sold
The World

November 2004 **With The Lights Out** *(multimedia box set)*
Dave Grohl appears on many tracks

November 2005 **Sliver (Best of the Box)**
Dave Grohl appears on several tracks

As **DAVID GROHL**
Album
1997 **Touch: Music From the Motion Picture**
1. Bill Hill Theme 2. August Murray Theme 3. How Do You Do
4. Richie Baker's Miracle 5. Making Popcorn 6. Outrage 7. Saints In Love
(Louise Post) 8. Spinning Newspapers 9. Remission My Ass 10. Scene
6 11. This Loving Thing (Lynn's Song) (John Doe) 12. Final Miracle
13. Touch (Louise Post)

FOO FIGHTERS
Singles

June 1995 **This Is A Call**
7-inch vinyl 1. This Is A Call 2. Winnebago
12-inch vinyl 1.This Is A Call 2. Winnebago 3. Podunk
CD: 1. This Is A Call 2. Winnebago 3. Podunk

September 1995 **I'll Stick Around**
7-inch vinyl 1. I'll Stick Around 2. How I Miss You
12-inch vinyl 1. I'll Stick Around 2. How I Miss You 3. Ozone
CD: 1. I'll Stick Around 2. How I Miss You 3. Ozone

November 1995 **For All the Cows**
7-inch vinyl 1. For All The Cows 2. Wattershed (Live)
CD: 1. For All The Cows 2. For All The Cows (Live) 3. Wattershed (Live)

March 1996 **Big Me**
7-inch vinyl 1. Big Me 2. Floaty 3. Gas Chamber
CD: 1. Big Me 2. Floaty (BBC Evening Session Recording) 3. Gas Chamber (BBC Evening Session Recording) 4. Alone+Easy Target (BBC Evening Session Recording)

April 1997 **Monkey Wrench**
7-inch vinyl 1. Monkey Wrench 2. The Colour And The Shape
CD1: 1. Monkey Wrench 2. Up In Arms (slow) 3. The Colour And The Shape
CD2: 1. Monkey Wrench 2. Down In The Park 3. See You (Acoustic)

July 1997 **Everlong**
7-inch vinyl 1. Everlong 2. Drive Me Wild
CD1: 1. Everlong 2. Drive Me Wild 3. See You (Live)
CD2: 1. Everlong 2. Requiem 3. I'll Stick Around (Live)

January 1998 **My Hero**
7-inch vinyl 1. My Hero 2. Dear Lover
CD: 1. My Hero 2. Baker Street 3. Dear Lover 4. Enhanced section

August 1998 **Walking After You**
7-inch vinyl 1. Walking After You 2. Beacon Light (by Ween)
CD: 1. Walking After You 2. Beacon Light (by Ween)

October 1999 **Learn to Fly**
7-inch vinyl 1. Learn To Fly 2. Have A Cigar
CD1: 1. Learn To Fly 2. Iron And Stone 3. Have A Cigar
CD2: 1. Learn To Fly 2. Make A Bet 3. Have A Cigar

May 2000 **Generator**
7-inch vinyl 1. Generator 2. Fraternity
CD: 1. Generator 2. Ain't It The Life (Live acoustic) 3. Floaty (Live acoustic)
4. Fraternity 5. Breakout (Live)

July 2000 **Breakout**
7-inch vinyl 1. Breakout 2. Stacked Actors (Live from Sydney)
CD1: 1. Breakout 2. Learn To Fly (Live from Sydney) 3. Stacked Actors (Live
from Sydney)
CD2: 1. Breakout 2. Monkey Wrench (Live in Australia) 3. Stacked Actors
(Live from Sydney)

December 2000 **Next Year**
7-inch vinyl 1. Next Year 2. Next Year (2 Meter Sessions)
CD1: 1. Next Year 2. Big Me (2 Meter Sessions) 3. Next Year (2 Meter
Sessions)
CD2: 1. Next Year 2. Baker Street 3. Enhanced section

October 2002 **All My Life**
7-inch 1. All My Life 2. Sister Europe
CD1: 1. All My Life 2. Sister Europe 3. Win Or Lose 4. All My Life (Video)
CD2: 1. All My Life 2. Danny Says 3. The One

January 2003 **Times Like These**
7-inch vinyl *(UK limited edition)* 1. Times Like These 2. Life Of Illusion
CD1: 1.Times Like These 2. Life Of Illusion 3. Planet Claire (Live)
4. Enhanced section
CD2: 1. Times Like These 2. Normal 3. Learn To Fly (Live) 4. Enhanced
section

July 2003 **Low**
7-inch vinyl *(UK limited edition)* 1. Low 2. Never Talking To You Again
(Live)
CD1: 1. Low 2. Enough Space (Live) 3. Low (Video)
CD2: 1. Low 2. Never Talking To You Again (Live) 3. Enhanced section

October 2003 **Have It All**
7-inch vinyl *(UK limited edition)* 1. Have It All 2. Disenchanted Lullaby
(Live/Acoustic)
CD: 1. Have It All 2. Darling Nikki 3. Disenchanted Lullaby (Live/Acoustic)

August 2005 **Best Of You**
7-inch vinyl 1. Best Of You 2. Spill
CD1: 1. Best Of You 2. I'm In Love With A German Film Star
CD2: 1. Best Of You 2. FFL 3. Kiss The Bottle 4. What An Honour
(Interview video)

September 2005 **DOA**
7-inch vinyl 1. DOA 2. Razor (Acoustic)
CD1: 1.DOA 2. I Feel Free
CD2: 1.DOA 2. Skin And Bones 3. I Feel Free 4. Best Of You (Video)

November 2005 **Resolve**
7-inch vinyl 1. Resolve 2. World (Demo)
CD1: 1. Resolve 2. DOA (Demo)
CD2: 1. Resolve 2. World (Demo) 3. Born On The Bayou 4. Resolve Take
Two (Video)

March 2006 **No Way Back**
CD: 1. No Way Back 2. Cold Day In The Sun 3. Best Of You (Live)

September 2006 **Miracle**
Released to radio only (not a physical single)

September 2007 **The Pretender**
7-inch vinyl 1. The Pretender 2. Bangin'
CD1: 1. The Pretender 2. If Ever
CD2: 1. The Pretender 2. Come Alive (demo) 3. If Ever 4. Monkey Wrench
(live from Hyde Park video)

December 2007 **Long Road To Ruin**
7-inch vinyl 1. Long Road To Ruin 2. Holiday in Cambodia (live MTV
Awards)
CD1: 1. Long Road To Ruin 2. Seda
CD2: 1. Long Road To Ruin 2. Keep the Car Running (live) 3. Big Me (live)
4. Long Road To Ruin (video)

September 2009 **Wheels**
CD: 1. Wheels 2. Word Forward

Albums

July 1995 **Foo Fighters**
1. This Is a Call 2. I'll Stick Around 3. Big Me 4. Alone + Easy Target
5. Good Grief 6. Floaty 7. Weenie Beenie 8. Oh, George
9. For All the Cows 10. X-Static 11. Wattershed 12. Exhausted

May 1997 **The Colour And The Shape**
1. Doll 2. Monkey Wrench 3. Hey, Johnny Park! 4. My Poor Brain 5. Wind
Up 6. Up in Arms 7. My Hero 8. See You 9. Enough Space 10. February
Stars 11. Everlong 12. Walking After You 13. New Way Home

November 1999 **There Is Nothing Left To Lose**
1. Stacked Actors 2. Breakout 3. Learn to Fly 4. Gimme Stitches
5. Generator 6. Aurora 7. Live-In Skin 8. Next Year 9. Headwires
10. Ain't It The Life 11. MIA

October 2002 **One By One**
1. All My Life 2. Low 3. Have It All 4. Times Like These 5. Disenchanted
Lullaby 6. Tired of You 7. Halo 8. Lonely As You 9. Overdrive 10. Burn Away
11. Come Back

June 2005 **In Your Honour**
1. In Your Honour 2. No Way Back 3. Best of You 4. DOA 5. Hell
6. The Last Song 7. Free Me 8. Resolve 9. The Deepest Blues Are Black
10. End Over End

November 2006 **Skin And Bones**
1. Razor 2. Over and Out 3. Walking After You 4. Marigold 5. My Hero
6. Next Year 7. Another Round 8. Big Me 9. Cold Day in the Sun
10. Skin And Bones 11. February Stars 12. Times Like These
13. Friend Of A Friend 14. Best Of You 15. Everlong

September 2007 **Echoes, Silence, Patience And Grace**
1. The Pretender 2. Let It Die 3. Erase/Replace 4. Long Road To Ruin
5. Come Alive 6. Stranger Things Have Happened 7. Cheer Up, Boys (Your
Make Up Is Running) 8. Summer's End 9. Ballad Of The Beaconsfield
Miners 10. Statues 11. But, Honestly 12. Home

November 2009 **Foo Fighters Greatest Hits**

1. All My Life 2. Best Of You 3. Everlong 4. The Pretender 5. My Hero
6. Learn To Fly 7. Times Like These 8. Monkey Wrench 9. Big Me
10. Breakout 11. Long Road To Ruin 12. This Is A Call 13. Skin And Bones
14. Wheels 15. Word Forward 16. Everlong (acoustic)

DVD

1. I'll Stick Around 2. Big Me 3. Monkey Wrench 4. Everlong 5. My Hero
6. Walking After You 7. Learn to Fly 8. Next Year 9. All My Life 10. Times
Like These (Acoustic version) 11. Low 12. Best Of You 13. DOA
14. Resolve (Non-glow version) 15. The Pretender 16. Long Road to Ruin
17. Wheels 18. Everlong (Live – Everywhere But Home DVD)
19. Breakout (Live from Hyde Park) 20. Skin And Bones (Live from
Hollywood – Skin And Bones DVD) 21. All My Life (Live – Live from
Wembley Stadium DVD) 22. No Way Back (Hidden bonus video)

Dave Grohl as **PROBOT**

February 2004 **Probot**

1. Centuries Of Sin (with Cronos of Venom) 2. Red War (with Max Cavalera
of Soulfly, Sepultura) 3. Shake Your Blood (with Lemmy of Motörhead)
4. Access Babylon (with Mike Dean of COC) 5. Silent Spring (with Kurt
Brecht of DRI) 6. Ice Cold Man (with Lee Dorrian of Cathedral/Napalm
Death) 7. The Emerald Law (with Wino of Place Of Skulls/The Obsessed)
8. Big Sky (with Tom G. Warrior of Celtic Frost) 9. Dictatorsaurus (with
Snake of Voïvod) 10. My Tortured Soul (with Eric Wagner of Trouble)
11. Sweet Dreams (with King Diamond of Mercyful Fate) 12. (exclusive
bonus hidden track)

THEM CROOKED VULTURES
Album

November 2009 **Them Crooked Vultures**

1. No One Loves Me & Neither Do I 2. Mind Eraser, No Chaser
3. New Fang 4. Dead End Friends 5. Elephants 6. Scumbag Blues
7. Bandoliers 8. Reptiles 9.Interlude With Ludes 10. Warsaw Or The First
Breath You Take After You Give Up 11. Caligulove 12. Gunman
13. Spinning In Daffodils

Additional appearances

Dave appeared on the *Backbeat* soundtrack (1994) and has guested as a
musician on albums by (among others): Killing Joke, Tony Iommi,
David Bowie, Puff Daddy, Mike Watt, John Doe, Queens of the Stone Age,
Garbage, Cat Power, Nine Inch Nails and Tenacious D.

Foo Fighters promotional videos

The video world welcomed Foo Fighters with open arms, not least because
of their ability to send themselves up. While it would have been easy to
concentrate on Nirvana-style performance videos the Foos have brought a
humorous dimension to their clips, not least with self-referential musical
jokes and the participation of Jack Black and Kyle Gass, collectively known
as Tenacious D.

Another theme that's recurred in the videos is a penchant for dressing
up in women's clothing. Dave traces this back to a comedy company from
Canada called *Kids in the Hall*. 'They're kinda like a *Saturday Night Live*
show and were the inspiration for out cross-dressing videos,' he confirmed. 'It was five or six guys, no women in the cast at all, so they had to
cross-dress to get female characters in their skits... fucking hilarious!'He
felt the 'habit' had the by-product of discouraging any homophobics
among the band's fans. 'It was important to Nirvana, it was important to
us, it's important to me. The people who are threatened by cross-dressing
or think it's strange to harbour a bit of that homophobic element... it
takes a big man to wear a dress.'

It took a while for their video career to take off, largely because Foo
Fighters did not exist when the first album of that name was released.

The tour bus is where bands traditionally watch a lot of videos while
travelling, and their taste often filters through into their promos. One of
Dave's perennial favourites is *Waiting For Guffman*, which he describes as
'basically *Spinal Tap* but based around regional theatre. You have to watch
it 15 times, it's just so good.'

The Foos have used a variety of directors to give their videos a unique
flavour. These have included Grohl himself. Gerry Casale, who directed
their first clip, was bass player for late-1970s/early 1980s new wave band
Devo, acclaimed as pioneers of the music video: their 'Whip It' became an
early staple of MTV, while many other video clips are landmarks in the
development of the genre. His track record as director included work with
Rush and Soundgarden.

'I liked working with the Foo Fighters,' said Casale, 'because at that
point they had never made a video. They were anti-video and it was really

low budget but it was fun because Dave decided okay, we're gonna do a video but we're kind of going to do a fucked-up video.' That was 'I'll Stick Around', the first of many Foo classics.

I'll Stick Around (1995)
Director: Gerry Casale

The most controversial track from first album *Foo Fighters* was, in director Casale's opinion, 'about Courtney Love – I know it was, though [Dave] will never admit it.' The clip, shot in August 1995, was 'An interesting non-video video.'

Big Me (1996)
Director: Jesse Peretz

Shot in Sydney, Australia, the clip for this single/first-album track won MTV's Award for Best Group Video that year as well as picking up nominations for Video of the Year, Best Alternative Video, Breakthrough Video and Best Direction. The clip is built around a spoof ad for Footos (Mentos) sweets, slogan 'The Fresh Fighter'.

'That was the first video that we had made that was like a parody of a music video. We did that in Australia. There is something that bothers me about musicians that rely on image in order to sell their music. That's never really been a part of what we do. As you can see, we are not really concerned with looking handsome or, you know, like a rock band. So we were like making fun of making videos. In some ways it's a necessary evil. But after doing that video we realised we could take the piss out of ourselves and it's funny.'

Monkey Wrench (1997)
Director: Dave Grohl

Nominated for Best Rock and Best Alternative Video in the 1997 MTV Video Music Awards, this was Dave Grohl's directorial debut. In the first of a recurring theme, a Muzak version of 'Big Me', recorded by the Moog Cookbook, was playing in the elevator scene. The track, first single from *The Colour and the Shape*, is 'a relationship in which you realise you are the source of all the problems.'

Everlong (1997)
Director: Michel Gondry

The second album's second single celebrated the fact that 'You've made you way around all those obstacles and you're not scared any more'. Its video, with Michel Gondry (*Eternal Sunshine of the Spotless Mind*) at the helm, picked up nominations for Best Rock, Best Director and Best Special Effects at the 1998 MTV Video Awards. Dig the hairdo!

My Hero *(1998)*
Director: Dave Grohl
Dave took the director's chair for the second time for a personal song: 'Most of my [childhood] heroes were ordinary people, friends of the family rather than [Kiss's] Gene Simmons or a basketball player'. This is the only video in which guitarist Franz Stahl appears – surprising, perhaps, as he has a track record in the genre as a production person.

Walking After You *(1998)*
Director: Matthew Rolston
Only Dave appears in this video, as the rest of the band preferred to be with their families – or in Nate's case, go snowboarding! Even so, its budget was on the wrong side of $300,000. It took two days to shoot. The song 'about someone leaving you', originally heard on *The Colour and the Shape*, appears in the *X-Files* movie, so Dave went for something fairly mysterious, appearing on the other side of a prison-style glass screen from his co-star. This was Arly Joven, who'd just finished filming *Blade* with Wesley Snipes, and was made up to look as if she'd been beaten up and dragged through a hedge.

Learn To Fly *(1999)*
Director: Jesse Peretz
Much loved by Foos fans, this had its world premiere on MTV on 7 October 1999 and was so well received it was a late inclusion on the album CD which appeared the following month. As well as picking up nominations for Best Group Video and Best Director in the following year's MTV Videos Awards, it won a Grammy for Best Short Form Video.

The airport workers are hiding drugs in the coffee pot are of course Tenacious D, though the band later claimed the 'secret powder' isn't drugs but 'World Domination brand Erotic Sleeping Powder'! The video originally featured a close-up of the package with that label, but in the end they opted to keep it vague. The joke of course was that the rock band, who preferred loading up on alcohol than coffee, had to land the plane after the crew fell asleep at the controls. Continuing the running gag, a version of 'Everlong' is playing on the plane at the beginning of the clip.

Breakout *(2000)*
Director: The Malloy Brothers
Another outstanding track from *There Is Nothing Left To Lose* followed 'Learn To Fly' into the UK Top 30. It stars Traylor Howard, from the ABC sitcom *Two Guys, a Girl and a Pizza Place*.

The self-referencing musical joke continues, as Generator is playing in the car as the clip begins.

Next Year *(2000)*
Director: Phil Harder
Shot over two long days at Universal Studios in Los Angeles, the video for the almost country-style third *Nothing Left* single was based on NASA's Apollo space project that put the first man on the moon in 1969. Over 15 costume changes were apparently involved.

Generator
Director: Unknown
Released as lead track of an EP in some territories, the video for this track was a live clip shot at the Chapel in Melbourne, Australia in February 2000. It was only shown on TV Down Under, but has since appeared on the reissue of *There is Nothing Left to Lose*. Careful listening will reveal, however, that the studio version of 'Generator' was used and cunningly synched with the live performance visual.

The One *(2001)*
Director: Jesse Peretz
Shot in Brooklyn, New York and featuring actress Amy Weaver, this was a clip for a single not released in all territories. Dave sports a nice line in headgear, while stringed instruments, pierrot costumes and leotards are also involved.

My Life *(2002)*
Director: Dave Grohl
Shot in Los Angeles with Dave again directing, the video for this rock anthem had 'Big Me' playing in the elevator when he enters.

Times Like These (2002)
Director: Liam Lynch/Marc Klasfeld/Bill Yukich
Three different clips were shot for the song. Klasfeld's piece was located in a desert in Victorville, California, while Yukich's was an acoustic version.

Low (2003)
Directors: Jesse Peretz and Les Dudis
Featuring Jack Black of Tenacious D, 'Low' was banned by MTV. Grohl and Black are two rednecks on a drinking spree who end up in a motel dressed in women's clothing. References to *Reservoir Dogs* and *Deliverance* abound for the cinephile's delight.

Have It All (2003)
Director: Unknown
Shot live in Toronto, Canada, this shows the Foos enjoying themselves in performance with a song Dave claimed featured 'a beautiful melody, like fucked-up Beach Boys or something.'

Shake Your Blood (2003)
Director: Unknown
The video from Grohl's side project, Probot, featured Motörhead's Lemmy, Obsessed founder Scott 'Wino' Weinrich and a host of half-naked girls, covered in tattoos and sporting multi-coloured hair. It just had to be mentioned!

Best Of You (2005)
Director: Mark Pellington
Shot on 27 April 2005 in an abandoned hospital in Los Angeles, this was the first single from fifth album *In Your Honour*.

DOA (2005)
Director: Michael Palmieri
This promo was shot in a gravity-defying rotating room. Chris Shiflett said: 'All video treatments kind of look the same – especially when you read like 20 of them in one sitting – they're all roughly the same. So we went for one that was, like, the anti-treatment.'

Director Palmieri who previously worked with the domino-inspired promo for the Bravery's 'An Honest Mistake', said. 'I was waiting to spring this idea on the right band... the whole thing is a combination of really high-tech stuff and the slow-motion tunnel sequence on *The Six Million Dollar Man*. It's full of physics and gravity. It makes no sense and it's completely ridiculous, but that's what it makes it fun.' Dave promptly dubbed the rotating room 'The Barf Ball'.

Resolve (2005)
Director: Michael Palmieri
There's Dave, the band, a bargain-basement sushi restaurant, a strangely familiar waitress, underwater high jinks and... well, let's just say you'll never see seafood in quite the same way again.

'No Way Back' (2006)
Director: Unknown
This video was shot in Amsterdam while the band were on their European tour. Taylor: 'We might do one of those Bon Jovi-on-the-road videos [where] you're sitting in the private jet. You know, before we go onstage, all slow motion. I just remember those videos back in the '80s. Bon Jovi's sitting on his private jet, [thinking] "I miss my mansion." Sorry, Bon. Got no beef with you. Like your videos. We're gonna rip them off.' The video turned out to be a rather tamer 'on the road' job.

The Pretender (2007)
Director: Sam Brown
A fairly ordinary beginning gave way to a memorable sequence in which forty-odd riot police face the band across an ice rink. As they advance, jets of red liquid erupt from a screen behind the band and the police are stopped in their tracks as the band play on.

Long Road To Ruin (2007)
Director: Jesse Peretz
After a dramatic video came the inevitable comedy clip sending up every hospital drama you've ever seen. More than that, it's a show within a show as the screened sequences are depicted in sepia while footage of the 'actors' (the Foos plus guest star/love interest Rashida Jones) are in 'normal' colour. Grohl plays Davy Grolton, who stars as the main doctor, Hansom Davidoff, and performs the song in cheesy fashion with his band in a shopping mall. The final scene sees him driving off a cliff as he chases the fleeing Jones.

Wheels *(2009)*
Director: Sam Brown

There are no fancy sets or comedy acts in this low-key video as it focuses on the band as they rock an empty club.

Index